CONTENTS

Photos follow page 234.

AUTHOR'S NOTE

THIS IS A TRUE STORY, A WAR STORY; at least that is how Elizabeth Cady Stanton and Susan B. Anthony described their long fight against beliefs, customs, and laws that oppressed and disenfranchised women. They wrote and spoke about "ammunition" and "bullets" to fire against the "enemy," and engaged in "combat" with "tyrants." They "met in councils of war" and "organized raw recruits" and "set squadrons in the field" to "seize the fort." They were called "Napoleon" and "General." And, without shedding any blood, they kept each other on the "war-path at the point of a bayonet" and led a "revolution" that transformed the lives of women.

Elizabeth and Susan came of age when the American Revolution was a recent event, one in which their grandfathers had fought. That perhaps could explain their use of war language. More likely, I think, it reflects their acute awareness of the scope of their unprecedented undertaking: "Night after night by the light of an old-fashioned fireplace," Elizabeth once wrote, "we plotted and planned the coming agitation, how, when, and where each entering wedge could be driven, by which woman might be recognized, and her rights secured. . . . Such battles were fought over and over again."

"Mode of Attack"

There is a mountain of primary source material about their "campaign" and "mode of attack"—letters, speeches, petitions, court decisions, reports, and newspaper and magazine articles. Elizabeth wrote her autobiography and kept a diary for the last twenty years of her life. Susan kept a diary and travel journals throughout her life. They were both prolific letter writers. Ida Husted Harper wrote Susan's three-volume biography with her cooperation. Elizabeth and Susan and Matilda Joslyn Gage edited the first three volumes of the monumental six-volume *History of Woman Suffrage.* Susan edited volume four with Ida Husted Harper, who edited the last two volumes alone. I spent several years immersed in that material. One summer I took a road trip to see places that were important in their lives. My house in Englewood, New Jersey, is a few miles from the house in Tenafly where Elizabeth lived for many years. Oftentimes I would walk up the hill to her house and think, "This is where they walked, and worked, and where Elizabeth tried to vote in 1880."

Elizabeth and Susan met in 1851 on a street corner in Seneca Falls, New York. Elizabeth, the prime mover of the first woman's rights convention in 1848, was thirty-five years old and the mother of four boys from the ages of nine years to three months. Susan was thirty-one years old and unmarried. She had recently retired from teaching and was involved in temperance work. Of course, that is where I could have started their story. But I was curious: What were their early experiences? Were there similarities or differences in their upbringings? I explore those questions in the prologue and in alternating chapters in Part I. The years from their meeting through the Civil War appear in Part II. What Elizabeth called the "dark hour of woman's struggle" is covered in Part III. Their final years, in which they go from ridicule to reverence, ostracism to embrace, are examined in Part IV.

Susan publicly called Elizabeth "Mrs. Stanton." Elizabeth called her "Susan." I choose to use their first names, in no way intending to be disrespectful. It is just that that was who they came to be to me as I wrote this book. In keeping with that style, I used first names for other people in the book. Throughout, I use the word *woman* in phrases such as "woman suffrage" because it is the term nineteenth-century reformers used to indicate equality with the word *man*. Typically, modern writers change it to *women*, but staying with their terminology helped me stay in the perspective of their time period.

This book is not an analysis, or a hagiography, or a polemic. It is a story, a true story, told chronologically through incidents and quotations that brought Elizabeth Cady Stanton and Susan B. Anthony and their friendship and their battles to life for me. I wrote this book to bring them to life for you too.

ELIZABETH CADY STANTON
and
SUSAN B. ANTHONY

*A Friendship That
Changed the World*

PROLOGUE
IMAGINE A TIME

Imagine a time in America—

When girls get much less education than boys do.

When girls' activities, especially for middle- and upper-class girls, are limited to "ladylike" endeavors.

When girls and women are considered naturally weaker and inferior to boys and men.

When it is considered shocking, outrageous, scandalous for a woman to give a speech in public, especially to audiences of both men and women.

When women who dare to speak in public are ridiculed, reviled, threatened, even attacked.

When women, especially middle- and upper-class women, are expected to confine their activities to a "separate sphere," or their homes, and to exhibit the virtues of religious piety, sexual purity, wifely submission, and motherly domesticity. And to always be escorted outside their home by a man.

When ministers—powerful shapers of cultural norms and public opinion—vigorously promote women's roles based on biblical verses, such as "Wives, submit yourselves unto your own husbands, as unto the Lord" and "But I suffer not a woman to teach, nor to usurp authority over the man, but to be in silence."

When a married woman does not have the legal right to own property, enter into contracts, sign legal documents, or control what happens to her wages or her children.

When women who do not get married or who have to earn money have very few job opportunities and are always paid less than a man who does the same job.

When the United States government successfully pressures the Cherokee Indians to eliminate women's traditional power in making tribal decisions.

When almost a million African women are held in chattel slavery.

When women are not allowed to vote.

"Once upon a Time"

Once upon a time in America, all the conditions you have just been imagining really existed. Why? They evolved from religious beliefs, entrenched customs, and legal traditions that early settlers brought with them to America. Throughout American history, countless numbers of women and men have fought to change these conditions. To write all their names we would need both sides and the top of the Great Wall of China. And, as is always the case, certain names would stand out—in particular, Elizabeth Cady Stanton and Susan B. Anthony, who are remembered for their fierce, relentless, groundbreaking leadership and their powerful friendship in the fight for woman's rights.

"On a Street Corner"

Elizabeth and Susan first met on a street corner on a spring day in 1851. "There she stood," Stanton later recalled, "with her good earnest face and genial smile. . . . I liked her thoroughly." Thus began a legendary friendship that lasted fifty-one years, a friendship that fueled and sustained the nineteenth-century fight for woman's rights, a fight they waged despite fierce opposition, daunting conditions, scandalous entanglements, and betrayal by their friends and allies.

Elizabeth Cady Stanton, a scintillating thinker, prolifically influential writer, and fearless orator, was born Elizabeth Cady on November 12, 1815. Susan Brownell Anthony, an indefatigable doer, an organizer and planner extraordinaire, and a principled pragmatist, was born four years and three months later, on February 15, 1820.

During their growing-up years, Elizabeth and Susan had some things in common. They both had fathers named Daniel and maternal grandfathers who fought in the American Revolution and who were elected to a state legislature. They were born in places of natural beauty, came from large families with lots of sisters, dealt with the deaths of siblings, and were precocious children. But most everything else during their early years was different.

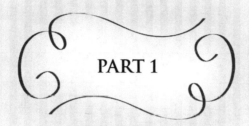

PART 1

1

"Ah, You Should Have Been a Boy!"

ELIZABETH CADY
1815–1832

ELIZABETH WAS BORN IN JOHNSTOWN, NEW YORK, a village forty miles northwest of Albany surrounded by the hills and meadows of the fertile Mohawk Valley. She grew up in a wealthy family and lived in a large house with servants. Recalling her childhood, Elizabeth wrote that she "keenly enjoyed outdoor life," from finding "pretty pebbles" in the Cayadutta, a stream that ran through one end of Johnstown, to playing in the snow outside the house. She and her siblings would "build statues and make forts" and climb up and down "huge piles of wood covered with ice, which we called the Alps."

A plump child with rosy cheeks, Elizabeth had bright blue eyes and two features she was particularly proud of—her very curly dark-brown hair and small feet. Her father, Daniel Cady, a prominent lawyer, was elected to one term in Congress and spent many years as a judge in the state of New York. He was a short man whom Elizabeth later described as "a man of firm character and unimpeachable integrity, and yet sensitive and modest." Her mother,

Margaret Livingston Cady, was a tall woman, almost six feet tall. Elizabeth remembered her as "courageous, self-reliant, and at her ease under all circumstances and in all places."

"What a Pity"

Margaret Cady gave birth to eleven children (Elizabeth was number eight) in eighteen years, five of whom died at a very young age. Elizabeth grew up with an older brother (Eleazar, who died at the age of twenty, the year Elizabeth turned eleven years old) and four sisters, two older (Tryphena and Harriet) and two younger (Margaret and Catharine). Margaret's birth was one of Elizabeth's earliest memories. She was four years old and puzzled because she "heard so many friends remark 'What a pity it is she's a girl!'" Of course, she knew that the new baby was the fifth girl, but at that time, Elizabeth later recalled, she did not understand "that girls were considered an inferior order of beings."

That lesson was seared into her soul when Eleazar died. The family was devastated, but Daniel was inconsolable. Eleazar was his pride and joy. He was the son who would follow in his footsteps.

In an effort to console her father, Elizabeth set about "to be all my brother was." She "pondered the problem of boyhood" and concluded that the "chief thing to be done in order to equal boys was to be learned and courageous." Throwing herself into embracing boyhood, she became a skilled equestrian and an excellent student, the only girl in a class of boys at the Johnstown Academy. When she won a prize for her skill in Greek, she raced home to tell her father, full of the hope that he would "recognize the equality of the daughter with the son." Her father, she later wrote, "kissed me on the forehead and exclaimed, with a sigh, 'Ah, you should have been a boy!' "

Judge Cady's law office was connected to their house. That is where Elizabeth spent a lot of time hearing sad stories about how the law negatively affected women, especially married women. Her father could not help them, he explained, because married women were considered legally dead under the law. Once a woman got married, any property she had owned legally belonged solely to her husband, as did any wages she earned during the marriage, her clothes, and their children. Taking law books down from the shelf, Judge Cady showed Elizabeth the statutes.

The young male law students who were studying with Judge Cady loved to tease her about the laws. One Christmas she happily showed one of the students her new coral necklace and bracelet. Under the law, if they were married, he told her, "I could take them and lock them up, and you could never wear them except with my permission. I could even exchange them for a box of cigars, and you could watch them evaporate in smoke."

Finally, Elizabeth decided to take her scissors and cut every one of the "odious laws . . . out of the books." Her father heard about her plan, and without letting her know that he knew what she was going to do, he explained that there were many lawyers and libraries and that even "if his library should burn up it would make no difference in woman's condition."

Elizabeth graduated from Johnstown Academy, the only girl in advanced classes in mathematics and languages. The boys she had studied with were all going to Union College in Schenectady, New York, the college her brother had attended. But girls were not admitted. "Again," she recalled, "I felt more keenly than ever the humiliation of the distinctions made on the grounds of sex." Instead, Elizabeth went to the Troy Female Seminary, a school founded by Emma Willard and the first one that offered an education similar to what men received in college. There she experienced another searing event—the religious revival meetings led by Charles Grandison Finney that, Elizabeth recalled, "swept over the city and through the seminary like an epidemic."

Elizabeth had been raised as a Scotch Presbyterian, a "gloomy" religion, she later wrote, in which a stern God had already decided who would go to heaven or hell. All a person could do was hope to be saved from hell, a fate that terrified Elizabeth.

"Searing Event"

Charles Finney was a leader of what historians call the Second Great Awakening, a period of fervent religious activity fueled by evangelical ministers who preached about human sinfulness and God's judgment and the devil and hell but who also promised that people could be saved if they repented of their sins and accepted Jesus as their Lord and Savior. (The First Great Awakening happened in the 1730s and 1740s.) Elizabeth's fear of hell and "vivid imagination" made her susceptible to his preaching, especially his graphic images of everlasting punishment for sinners. He was "a terrifier of human souls," Elizabeth later wrote. "I can see him now, great eyes rolling around the congregation and his arms flying about in the air like those of a windmill."

The intensity of trying to achieve salvation was too much for her. She became distraught, haunted by her fears, unable to sleep. "Returning home," she later wrote, "I often at night roused my father from his slumbers to pray for me, lest I should be cast into the bottomless pit."

Deeply concerned about Elizabeth's state of mind, her father took her on a trip to Niagara Falls, along with her sister Tryphena and her husband, Edward Bayard, a man with whom Elizabeth loved to discuss books and ideas, such as skepticism, logic, and reason. For six weeks, they traveled, saw new sights, and talked. In time, Elizabeth later reported, "religious superstitions gave place to rational ideas based on scientific facts, and . . . as I looked at everything from a new standpoint, I grew more and more happy."

In her autobiography, *Eighty Years and More*, Elizabeth highlighted her youthful awareness of the inferior status of women and her traumatic encounter with religion as having profound influences on her life. Let us now find out about Susan. What were the salient influences in her life from her birth in 1820 until 1832?

2

"An Affectionate Family"

SUSAN B. ANTHONY
1820–1832

SUSAN WAS BORN IN A FARMHOUSE in Adams, Massachusetts, a village built on the Hoosic River in the Berkshire Hills, an area still famed today for the beauty of its forests, fields, gorges, and streams. To the west of Adams stands the stately Mount Greylock, the highest point in Massachusetts. Susan lived there until she was six years old and never forgot the joy of wandering in the woods, picking wildflowers, and studying wildlife. Her favorite memory was about how she would sit quietly and watch the sun set behind Greylock's dome-shaped summit, which has inspired generations of writers and poets. "Come here where Greylock rolls," wrote the poet Julia Taft Bayne, "Itself toward heaven; in these deep silences."

A tall, lean child, Susan had angular features, including "the Anthony Nose" that her great-niece and namesake described as a "thin, convex, high nose with a bump on the bridge, which had been inherited from centuries of Anthonys." Her dark-brown hair was thick and straight. One of her eyes turned slightly outward, a condition known as strabismus. The explanation, according to her family and repeated by Susan and later biographers, was that her eye problem resulted from too much reading at a young age. (Curious about this story, I consulted with an ophthalmologist, who said, "Although we do not know the exact cause of this condition, we do know that it's not caused by too much reading.")

"Different Religions"

Susan's parents had been raised in different religions—Lucy as a Baptist, Daniel as a Quaker. Both religions developed in the 1600s in England. Quakers (officially known as the Society of Friends) believed that an Inner Light, or God's spirit, dwelled within each person, regardless of sex, race, or class. They attended meetings where they sat in silence, listening for God's presence and sharing out loud if they heard something. Members with a gift for hearing and speaking were recognized as elders and ministers, including women such as Lucretia Mott, who would eventually inspire both Elizabeth and Susan. Quakers stressed education for both boys and girls, pacifism, and social justice. Living differently than other people, Quakers wore plain clothes, used "thou" and "thy" in their speaking and writing, and did not dance, sing, attend parties, drink hard liquor, or marry a non-Quaker without permission from the Quaker assembly. Most of them refused to vote because they did not want to participate in a government that waged war.

Freedom of conscience, or the right to think for yourself, was important to the Baptists. In their church services, they listened to a minister preach, prayed out loud, and sang hymns. As a Baptist, Lucy, a tall girl with glossy brown hair and blue eyes, was allowed to express her love of singing, dancing,

13 ∾

wearing pretty clothes, and going to parties. She gave all that up to marry Daniel, but not before she danced until four in the morning a few days before the wedding while Daniel sat on the sidelines watching his bride-to-be have her last fling. Susan retold this story to her biographer without an explanation of what the story meant to her. Perhaps, for her, it served as a lesson in self-discipline and self-denial, characteristics that Susan herself would later exhibit many times in the course of her life.

Because Quakers valued education for both boys and girls, Susan and her sisters received the same education as their brothers. All of them were encouraged to be self-reliant, self-confident, and concerned about social issues, in particular temperance, or the movement against drinking alcohol, and abolition, the fight against slavery. Daniel insisted that his children abide by the Quakers' rules against singing, dancing, and drinking. Occasionally, however, he violated a rule; for instance, he married Lucy without getting permission from the Quaker assembly. In order to remain a Quaker, he had to apologize, which he did.

Susan's father owned a small textile mill in Adams that made cotton cloth. In the corner of the house that he built, there was a small store where their neighbors bought supplies. A well-educated, confident man, his independent-mindedness eventually got him dismissed from the Society of Friends, but not until Susan was an adult. During her growing up, she knew her father struggled to follow the rules of a religious society that he said he "revered most," and also to be true to himself.

Lucy never joined the Quakers, although she did adopt their simple lifestyle. Every now and then, however, she would add a brightly colored piece of fabric or ribbon to her children's clothing. When they were older, she would arrange for them to stay overnight with friends and attend parties to watch the dancing. Over a period of thirteen years, she gave birth to eight children (Susan was number two). Six of them were girls (one was stillborn)—Guelma, Susan, Hannah, Mary, Eliza—and two were boys—Daniel and Jacob Merritt, known as Merritt. When Susan was twelve years old, Eliza died at the age of two. Unlike Elizabeth's mother, Susan's did not have any regular household help, just the older children to help care for the younger children and pitch in with the cooking, sewing, washing, gardening, sweeping, butter and cheese making, and many other chores.

Although her mother was described as "very timid" (a stark contrast to her unmarried personality), Susan never forgot her mother's "wise counsel, tender watching, and self-sacrificing devotion." A young cousin who lived with the Anthonys for a year would later write that she basked in the home life of the affectionate family.

Susan's grandparents lived nearby; in particular, she liked to visit Grandmother Anthony, who had a house full of special treats, such as a tub of maple sugar that she kept under the parlor stairs. Then there was the "hasty pudding" that Susan relished most of all. Made by slowly cooking cornmeal in water until it thickened, this delectable dish was served in the shape of a volcano filled with sweet, fresh butter and honey or maple syrup.

"First Move"

About 1826, Daniel did something unusual for that time. He uprooted his family from the place where he and Lucy had grown up, and where their parents still lived, and moved to Battenville, New York, to manage a larger textile mill. This would be the first of several moves that Susan would experience during her childhood, perhaps preparing her for the itinerant life she would live as an adult.

A precocious child, Susan had learned to read at an early age. In Battenville, she attended the local school until she had a run-in with a male teacher who told her that girls did not need to learn long division. That is when Daniel opened a private school and hired teachers who had new ideas, such as using books with pictures and teaching girls long division and calisthenics.

The Anthony family prospered. Daniel successfully managed the mill. He supervised the building of a large store, a sawmill, a gristmill, and small wood houses for his workers. He hired brick makers to build a large house for his family. Since Lucy was busy with a new baby, Susan, Guelma, and Hannah cooked and served the food for the brick makers. Throughout her life, Susan never hesitated to work hard. When a mill worker got sick, she eagerly filled in, despite the long hours and grueling work. With the money she earned—three dollars for two weeks of work—she bought six delicate coffee cups and saucers for her mother.

3

"ROUSING ARGUMENTS"

ELIZABETH CADY
1833–1839

ELIZABETH GRADUATED FROM EMMA WILLARD'S SCHOOL in 1833 and returned home to what she later wrote were "the most pleasant years of my girlhood." Her life was a blur of activities: riding her horse; taking long walks; dancing, playing the guitar and the piano, and singing; reading stacks of books and giving recitations; playing practical jokes and games, including chess; and entertaining a large circle of friends. Her social life, however, paled in light of what she experienced during her visits with her cousin Gerrit Smith (his mother and her mother were sisters) and his wife, Ann, known as Nancy, in Peterboro, New York. Although the Smiths' daughter, who was also named Elizabeth (but often called Libby), was seven years older than Elizabeth, the girls were close friends.

A hulk of a man, Gerrit was eighteen years older than Elizabeth. He had accumulated great wealth and used his money to support the radical causes of the day. His mansion was a meeting place for a kaleidoscope of passionate reformers who vigorously discussed and debated issues, such as the Sunday school movement, prison reform, capital punishment, temperance, slavery, and woman's rights, including suffrage, or the right to vote. This was in stark contrast to Elizabeth's home, where her conservative parents shunned reform movements.

"The rousing arguments of Peterboro," Elizabeth wrote, "made social life seem tame and profitless." During her yearly visits that lasted for weeks, she experienced "an atmosphere of love and peace, of freedom and good cheer." She met "scholars, philosophers, philanthropists, judges, bishops, clergymen, statesmen," and members of the nearby Oneida Indian tribe. She listened, learned, participated, and observed how people conducted themselves. Gerrit, she noted, was "cool and calm in debate."

Gerrit and Nancy were abolitionists, or people who wanted to end slavery, and their mansion was a station on the underground railroad, a complex system of secret routes and safe places that slaves used to escape to freedom in the North and in Canada. One day, when Elizabeth and a group of girls were socializing and singing together in the parlor, Gerrit appeared. Swearing them to secrecy for at least twenty-four hours, he led them to the third floor. There they met a runaway slave named Harriet Powell. "I have brought all my young cousins," Gerrit told her. "I want you to make good abolitionists of them by telling them the history of your life—what you have seen and suffered in silence."

For two hours, the girls listened to Harriet's tragic story of being separated from her family and sold to a master who wanted her for her beauty. "The details of her story," Elizabeth later wrote, "I need not repeat. The fate of such girls is too well known to need rehearsal." The girls "wept together," and by the time Gerrit returned, they were all "earnest abolitionists." That night Harriet, disguised in the plain clothes and bonnet of a Quaker, traveled in a carriage driven by a trusted friend to Lake Ontario, where she would cross into Canada.

She had escaped from her master when he was staying at a hotel in nearby Syracuse. In hot pursuit of her, he tracked her to Peterboro and knocked on the Smiths' door. Gerrit welcomed him, assured him that he was not harboring a slave, offered to let him search the house, and invited him for dinner. Obviously disarmed by his hospitality, the slave owner stayed for dinner, thus allowing Harriet even more time to reach safety in Canada. Later, Gerrit addressed a letter to Harriet's master and published it in a national newspaper informing him that Harriet "was now a free woman. . . . I had the honor of entertaining her under my roof, sending her in my carriage to Lake Ontario, just eighteen hours before your arrival."

"An Explosive Issue"

Slavery was an explosive issue by the mid-1830s. Antislavery forces intensified their efforts to end slavery, as proslavery forces advocated for the expansion of slavery into western states and territories.

From St. Louis, Missouri, to Bangor, Maine, abolitionists formed local antislavery societies. They held conventions; published persuasive tracts; signed petitions; recruited new members; and hired agents, passionate and brave public speakers who traveled far and wide arousing public sentiment against slavery. More and more people were reading the *Liberator*, an antislavery newspaper edited by the fiery abolitionist William Lloyd Garrison, who also was a cofounder of the American Anti-Slavery Society (AASS).

Outstanding abolitionist women, including Lucretia Mott, a petite woman with a prominent forehead and resolute personality, were invited to attend AASS's first convention in Philadelphia, Pennsylvania, as spectators, instead of as equal participants because as Lucretia later explained, "there was not, at that time, a conception of the rights of women." The AASS also invited the women to form an auxiliary organization.

Lucretia and other white and black women founded the Philadelphia Female Anti-Slavery Society. Having "no idea of the meaning of preambles and resolutions and votings," she later recalled, "there was not a woman capable of taking the chair and organizing that meeting in due order; and we had to call on James McCrummel, a colored man, to give us aid in the work." (McCrummel was a dentist and the husband of Sarah, a black woman who signed the Society's constitution.) Quickly learning what they needed to know, the women ran a highly effective organization and recruited many other women to the antislavery cause. In time, they would also embrace the concept of woman's rights.

Proslavery forces, who reaped huge profits—Northern ship owners, bankers, insurance agents, and merchants; and Southern slave traders and owners—fought back. They preyed on the fears of unemployed and minimally employed white people that ending slavery would flood the job market with free black people. Proslavery members of Congress passed a "gag rule" that stopped Congress from considering antislavery petitions, or documents with the signatures of scores of abolitionists.

Riots were instigated against abolitionists in New York City and Utica, New York; in Boston; and in Philadelphia. The homes and businesses of free black people were burned down.

Crazed crowds hooted, hissed, and booed during antislavery meetings. They threw chairs, smashed windows, destroyed speaking platforms, released greased pigs in the audience, and pelted stones, eggs, sticks, and other debris at antislavery speakers.

In Philadelphia, a proslavery rabble-rousing mob disrupted a convention of a new national organization of women, the Anti-Slavery Convention of American Women. Undeterred, Angelina Grimké, a tall, slender woman who had left her prominent slave-owning family in South Carolina and joined the abolitionist movement, raised her voice over the catcalls and calmly addressed the nervous audience: "What if that mob should burst in upon us, break up our meeting, and commit violence upon our persons—would this be anything compared with what the slaves endure?"

The next day, as the women started their meeting in Pennsylvania Hall, a brand-new building, the mob broke down the door and started a fire. All the women escaped, but the building was destroyed. As the fire burned, Lucretia and many black and white friends gathered at her house. Before long, they heard the sounds of the mob growing closer, but then heading off in another direction. Later they learned that a friend had managed to get to the head of the mob and lead them astray.

"Take Their Feet from Our Necks"

Angelina and her older sister, Sarah, had started their antislavery work by writing tracts, or pamphlets. In 1836, Angelina wrote *An Appeal to the Christian Women of the South*. "A pretty bold step, I know and one of which my friends will highly disapprove," she wrote to Sarah in a note she sent along with a copy of her tract. A few months later, Sarah published *Epistle to the Clergy of the Southern States*. Although widely read in the North, in the South copies of *Appeal* and *Epistle* were confiscated and burned. Keeping within the limits of acceptable womanly behavior, they started speaking to small groups of women in private parlors. Soon, however, their unique perspective as Southerners and Angelina's gifts as a speaker propelled them into the public, or male, spaces as their audiences grew to include both black and white women and men.

In May 1837, Angelina and Sarah set off on an extensive lecture tour across Massachusetts. Large crowds of curious and enthusiastic men and women, white and black, attended their lectures. Their breach of propriety—crossing over from the female to the male sphere—infuriated a group of prominent clergymen and Catharine Beecher, a popular commentator on women's proper roles in society. A woman who spoke in public, she wrote, was "intolerably offensive and disgusting." Such women, the clergy wrote in a pastoral letter that was read in churches throughout Massachusetts, would fall in "shame and dishonor in the dust." (When Lucy Stone, a future fighter for woman's rights, and her cousin heard the pastoral letter read in their church, Lucy's "indignation blazed." As for her cousin, she reported that she was "black and blue from Lucy's jabs and nudges.")

"Turning the World Upside Down"

Unrepentant, the Grimkés responded to their critics. Angelina expressed her "indignation at the view she [Beecher] takes of woman's character and duty" in a series of letters titled *Letters to Catharine Beecher* that were published in the *Liberator*. Sarah wrote *Letters on the Equality of the Sexes and the Condition of Woman* that appeared in various publications. Boldly she declared, "I ask no favors for my sex. I surrender not our claim to equality. All I ask of our brethren is, that they will take their feet from our necks and permit us to stand up right on that ground which God assigned us to occupy."

The Grimkés' public role also troubled some abolitionists who feared that the controversy would detract from the main cause—ending slavery. Their anxiety increased as other women crossed over into the public sphere to speak out against slavery and for woman's rights. Angelina was correct when she said, "We Abolition Women are turning the world upside down."

Following all these events—antislavery activities, proslavery backlash, debates about the "woman question," a commonly used phrase—at Peterboro, Elizabeth described this intense time as "white hot." Little did she know that the people she was hearing about—Lucretia Mott, William Lloyd Garrison, Angelina and Sarah Grimké—would play important roles in her future life. For now, she read, listened, and learned.

"Mingled Emotions"

Elizabeth had "a passion for oratory," or public speaking; she loved attending antislavery conventions where she heard the "thrilling oratory, and lucid arguments of the speakers." In particular she was impressed by Henry Stanton, an agent for the American Anti-Slavery Society. "He could make his audience both laugh and cry," she wrote.

Elizabeth and Henry met at Peterboro in 1839. Ten years older than Elizabeth, he was "a fine-looking, affable young man, with remarkable conversational talent," a talent that Elizabeth herself possessed. One day in October, during a horseback ride, Henry proposed. Elizabeth accepted with "mingled emotions of pleasure and astonishment." That night she broke the news to her cousin Gerrit, who warned her that her father would object to Elizabeth's choice of an abolitionist, especially one with no other means of providing financial support.

Gerrit was right. Judge Cady adamantly opposed her choice. Edward Bayard, her brother-in-law, reminded her of the "odious laws" that curtailed married women's rights. Her friends, who had been recommending other suitors for her, now told her that men were "depraved and unreliable." Elizabeth's engagement, she later wrote, "was a season of doubt and conflict."

4

"HARDSCRABBLE TIMES"

SUSAN B. ANTHONY
1833–1839

B Y 1833, SUSAN'S FATHER WAS A WEALTHY MAN (remember, her mother could not legally own anything); again he did something unusual. Instead of expecting his daughters to rely on a husband for financial support, he encouraged them to be self-sufficient as teachers, one of the few professions for women at that time (and the most acceptable). The summer Susan was fifteen years old, she taught the younger children in her father's private school. Two years later, during the winter months, she lived with a family and tutored their children for room and board and one dollar a week. That summer she taught in a local school for a dollar fifty a week. In the fall, Daniel paid the tuition for Susan to continue her own education at Deborah Moulson's Female Seminary, a Quaker boarding school near Philadelphia.

"I Have Been Guilty"

There she eagerly learned about philosophy, chemistry, physiology, and literature. In letters to her parents, she wrote about "the pleasure" of looking through a microscope at the wings of a butterfly. She described a trip to the Academy of Arts and Sciences in Philadelphia. On seeing the "splendid scene" of the metamorphoses of insects, she wrote, "I was ready to exclaim, 'O, Miracle of Miracles.'"

Deborah Moulson insisted that her students also learn "the principles of Humility, Morality and a love of Virtue." She closely monitored everything her students did, from scrutinizing the letters they wrote to critiquing their behavior. "O, may the many warnings which we every day receive," Susan wrote in her diary, "tend to make me more attentive to what is right!"

Despite her efforts to measure up, Susan repeatedly incurred Deborah's displeasure. "I have been guilty of much levity and nonsensical conversation," she confessed in her diary. In another entry, she described an afternoon when Deborah examined their handwriting: "I, thinking I had improved very much, offered mine for her to examine. . . . She asked me the rule for dotting an i. I acknowledged that I did not know. She then said it was no wonder she had undergone so much distress in mind and body, and that her time had been devoted to us in vain." Devastated by Deborah's reaction, Susan rushed to her room and cried. In her diary, she concluded that she was a "vile sinner. . . . Indeed I do consider myself such a bad creature that I can not see any who seems worse."

"Calamitous News"

On her birthday in 1838, Susan wrote in her diary, "2nd mo. 15th day.—This day I call myself eighteen. It seems impossible that I can be so old, and even at this age I find myself possessed of no more knowledge than I ought to have had at twelve." Within a few months, her frustration with her lack of knowledge would pale in comparison with her father's calamitous financial news. He was bankrupt.

Daniel Anthony lost everything—the factory, store, brick house—because of the Panic of 1837, a devastating widespread economic depression that would last five years. In the summer of 1838, the family's possessions were auctioned off to pay outstanding bills. The inventory of items to be sold listed everything: furniture; silverware and china; the flour, tea, coffee, and sugar on their shelves; schoolbooks; Mr. and Mrs. Anthony's eyeglasses; and underclothes belonging to Susan and her sisters and mother. Susan's uncle, Joshua Read, bought back some of the personal items for the family. But most were sold. Susan never forgot this grim time.

"Be the Future What It May"

The Anthony family moved to Hardscrabble, New York, a nearby village with an appropriate name, given their dire finances. Daniel owned two small heavily mortgaged mills and some land with timber there. He and his sons set about to make them profitable. Susan and her sisters helped her mother: "baked 21 loaves of bread," she wrote in her diary, "wove three yards of carpet yesterday. . . . got my quilt out of the frame. . . . The new saw-mill has just been raised; we had 20 men to supper." But soon Susan realized that she needed to do more. She had to earn money and help her father pay his debts.

In 1839 (the same year that Elizabeth was torn between Henry's marriage proposal and her father's disapproval), Susan took the first of what would be a series of positions as a teacher. For now, she accepted the fact that women teachers were paid much less than men. She was concerned about other serious issues—temperance, slavery, the fate of the country. "Be the future what it may," she wrote in her diary, "our happiness in the present is far more complete if we live an upright life."

Then there were the men who were courting her. They ranged from a "noble-hearted fellow" to "a real soft-headed old bachelor" to a suitor who sent her "a piece of poetry on Love and one called 'Ridin' on a Rail,' and numerous little stories and things equally as bad. What he means I can not tell, but silence will be the best rebuke." In another entry, she wrote, "Last night I dreamed of being married, queerly enough, too, for it seemed as if I had married a Presbyterian priest, whom I never before had seen."

"An Absurd Notion"

For fifteen weeks, Susan taught at a Quaker girls' boarding school in New Rochelle, New York. There she witnessed Quakers refuse to welcome a freed black man in their meetinghouse. (In 1827, Quakers split over the issue of whether or not to follow the teachings of Elias Hicks, an abolitionist preacher. Those who did, including Lucretia Mott, were known as Hicksite Quakers; others, such as the ones whom Susan encountered in New Rochelle, were known as Orthodox Quakers.) "What a lack of Christianity is this!" she wrote in a letter to Aaron McLean, her sister Guelma's fiancé. Aaron warned her to "be prudent in your remarks" and do not try to integrate "the good old Friends about you." Undeterred, Susan described her "unspeakable satisfaction of visiting four colored people and drinking tea with them."

 28

On a visit to nearby New York City, Susan heard a woman preacher. "I guess if you could hear her," she wrote to Aaron, "you would believe in a woman's preaching. What an absurd notion that women have not intellectual and moral faculties sufficient for anything but domestic concerns." In another letter, she railed against President Martin Van Buren because he attended the theater in New York—"one of the most heinous crimes or practices with which our country is disgraced." Although later in life Susan would change her mind about the theater, she never changed her habit of zealously forming and expressing strong opinions.

Susan was homesick in New Rochelle. She wrote about her longings for home and her mother's currant pie. She consoled herself with long walks to Long Island Sound, where she would watch the sunset and pine for her family. She was distressed by her sister Guelma's upcoming marriage to Aaron. In August, she wrote to Aaron, "I have no loved sister to whom I can freely open all my heart and in whom I can confide all my little griefs." Although it was painful for her, she finally returned home just in time for Guelma's wedding in September.

At the end of the 1830s, Susan and Elizabeth were living very different lives. One was an unmarried, self-sufficient teacher. The other was engaged to be married. During the next decade, how would their lives unfold?

5

"A NEW WORLD"

ELIZABETH CADY STANTON
1840–1847

HENRY WAS A ROMANTIC SUITOR. In a letter to his "own beloved Elizabeth," dated January 1, 1840, he copied a poem by the Irish poet Thomas Moore.

The heart that loves truly, love, never forgets,
But as truly loves on to the close,
As the sun-flower turns to her god as he sets,
The same look that she turned when he rose.

There was much about Henry to attract Elizabeth. Like her, he was good-natured and witty; he loved to dance and to discuss politics. He was handsome, charismatic, and gave her access to a stimulating circle of intellectuals and reformers. He appeared to support woman's rights.

Despite all that, Elizabeth broke their engagement in February after "months of anxiety and bewilderment." She explained in a letter to her cousin Nancy Smith that "much since then has convinced me that I was too hasty" in accepting Henry's proposal. She and Henry were "still friends and correspond as before." She hoped that they would be even "dearer friends" once the "storm blows over."

In the spring, Henry told Elizabeth he was going to London, England, as a delegate to the World's Anti-Slavery Convention to be held in June. With that news, she decided to marry him because she "did not wish the oceans to roll between us." There was perhaps another reason. A story has been handed down through the Stanton family that Elizabeth's brother-in-law Edward Bayard was in love with her. He wanted to run away with her. There is little evidence to verify this story. However, years later, one of Elizabeth's daughters said, "Yes, no doubt my mother was as much in love with Edward Bayard as he was with her."

"As Speedily As Possible"

Elizabeth and Henry were married in Johnstown, New York, on May 1, 1840. There is no record that her family attended, just a few friends. She insisted that the minister omit the word *obey* from her wedding vows. "I obstinately refused to obey one with whom I supposed I was entering into an equal relation," she later wrote. They spent that night and the next with Gerrit and Nancy Smith in Peterboro. Then they went to New York City. From there, Henry took Elizabeth to Belleville, New Jersey, where they stayed for several days with Angelina and Sarah Grimké and Angelina's husband, Theodore Weld, an abolitionist and Henry's best friend. Elizabeth was thrilled to meet them. In a letter, she wrote, "Dear friends, how much I love you!! What a trio! For me to love!"

On May 12, Elizabeth and Henry boarded the sailing ship *Montreal*. Her sister Madge, who Elizabeth wrote "had stood by me bravely through all my doubts and anxieties," came to see them off. Her sister Harriet and her husband, Daniel C. Eaton, were there too. Daniel and Elizabeth played tag. Her playfulness, competitiveness, disregard for the rules of "polite society" (remember, she was a married woman), and warmth are evident in her recollection of that game: "He and I had had for years a standing game of 'tag' at all our partings, and he had vowed to send me 'tagged' to Europe. I was equally determined that he should not. Accordingly, I had a desperate chase after him all over the vessel, but in vain. He had the last 'tag' and escaped. As I was compelled, under the circumstances, to conduct the pursuit with some degree of decorum, and he had the advantage of height, long limbs, and freedom from skirts, I really stood no chance whatever. However, as the chase kept us all laughing, it helped to soften the bitterness of parting."

Henry's friend James G. Birney, who was also a delegate, was traveling with them. Elizabeth's irrepressibly high-spirited personality greatly distressed him. "I soon perceived that he thought I needed considerable toning down before reaching England," she recalled. Noting that he expressed his displeasure in roundabout rather than direct ways, Elizabeth good-naturedly invited him to "polish" her up "as speedily as possible." One night after beating him at chess, she asked if he had any criticisms.

To which he replied, "You went to the masthead [the top of the mast] in a chair, which I think very unladylike, I heard you call your husband 'Henry' in the presence of strangers, which is not permissible in polite society. You should always say 'Mr. Stanton.' You have taken three moves back in this game."

"Goes for Woman's Rights"

The day after Elizabeth and Henry and James Birney had settled into a boardinghouse in London, another group of delegates from the United States joined them: Lucretia Mott and her husband, James, Sarah Pugh, and Elizabeth Neall from Philadelphia and Wendell Phillips and his wife, Ann, from Boston. Elizabeth later wrote that these were the first women she ever met "who believed in the equality of the sexes."

Even before the convention began, male delegates badgered the women in an effort to dissuade them from attending it. They claimed that women delegates would bring ridicule upon the convention and violate God's will. Lucretia was warned that women "are constitutionally unfit for public meetings with men." To which she replied in the language of the Quakers, "It's interesting that thou should put it that way. Hast thou ever heard slaveowners talk? They use that phrase to say the colored men are constitutionally unfit to mingle with whites."

The convention opened on June 12, with Elizabeth, wearing a cut silk dress, and the Quaker women, in their plain gray dresses and white caps and kerchiefs, seated behind a railing with a low curtain in the back of the hall. For the first order of business, Wendell introduced the motion to admit the women delegates. "No shilly-shallying, Wendell!" his wife had admonished him. "Be brave as a lion." The debate raged for hours. James Birney spoke against the motion. Henry spoke for it, which pleased Elizabeth. In the end, the motion was overwhelmingly rejected. Elizabeth always believed Henry voted for it, although James Birney and others said that Henry voted against it.

The men did, however, agree to allow the women delegates to remain seated in what was called "the ladies' portion of the hall," a big concession, the men thought.

When William Lloyd Garrison arrived several days later, he chose to sit with the women because he could not condone barring women after "battling so many long years for the lib-eration of African slaves." That was how Elizabeth met the legendary abolitionist, and they quickly became good friends. "Mrs. Stanton is a fearless woman," he wrote in a letter to his wife, "and goes for woman's rights with all her soul." Lucretia sat in the middle of the front row. "Nobody doubted that Lucretia Mott was the lioness of the Convention," a reporter for the *Dublin Weekly Herald* wrote. (Upon reading this, Lucretia commented, "As to the lion part, we felt much more that we were created as sheep for the slaughter.")

Elizabeth had never met anyone like Lucretia. A brilliant, quick-witted, uncompromising Quaker preacher, she was twenty-two years older than Elizabeth and the mother of six children. By all accounts, she and her husband, James, had a marriage based on Lucretia's precept that "the independence of the husband and the wife is equal, their dependence mutual, and their obligations reciprocal." A lifelong activist, Lucretia Mott embraced a variety of reform movements: abolition, school and prison reform, tem-perance, peace, the rights of Native Americans, and woman's rights.

"I sought every opportunity to be at her side, and continu-ally plied her with questions," Elizabeth later wrote. Lucretia encouraged her to think for herself, to trust her own opinions, beliefs, and ideas. A new world opened up to Elizabeth. She "felt a new born sense of dignity and freedom."

Before they parted, Elizabeth and Lucretia "resolved to hold a convention as soon as they returned home . . . to advocate the rights of women."

Henry and Elizabeth spent several months traveling in Scot-land, Ireland, and France, where he gave lectures to earn money. On one occasion they were joined by a conservative minister who criticized Lucretia. "In all my life I never did desire so to wring a man's neck as I did his," Elizabeth wrote in a letter to a friend. Thoroughly annoyed, she returned to London and spent ten days alone. Although some of her letters reveal that Henry occasionally chastised her for what he considered her impolite behavior, other people delighted in her. After meeting her, Richard D. Webb, a leading English reformer, wrote to his friend Lucretia, "Mrs. Stanton is one in ten thousand. I have met very few women I considered equal to her—such eloquence . . . clearsightedness, candor, openness, such love for all that is great and good." His wife, he added, was "highly delighted" with her and found her "a brave upholder of woman's rights." Elizabeth was "bright, open, lovely," Lucretia replied. "I love her now as belonging to us."

"Neither Spanking, Shaking, nor Scolding"

Elizabeth and Henry returned home on the *Sirius*, one of the first steamships to cross the Atlantic, and arrived in time to spend Christmas with Harriet and Daniel Eaton. After making the rounds to visit friends, they returned to Johnstown, where her parents and sisters Cate and Madge warmly welcomed them. Undoubtedly the many letters she had written to them after her precipitous marriage facilitated their return. They remained in Johnstown for two years while Henry trained to be a lawyer under Judge Cady's supervision.

Elizabeth enjoyed her sisters' company, devoted herself to studying "law, history, political economy," and kept up a lively correspondence with old and new friends, including the women she had met in London. As was typical of letters between reform-minded people, she discussed public events and engaged in ongoing discussion about the issues of the day. In 1841 she wrote to

Lucretia, "The more I think of the present condition of woman, the more I am oppressed with the reality of her degradation." That same year, she gave her first public speech. It was on temperance, with a "dose" of woman's rights. "I was so eloquent in my appeals as to affect not only my audience but myself to tears," she wrote to Elizabeth Neall.

Elizabeth gave birth to Daniel Cady Stanton, known as Neil, at the Cadys' house in 1842. Preparing for motherhood, she read scores of books and consulted doctors for advice, most of which she rejected, including tightly wrapping newborn babies in "bandages," or strips of cloth, and feeding them only one tablespoon of milk a day because their stomachs were so small. (Their friends Theodore and Angelina did the latter, until Angelina's sister, Sarah, dared to give the baby a pint of milk, thus saving it from starvation.) Instead she relied on her own observations and common sense. Motherhood taught her "another lesson in self-reliance," she later wrote. "I trusted neither men nor books absolutely after this, either in regard to the heavens above or the earth beneath."

Throughout her life, Elizabeth would offer to help exasperated parents. In her autobiography, she related one incident during a train ride when she offered her assistance to young parents who were shaking and slapping a crying child:

"Let me take your child," she told the parents, "and see if I can find out what ails it."

"Nothing ails it but bad temper," replied the father.

"The child readily came to me," she wrote. "I felt around to see if its clothes pinched anywhere, or if there were any pins pricking. I took off its hat and cloak to see if there were any strings cutting its neck or choking it. Then I glanced at the feet, and lo! there was the trouble. The boots were at least one size too small. . . . I rubbed the feet and held them in my hands until they were warm, when the poor little thing fell asleep. I said to the parents: 'You are young people, I see, and this is probably your first child.'" They said yes. "'Now,' said I, 'let me give you one rule: when your child cries, remember it is telling you, as well as it can, that something hurts it, either outside or in, and do not rest until you find what it is. Neither spanking, shaking, nor scolding can relieve the pain.'"

"The Then New Gospel of Woman's Rights"

Henry joined a law firm in Boston in the fall of 1842. Elizabeth alternated between living with him in a boardinghouse and with her family in Johnstown or in Judge Cady's town house in Albany where he served in the state legislature. She was at the town house when she gave birth to Henry Brewster Stanton, Jr., known as Kit, in 1844. Finally, she and Henry and their two children settled down in a house Judge Cady bought them in the Chelsea Hills, a section of Boston with a view of Boston Harbor. The Stantons' third son, Gerrit Smith Stanton, known as Gat, was born in 1845. With the help of two servants, Elizabeth reveled in raising her children and managing her own house.

Boston, with its plethora of cultural offerings, was paradise for Elizabeth. "I had never lived in such an enthusiastically literary and reform latitude before, and my mental powers were kept at the highest tension," she later reflected. She delighted in the theaters, museums, concerts, and "all sorts and sizes of meetings and lectures" on temperance, abolition, peace, and prison reform. The Quaker poet John Greenleaf Whittier was a regular visitor in her home. On Sundays, she walked two miles to hear the controversial minister Theodore Parker pray to "the Father and Mother of us all" and preach about an individual's right to determine God's will.

Many preeminent intellectuals and reformers lived in Boston, and Elizabeth made important new friends—Lydia Maria Child, Maria Chapman, Parker Pillsbury, Charles Hovey, and Joseph and Thankful Southwick. During a gathering at the Southwicks' house, she met Frederick Douglass, an escaped slave who would become a lifelong friend and ally. At their first meeting, he later recalled, she "did me the honor to sit by my side and by the logic of which she is master, successfully endeavored to convince me of the wisdom & truth of the then new gospel of woman's rights."

These happy years ended when Henry decided to move because Boston's winters were too hard on his health.

"The Real Struggle Was upon Me"

Their new home, they decided, would be in Seneca Falls, a town of four thousand people and many small factories and mills in central New York. It was near Rochester, the home of many reform-minded people. The prospects for Henry to fulfill his political ambitions were good. Elizabeth's sister Tryphena and her husband, Edward Bayard, lived there. Her father owned various properties in the area, including a house that had been unoccupied for several years.

Judge Cady gave her the house and a check to fix it up. "With a smile," she later recalled, he said, "You believe in woman's capacity to do and dare; now go ahead and put your place in order." While her children stayed in Johnstown and Henry remained in Boston, she supervised "carpenters, painters, paperhangers, and gardeners." Within a few months, they moved into a renovated house with a new kitchen.

However, all was not well with Elizabeth.

Henry was away a lot. Her children, ages five, three, and almost two, were a handful. Well-trained servants were impossible to find. Her house was on the outskirts of Seneca Falls, and the road to town was usually muddy—except in the summer, when it was dusty. Before long, she found herself living a "solitary" and "somewhat depressing" life. Matters got worse when her children were stricken with malaria. There is some evidence that she might have had a miscarriage. Her previous life, she later wrote, had "glided by with comparative ease, but now the real struggle was upon me."

Her misery and "tempest-tossed condition of mind" transformed Elizabeth. Finally, she "fully understood the practical difficulties most women had to contend with . . . the chaotic conditions into which everything fell without her constant supervision, and the wearied, anxious look of the majority of women." She resolved that something had to be done. But what? Her only thought, she later wrote, "was a public meeting for protest and discussion." However she was too isolated and overwhelmed to plan such an event by herself.

6

"Sink or Swim"

SUSAN B. ANTHONY
1840–1847

For Susan the 1840s were relatively uneventful compared to Elizabeth. But she had her share of challenges. She spent most of the decade as a schoolteacher. First she accepted a position in a country school near her family's home in Hardscrabble, now called Center Falls. (Her father changed the name after he was appointed the postmaster.) Her salary was two and a half dollars plus board a week, one-fourth less than what the male teacher had been paid. Then she taught a summer term in Cambridge, New York.

For several years, she worked as a tutor and governess for the reform-minded Taylor family in Fort Edward, New York. There she was exposed to new ideas, people, and experiences. She spent time with the Taylors' friend Abigail Mott, an abolitionist and operator in the Underground Railroad. Abigail, a former Quaker who had joined the Unitarian Church, introduced her to Unitarianism, with its emphasis on rationality and involvement in social reforms. Mr. Taylor took her to the Whig Party Convention, a political party formed in 1833 to oppose the policies of President Andrew Jackson. It was her first political convention, and she "enjoyed every moment of it."

"Yes, Here Is the Conflict"

In her diary, Susan recorded her social life of suppers and dances and horse-and-buggy rides. An excursion to Saratoga Springs, an idyllic town with many natural mineral springs, was not as much fun as she anticipated because the young man she liked invited another young woman to ride in his buggy. Susan ended up riding in the buggy of a man she considered far less appealing. Nevertheless, she tried to be "agreeable," until he pressed her to give up teaching and marry him.

She spent several months in Vermont with relatives and recruited her cousin Moses Vail to teach her algebra. Hearing about her accomplishment, her brother-in-law Aaron McLean said that he preferred that she continue to bake her delicious biscuits.

"I'd rather see a woman make such biscuits as these than solve the knottiest problem in algebra," Aaron told her.

"There is no reason why she should not be able to do both," Susan replied.

In the summer of 1845, she rejected another marriage proposal, this one from a wealthy widower who tried to entice her with visions of his fine farm, large house, and sixty dairy cows. He was taken with her, he said, because she reminded him of his dead wife. That same summer her sister Hannah announced her engagement to Eugene Mosher. As with Guelma's marriage, Susan struggled with her feelings of loss of her intense sisterly bond with Hannah. In a letter to her parents, she first expressed her concern that Hannah "seems so swallowed up" in herself.

But in her typical self-reflective way, she ended her letter with the insight that she needed to accept Hannah's love for someone outside their tight family circle: "Yes, here is the conflict, I hope after having seen her and Eugene I shall feel different and give it up." In time she accepted Eugene, although she continued to think that "no one is good enough for my Hannah."

"Cold and Cheerless Day"

For five years, the Anthonys struggled to recover from bankruptcy. Daniel tried to earn a profit from two small mills and a logging camp. Lucy took in boarders. She spent weeks at the camp and cooked for the workers. Susan sent him money from her meager salary. But to no avail. In search of new opportunities, Daniel traveled to Michigan and Virginia, but found nothing.

Finally Lucy's brother Joshua Read (who had saved their essential items from the bankruptcy auction) suggested they look at a farm for sale near Rochester, New York. They liked it, and Joshua used money for the down payment that Lucy would have inherited from their parents if she had not been a married woman.

Susan, her sister Mary, her brother Merritt, and their parents moved in early November. They went by stage and railroad to visit Joshua and his family in Palatine Bridge, New York, a village on the Mohawk River. From there they boarded a "line-boat" that was loaded with all their possessions, including their "old gray horse" and their wagon, to travel on the Erie Canal to Rochester. Arriving late on a "cold and cheerless day" and unable to afford a hotel, they hitched the horse to the wagon and headed to their farm, three miles to the west. The "roads were very muddy," Susan later recalled, and it was "quite dark" when they arrived. For dinner, Lucy made "a kettle of mush" from cornmeal and milk. That night, she and Daniel shared the only bed. Susan and her siblings slept on the floor. Beds and other household goods were delivered the next day. Soon a "long and lonesome," cold and snowy winter arrived. For months, Susan and her family felt "very sad and home-sick."

Springtime boosted their spirits. The fruit trees and bushes—peach, cherry, quince, currant, and gooseberry—bloomed. They were befriended by Quakers from Rochester who shared their antislavery sentiments. Their house soon became a popular gathering place for reformers and abolitionists.

In 1846, Susan moved to Canajoharie, New York, a town across the Mohawk River from Palatine Bridge. The Mohawk chief, Joseph Brant, had translated "Ca-na-jo-ha-rie" to mean in English "the pot that washes itself," an apt description of a large circular pothole carved by rushing water in the Canajoharie Creek Gorge. Susan accepted an offer to head the Female Department of the Canajoharie Academy, a private high school with forty boys and twenty-five girls. Her uncle Joshua was a trustee of the school. She worried about doing a good job. Did she know enough to teach older students? Would she disappoint Uncle Joshua? What about the parents? Uncle Joshua reassured her. The secret to success, he said, was "thinking you know it all."

"There Were Plenty of Them"

Susan spent three transformative years in Canajoharie. She gained confidence in her ability to teach a variety of subjects: reading, spelling, writing, grammar, arithmetic, botany, philosophy, and history. Her students excelled at the regular public examinations that were attended by the principal, trustees, and parents. She took them on field trips to "the pot that washes it-self" and other local sites. One year she directed her students in a play about the difference between country and city girls. She assembled the costumes—plain ones for the country girls and fancy ones with "splendid hats, trimmed with wreaths and plumes," for the city girls. The play was a hit.

"Can you begin to imagine my excitement?" she wrote to her parents. "Who ever thought that Susan Anthony could get up such an affair? I am sure I never did, but here I was; it was sink or swim, I made a bold effort and won the victory."

She no longer had to send money home because her father had gotten a job with an insurance company in Rochester. With the highest salary she had ever earned, $110 dollars a year (about $2,967 in today's dollars), Susan discovered she had a flare for fashion. She bought a "new pearl straw gypsy hat trimmed in white ribbon with fringe on one edge and a pink satin stripe on the other, with a few white roses and green leaves for inside trimming." For winter wear, she purchased a broché shawl, a gray fox muff, and a white ribbed-silk hat, and had a new dress made out of plum-colored merino wool. The hat, she told her parents, made "the villagers stare."

Her embrace of fashion was very un-Quaker-like. She also took up dancing. Susan, however, did not start drinking liquor. After one escort drank too much and made "a fool of himself," she vowed that she would only attend events with "a total abstinence man."

She was not lacking for suitors. Soon after her arrival in Canajoharie, she spent an evening with a Mr. Loaux. "Well, I passed the fiery ordeal," she reported to her parents, "no doubt he thought I was <u>handsome</u>." Later she mentioned a Mr. Wells, Mr. Stafford, and Dan S., but provided scant information about them. Many years later, her biographer, Ida Husted Harper, asked her why her diaries were not "full of 'beaux' as most girls' were."

Susan replied, "There were plenty of them, but I never could bring myself to put anything about them on paper."

7

"TO DO AND
DARE ANYTHING"

ELIZABETH CADY STANTON
1848–1850

D<small>URING THE SUMMER OF</small> 1848, Lucretia and James Mott were in the Seneca Falls area. They attended a Quaker meeting, traveled to communities of escaped slaves in Buffalo, New York, and Canada, spent time with the Seneca Indians in Cattaraugus, New York, visited prisoners in the penitentiary in Auburn, New York, and stayed with Lucretia's sister Martha Coffin Wright, who lived with her husband and seven children in Auburn, where she was active in the Underground Railroad.

Early in July, Elizabeth had tea with Lucretia, Martha, Jane Hunt, and Mary Ann M'Clintock at the Hunts' house in nearby Waterloo, New York. In the presences of such "earnest, thoughtful women," Elizabeth expressed her anguish with such "vehemence and indignation" that she stirred herself "as well as the rest of the party, to do and dare anything." And they did; together they wrote a call, or an announcement, of "a convention to discuss the social, civil, and religious condition and rights of woman" to be held in Seneca Falls on July 19 and 20.

Three days before the convention, Elizabeth took her draft of an opening statement and resolutions to the M'Clintocks' house in Waterloo. She sat at a small, round mahogany table and, with input from the M'Clintocks, worked to produce the Declaration of Sentiments. Using the Declaration of Independence as a model, she revised the famous five words, "all men are created equal," to read "all men and women are created equal," then described eighteen grievances and ended with eleven resolutions, including woman's "sacred right to the elective franchise," or the right to vote.

"With the Merry Eye"

Elizabeth was well prepared for her role. For years she had studied law, economics, history, and politics. She had read books by the great writers and philosophers on woman's rights—Mary Wollstonecraft's *A Vindication of the Rights of Women,* Sarah Grimké's *Letters on the Equality of the Sexes, and the Condition of Woman,* and Margaret Fuller's *Woman in the Nineteenth Century.* She read Judge Elisha Powell's essays strongly supporting woman's rights, and Reverend Samuel J. May's sermon "The Rights and Conditions of Women." In the mid 1840s, she, along with Ernestine Rose and Paulina Wright Davis, had lobbied New York legislators to pass an act allowing married women to retain property they brought into the marriage or inherited during it. The act—the Married Women's Property Act—had just been approved by the state legislature, the first in the country to take this step.

Lucretia warned Elizabeth that people might not attend "owing to the busy time with the farmers' harvest." But hundreds came. Some walked; others rode horses or traveled in horse-drawn vehicles—surreys, heavy farm wagons, and democrat wagons (lightweight flat-bottom wagons with two or more seats).

Thirteen-year-old Mary Bascom was there with her parents. Years later she remembered the scene "as vividly as if yesterday,—the old chapel with its dusty windows . . . the wooden benches or pews, and the platform with the desk and communion-table, and the group gathered there; Mrs. Stanton, stout, short, with her merry eye and expression of great good humor; Lucretia Mott, whose presence then as now commanded respect wherever she might be; Mary Anne McClintoc [sic], a dignified Quaker matron with four daughters around her, two of whom took active part in the proceedings."

"So Timely, So Rational, and So Sacred"

For two days, they listened, discussed, debated. The Declaration of Sentiments was adopted and signed by sixty-eight women and thirty-two men. Only one resolution caused a bit of a stir, and that was the one Elizabeth insisted on—the right of suffrage. Henry said he would leave town if she proposed it. She did, and he absented himself. Lucretia worried that it was too radical. Frederick Douglass, however, supported Elizabeth's demand for the vote and spoke up during the debate. "In due time," she said, "Douglass and I carried the whole convention."

It was inconceivable to Elizabeth that a convention that she considered "so timely, so rational, and so sacred" would be the brunt of "sarcasm and ridicule." But it was. Hyperbolic accounts appeared in newspapers across the country: The convention was "a most insane and ludicrous farce" and the participants were "erratic, addle-pated comeouters." The women's demands would "prove a monstrous injury to all mankind."

Some newspapers heralded the convention. The editor of the *Herkimer Freeman* wrote, "Success to the cause in which they have enlisted! . . . I hail it as a great jubilee of the nation." The *St. Louis Reveille* proclaimed, "The flag of independence has been hoisted for the second time on this side of the Atlantic . . . by a convention of women at Seneca Falls, New York." Horace Greeley, editor of the widely read *New York Tribune*, wrote, "It is easy to be smart, to be droll, to be facetious in opposition to the demands of these Female Reformers." But, he conceded, although their demands are "unwise and mistaken," they are based on the "assertion of a natural right," as are the words "all men are created equal" in the Declaration of Independence.

"The Right Is Ours"

Energized by the Seneca Falls convention, Amy Post, a prominent reformer, organized another one that was held two weeks later in Rochester. Although Elizabeth later said she attended "with fear and trembling" because of the hostile press, she was there, along with Lucretia and Frederick. Whereas men had presided at the Seneca Falls convention, Amy nominated her friend, the activist Abigail Bush, as president. Worried by such unwomanly behavior, Elizabeth and Lucretia left the platform and sat in the audience. Undeterred by their action, Abigail competently performed her duties. Afterward, Lucretia tenderly held Abigail in her arms and thanked her for presiding. Elizabeth wrote an apology to Amy: "I have so often regretted my foolish conduct." Her behavior, she said, was due to a lack of experience in seeing women "act in a public capacity."

The success of both conventions gave Elizabeth "great encouragement to go on." The question she asked was "What are we next to do?"

The answer was a whirlwind of activity. She printed the directions "Read and Circulate" on copies of the minutes of the Seneca Falls convention and sent them to her friends. She wrote letters to newspapers, organized a petition campaign, and gave her first major speech on woman's rights at a Quaker meetinghouse in Waterloo. Again she called for the right to vote—"The right is ours. Have it we must. Use it we will." After giving that speech a few times, she tied a ribbon in her favorite color—pale blue—around the manuscript and put it away. Years later she gave it to her two daughters with the hope that "they will finish the work which I have begun."

No longer intimidated by hostile press, Elizabeth cut out articles and pasted them in a small red-backed scrapbook (which is now in the Library of Congress). She welcomed any publicity because it spread their ideas and that would "start women thinking, and men too; and when men and women think about a new question, the first step in progress is taken. The great fault of mankind is that it will not think."

Her house was a place where young people gathered to talk and dance. On Saturday nights, people met for "conversationals," or discussion groups, on a different topic each week. She put a billiard table in the barn, started a dancing school, and put up swings and bars for exercise (a novel idea at the time). Years later, her children described her as "a most devoted mother; she sang and played for us on both piano and guitar, and told us wonderful stories."

"Great Effort and Patience"

Elizabeth had a miscarriage in March 1849. We know that from a letter Martha Wright wrote to her sister Lucretia with the news that Elizabeth "has miscarried at 5 mo. with a little girl—a great disappointment." Despite her sadness, Elizabeth kept up her whirlwind of activities.

Since January, she had been writing articles for the *Lily*, a temperance newspaper published by Amelia Bloomer, the deputy postmaster of Seneca Falls (her husband was the post-master). Amelia had attended the Seneca Falls convention, but she had not signed the Declaration; instead she had "stood aloof and laughed." Undeterred and characteristically strategic, Elizabeth set about with "great effort and patience" to infuse the *Lily* with woman's rights ideas. Within a year, she published "Woman," the first of many provocative articles about every aspect of women's lives—voting, housekeeping, dating, and sewing.

Her writing style was as bold, good-natured, and as colorful as her personality. Typically in both her writing and speaking, she posed questions, undoubtedly to provoke readers to think. In "Sewing," she wrote, "What use in all the flummering, puff-ing, and mysterious folding we see in ladies' dresses? What use in ruffles on round pillow cases, night caps, and children's clothes? . . . It will be a glorious day . . . when men and boys make their own clothes, and women make theirs in the plainest possible manner."

"The Point to Attack"

In Ohio in 1850, a group of delegates—all men—was slated to meet to revise the state constitution. Determined to convince them to add woman suffrage to the constitution, a group of women held the first Ohio Women's Convention on April 19 and 20 in Salem, Ohio. Elizabeth was invited to speak. Thrilled by the invitation, but not free to leave her children, she wrote a letter that was read to the convention. In it she underscored both the importance of and resistance to woman suffrage: "Depend upon it, this is the point to attack the stronghold of the fortress—*the one* women will find the most difficult to take, *the one* man will most reluctantly give up."

Although men had been allowed to participate in the conventions in Seneca Falls and Rochester, they were silenced in Salem by President Betsey Mix Cowles, a pioneering kindergarten teacher, operator in the Underground Railroad, and one of the Cowles Family Singers, along with her sister Cornelia and brother Lewis. "No men were allowed to sit on the platform, to speak or vote," recalled one participant. "They implored just to say a word; but no, the President was inflexible. . . . For the first time in the world's history, men learned how it felt to sit in silence. . . . They gamely founded their own suffrage association, where they promptly endorsed all that the women had said and done." (These efforts, plus petitions with eight thousand signatures, failed to get woman suffrage into the state constitution.)

Six months later, the First National Woman's Rights Convention was held in Worcester, Massachusetts. More than a thousand people attended. But not Elizabeth; again she wrote a letter that was read to the convention and published in the *Lily*. Why was she unable to attend? She was five months pregnant with her fourth child.

8

"OUT OF SORTS WITH THE WORLD"

SUSAN B. ANTHONY
1848–1850

ALTHOUGH SUCCESSFUL IN CANAJOHARIE, Susan was increasingly discontented. In the spring of 1848, she wrote to her parents, "a weariness has come over me." She was feeling "out of sorts with the world." What could she do? A new hat did not lift her spirits; neither did a visit home. She had little energy left for teaching, having taught since she was fifteen years old, always for less than what men were paid. Marriage did not appeal to her. Susan was restless and unfocused. News of the gold rush in California prompted her to wish "Oh, if I were but a man so that I could go!"

The year itself—1848—was unsettled. Revolutions swept Europe: Sicily, France, Germany, Hungary, and the Hapsburg Austrian Empire. Ireland was still in the throes of the Great Famine that killed a million people and forced hundreds of thousands to immigrate to America. Mexico lost the Mexican-American War and ceded vast territory, including California, in the Treaty of Guadalupe Hidalgo.

By 1848, the country was connected by thousands of

miles of canals and railroads. Trips that used to take days, now took hours. In 1844, communications had been transformed by the introduction of the telegraph that instantaneously transmitted messages, information, and news. By 1848, a telegraph line connected New York City and Chicago.

The rapid industrialization, growth of cities, westward migration, and huge influx of immigrants brought new opportunities for Americans. These changes intensified a range of existing problems: wretched living conditions, abject poverty, drunkenness, and vices such as prostitution, lewdness, and gambling. A reform movement rooted in religious revivals arose to ameliorate these problems. Women were the backbone of the movement; they formed hundreds of moral reform societies that focused on everything from helping prostitutes to establishing orphanages.

"There Is No Neutral Position"

By the 1840s, involvement in a reform movement seemed to offer educated women like Susan an alternative to marriage or teaching. Perhaps that was why she decided during her unsettled time to join the Canajoharie Daughters of Temperance. It was a logical choice. She had grown up in a temperance household. Her father had been involved in the movement for years. On March 1, 1849, she gave her first public speech to two hundred people at a supper sponsored by the Daughters of Temperance. On one wall of the Hall of Temperance, her name was "printed in large capitals of evergreen [branches]." She told her audience that "all that is needed to produce a complete Temperance and Social reform in this age of Moral Suasion, is for our Sex to cast their United influences into the balance. Ladies! there is no Neutral position for us to assume."

The next day the streets were abuzz with the opinion that "Miss Anthony is the smartest woman who ever had been in Canajoharie."

Susan lived in Canajoharie with her cousin Margaret and her husband and three children. Margaret was like a sister to her, supporting and encouraging her. She helped Susan get ready for a public examination of her students. She braided Susan's hair in four long braids and wound them around a big shell comb. She pinned her watch with a gold chain and pencil to Susan's dress.

"I Have Lost the Only Friend"

On March 7, six days after Susan's successful speech, Margaret gave birth to a baby girl. It was a difficult birth. Afterward Susan wrote to her mother, "It is rather tough business, is it not Mother. Oh, I am so glad she is through with it." Susan devotedly tended to Margaret for seven days, but then she died. Susan wrote to Hannah, "Sister, I feel that I have lost the only friend that I had (out of our own family circle) who loved me because of union of soul, of sympathy, of spirit, but that friend is gone."

Susan resigned her position. That summer she visited friends. In the fall, she returned to Rochester to run the farm for a while. She wanted to make temperance reform her life's work. How could she do that and be self-sufficient? That question was on her mind as she tended the fruit trees and gardens, cooked and cleaned, and cared for her ailing mother.

On Sundays, abolitionists and reformers gathered at the Anthonys' house to eat and talk. Susan developed important friendships with people like Frederick Douglass, who was a close friend of her father and Amy Post. She heard talk about the woman's rights conventions in Seneca Falls and Rochester and Worcester. In fact her parents and sister Mary had attended the Rochester convention. Her cousin Sarah Anthony Burtis had been the secretary. They had all signed the Declaration of Sentiments. Although Susan thought temperance and abolition were more important than woman's rights, she was intrigued by all the praise she heard about a woman named Elizabeth Cady Stanton.

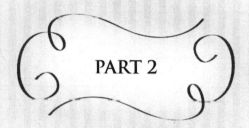

PART 2

9

"An 'Intense Attraction'"

Elizabeth and Susan
1851–1853

Susan B. Anthony and Elizabeth Cady Stanton had many mutual friends, including Amy Post, Frederick Douglass, and Amelia Bloomer. Eventually one of them was bound to introduce them. It was Amelia who invited Susan to visit and attend an antislavery meeting in Seneca Falls, in May 1851. The speakers were William Lloyd Garrison and George Thompson. Elizabeth, who had given birth in February to her fourth son, Theodore Weld Stanton, known as Theo, also attended.

After the meeting, Elizabeth encountered Amelia and Susan, who were standing on the corner of the street waiting to greet her. Amelia and Elizabeth were wearing bloomers, the new, comfortable but controversial fashion of a below-the-knee-length skirt worn over pants that dress reformers were promoting.

Years later, Elizabeth vividly recalled her first impression of her "future friend and coadjutor" and wrote, "There she stood, with her good, earnest face and genial smile. . . . I liked her thoroughly."

Susan later recalled that there was an "intense attraction" between them. She did not, however, yet share Elizabeth's passionate commitment to woman's rights.

Susan's lesser commitment to woman's rights was the result of several factors. Her Quaker upbringing had inoculated her with the idea of equality between women and men. Unlike Elizabeth's father, Susan's father did not value his sons more than his daughters; both were expected to be self-sufficient. Her parents supported her decision to leave teaching and take up reform work, including providing financial backing. As for voting, Quakers traditionally disavowed involvement in partisan politics. As pacifists, many Quaker men refused to vote as a protest against governments that engaged in wars.

Another factor was that Susan was just beginning to be immersed in the whirlwind of political debates, stimulating conversations, and new ideas that Elizabeth had been exposed to much earlier. Recently she had written to her father that she wanted to be "associated with those whose ideas are in advance of my own" because then she would "develop so much faster."

Of course, Susan had experienced some of the inequalities; she herself had been paid much less than male teachers. She knew that although her mother's money provided the down payment for the farm, her name could not be on the deed. Her organization, the Daughters of Temperance, was considered merely an auxiliary to the Sons of Temperance. But, unlike Elizabeth, Susan had not yet thoroughly delved into understanding the legal, social, civil, and religious status of women, and had not personally dealt with the "practical difficulties" of managing a household and raising children.

Susan was also well aware of the other great social movement: antislavery. But of the three—antislavery, temperance, and woman's rights—she remained most committed to her temperance work. That is where she thought she could make a difference. She soon learned otherwise.

"Come and Stay with Me"

Susan's first jolt of awareness came at a Sons of Temperance meeting. She was there because the Sons had invited the Daughters to send delegates. The women were welcomed, until Susan stood up to speak. "The sisters were not invited there to speak," the presiding officer told her, "but to listen and learn." Uncowed and indignant, Susan walked out. A few women followed her, but most remained seated, some remarking that Susan and the women who left with her were "bold, meddlesome disturbers."

The upshot of the incident was Susan's decision to organize an independent organization, the Women's New York State Temperance Society. She recruited Elizabeth to write her a lecture and to serve as president. "I will gladly do all in my power to aid you. Work down this way, then you come & stay with me, . . ." Elizabeth responded. "I have no doubt a little practice will make you an admirable lecturer. I will go to work at once & write you the best lecture I can. Dress loose, take a great deal of exercise & be particular about your diet, & sleep enough, the body has great influence upon the mind. In your meetings if attacked be good-natured & cool, for if you are simple & truth loving no sophistry can confound you."

As for her own speech as president, Elizabeth warned Susan that "anything from my pen is necessarily radical." If Susan needed to dissociate herself from what she said, that was all right; Elizabeth was "ready to stand alone." She did not "write to please any one . . . but to proclaim my highest convictions of truth."

"Half Man and Half Woman"

The convention met in Corinthian Hall in Rochester, New York, on April 20, 1852. More than five hundred women showed up, a testament to Susan's remarkable skills in organizing events: She had written countless letters, gotten press coverage, traveled to spread the news by word of mouth, invited prominent speakers who would attract a crowd, secured a hall, and supervised every detail from the program to the flowers. Men were there too, although they were not permitted to hold office or vote.

Elizabeth was elected the president. Wearing bloomers and with her hair newly cut short in a bob, she gave a "powerful speech," parts of which "acted as a bombshell not only at this meeting, but in press, pulpit and society." She proposed that women be permitted to divorce a "drunkard," at a time when divorce was a taboo subject. She also urged women to shift their support of religious charitable work from missionary work in other countries to "the poor and suffering around us," a heretical proposal at that time. Despite the uproar about Elizabeth's words and her bloomers and her bob, Susan stood with Elizabeth.

Two months later, Susan and Amelia were invited to another Sons' meeting. Their friend and supporter Samuel J. May had assured them that they would be welcomed; instead when they arrived in the hall their presence was denounced by others in the group. One particularly agitated clergyman proclaimed that they, indeed all women involved in temperance work, were "a hybrid species, half man and half woman, belonging to neither sex."

"A Brilliant Galaxy"

After the Seneca Falls convention, woman's rights conventions had been held in Ohio, Indiana, and Pennsylvania. Delegates from many states and Canada attended two national conventions in Worcester, Massachusetts. Although too busy with her children to go to any of them, Elizabeth was never too busy to write a letter that was read aloud to the audience. In the fall of 1852, Susan attended her first woman's rights convention, the third national one, which was held in Syracuse, New York. Elizabeth, who was eight months pregnant with her fifth child, asked her to read the letter.

By this time, Elizabeth was widely known and greatly admired; so the fact that Susan stood on the speakers' platform and read her letter to the audience added to the cachet she had already acquired through her temperance work. It also associated her with Elizabeth's radical ideas, such as proposing that colleges accept women, which "raised the usual breeze in the convention." Unconcerned by controversy, Susan chose to stand by Elizabeth, and she read the letter with "hearty approval."

It was perhaps easy for Susan to support Elizabeth because she too was bold and willing to stand alone when necessary. That was how she blocked the election of Elizabeth Oakes Smith as president of the convention.

An elegantly stylish woman, Elizabeth Oakes Smith was a

poet, novelist, and lecturer. She and her close friend Paulina Wright Davis, who had organized the convention, arrived wearing matching short-sleeved, low-necked white dresses with loose jackets, one embroidered in pink, the other in blue. Susan, like most women, shrouded herself in layers of clothes because it was unthinkable at that time for a woman to bare her arms and neck in public. When Paulina nominated Elizabeth Oakes Smith for the presidency, Susan objected because "nobody who dressed as she did could represent the earnest, solid, hardworking women of the country." Although no one else spoke up, Susan clearly prevailed—the plain-dressing Quaker Lucretia Mott was elected president.

Lucretia was just one of the many extraordinary people Susan met and listened to at the convention. Lucy Stone, a graduate of Oberlin College and a spellbinding orator; Matilda Joslyn Gage, a freethinker with a dry wit; and the charismatic Ernestine Rose, known at the time as "the queen of the platform," were among the many dynamic speakers. All in all, it was a "brilliant galaxy of men and women" who discussed woman's rights from "every conceivable standpoint."

By the time the convention ended, Susan had embraced the centrality of suffrage. She had realized that, without the vote, women were powerless to influence politicians and to effect changes in laws and policies. Although she continued her temperance work, her focus had shifted.

"Oh! How I Wish"

Whenever Elizabeth had a baby, so the story was told, she flew a flag—red for a boy, white for a girl. Her first white-flag baby was born in 1852. She named her Margaret Livingston, after her mother. "Rejoice with me all womankind," she wrote to Lucretia, "for lo! a champion of thy cause is born." She recounted how, with the help of Amelia Willard, her full-time housekeeper, she gave birth in about fifteen minutes.

With four boys ranging in age from ten years to twenty months, a newborn, and a frequently absent husband, Elizabeth had her hands full. Rejecting the strict parenting style that was in vogue, she had developed her own commonsense approach. Shunning physical punishment, she stressed self-control and self-discipline. By the time Margaret, known as Maggie, was born, Neil and Kit were spending the school year at a coeducational boarding school run by Angelina and her husband Theodore Weld and her sister Sarah who lived with them and taught at the school.

The boys received long letters from their mother full of love and advice. In one, Elizabeth responded to Neil's request that she not wear her bloomers when she visited them at school. First in her letter, she asked him to imagine that they were walking in a field and a bull began chasing them. While Neil could run away fast unencumbered by petticoats, she could not. "Then you in your agony, when you saw the bull gaining on me, would say: 'Oh! how I wish mother could use her legs as I can.' Now why do you wish me to wear what is uncomfortable, inconvenient, and many times dangerous? I'll tell you why. You want me to be like other people. You do not like to have me laughed at. You must learn not to care for what foolish people say."

"Bigger Fish to Fry"

Throughout the 1850s, Elizabeth's domestic responsibilities constrained her ability to think and write and speak on woman's rights. Although she had the invaluable help of Amelia, she needed a physical link to the outside world to avoid being "wholly absorbed in a narrow family selfishness." That link was Susan, who not only brought her firsthand reports, but also willingly relieved her of her domestic demands and duties so that she could think and write. "But for her pertinacity I should never have accomplished the little I have," Elizabeth reflected years later. In turn, Susan loosened up under Elizabeth's influence. In December 1852, she started wearing bloomers; then she got her hair cut in a bob.

Susan and Elizabeth wore their bloomers to the first anniversary meeting of the Women's New York State Temperance Society in June 1853. It now had over two thousand members, thanks to Susan's hard work. As the president, Elizabeth addressed the hotly debated issue of talking about woman's rights at a temperance meeting. It was necessary, she said, because many people questioned whether women should be allowed to talk on any subject. She also raised the inflammatory divorce issue again.

Then a motion was made to change the constitution and allow men to be elected as officers. Elizabeth and Susan supported the change with the hope that the men "would modestly permit women to continue the work she had so successfully begun." That was not to be. The men, with the support of many women, took over. They changed the name to the People's League and rejected any connection to woman's rights. Elizabeth was defeated for reelection as president, and she refused the vice-presidential position that she was offered instead. Susan refused her reelection as secretary. Together they walked away from the organization that Susan had founded.

Susan returned to her home in Rochester disheartened and worried that Elizabeth was "plunged in grief" by her defeat. Not to worry, Elizabeth reassured her. She was happy to shed the responsibility and satisfied that she had brought up the divorce issue. "Now, Susan," she wrote in a letter, "I do beg of you to let the past be past, and to waste no more powder on the Women's State Temperance Society. We have other and bigger fish to fry."

10

"Do You Not See?"

A WOMAN'S RIGHTS POINT OF VIEW
1853–1854

Elizabeth had ambitious goals, but first she needed a break. "I forbid you to ask me to send one thought or one line to any convention, any paper, or any individual," she wrote to Susan, "for I swear by all the saints that whilst I am nursing this baby I will not be tormented with suffering humanity."

For now Susan heeded her friend's admonition and joined forces with Lucy Stone to organize a temperance convention where both women and men could speak. Her idea was to schedule it to coincide with the World's Temperance Convention in September 1853 or, as Susan put it, when "the Old Fogies hold their convention." The "Old Fogies," of course, were the people who refused to allow women to speak. But, first, Susan wanted to stir up the women at the New York State Teachers' Convention.

"I Wish to Speak"

The teachers' meeting was held in August in Corinthian Hall in Rochester. Anyone who paid a dollar could participate. Susan paid and sat without saying anything for a day. She later described her "grief and indignation" that although two-thirds of the five hundred attendees were women, they did not even try to participate in the proceedings; the handful of men teachers did everything: presiding, pontificating, debating, and voting. That was bad enough, but what was worse for Susan "was to look into the faces of those women and see that by far the larger proportion were perfectly satisfied with the position assigned to them."

On the second day, she stood up and said, "Mr. President," causing shockwaves to ripple through the audience.

"What will the lady have?" replied the president, Charles Davies, a professor at West Point who was wearing his full-dress uniform.

"I wish to speak to the question under discussion," she said.

"What is the pleasure of the convention?" he asked the group.

"I move she shall be heard," one man said; another man seconded the motion, which was then debated for half an hour. Susan remained standing, afraid to appear to be giving up by sitting down. Finally the men voted and by a small margin the motion passed. Susan had permission to speak on the question under discussion, which was "Why the profession of teacher is not as much respected as that of lawyer, doctor or minister."

In a voice that carried to every part of the hall, she said, "It seems to me you fail to comprehend the cause of the disrespect of which you complain. Do you not see that so long as society says woman has not brains enough to be a doctor, lawyer or minister, but has plenty to be a teacher, every man of you who condescends to teach, tacitly admits . . . that he has no more brains than a woman?"

Susan was not greeted with applause; instead she heard comments such as "Did you ever see such a disgraceful performance?" and "I was never so ashamed of my sex." Two teachers, however—Mrs. Northrop and her sister Mrs. J. R. Vosburg—told Susan that she had "taught us our lesson and we propose to make ourselves heard." They did just that the next day by offering two resolutions. One recognized the rights of women teachers to fully participate in the organization, and the other dealt with providing equitable pay for women teachers. To Susan's satisfaction and Charles Davies's shock, both resolutions passed.

"The Uproar Was Indescribable"

New York City was abuzz with excitement in September; huge crowds were attending the Exhibition of Industry of All Nations in the Crystal Palace, a spectacular new building made of glass and iron with a dome one hundred feet in diameter. Over five thousand exhibitors from every part of America and twenty-three foreign countries were showing off steam-powered machines, marble statues, fancy home furnishings, paintings, and specimens of ores and minerals, including California gold.

Hoping to attract the crowds to their cause, various reform groups held their conventions at the same time—two temperance, one antislavery, and one woman's rights. The temperance convention organized by Susan and Lucy was a great success. The other one, the World's Temperance Convention (or the Half-World's Temperance Convention, according to Susan and Lucy), spent most of its time arguing over whether or not to allow Antoinette Brown, the first woman to be ordained a minister, to speak. As one newspaper described it, "This convention has completed three of its four business sessions and the results may be summed up as follows: First day—Crowding a woman off the platform; second day—Gagging her; third day—Voting that she shall stay gagged."

As usual there were aggressive rowdies at all the conventions, especially at the two-day woman's rights convention. Hostile spectators hissed, whistled, and cried "shut-up" and "get out." Susan later told her biographer that the "uproar was indescribable, with shouting, yelling, screaming, bellowing, stamping and every species of noise that could be made." Henceforth it would be known as the "mob convention."

"A Purse of Her Own"

That fall Susan attended one more convention, the Fourth National Woman's Rights Convention in Cleveland, Ohio. In dramatic contrast to the "mob convention," it was peaceful and orderly. She was appointed to a committee on finance and business. Now fully committed to work for woman's rights, she revisited the counties in New York where she had already organized women to work for temperance. But all the groups had fallen apart. The reason, she was told, was that the women, all wives, had no money of their own to continue the work. She wrote in her journal that as she traveled "from town to town," she "was made to feel the great evil of woman's utter dependence on man for the necessary means to aid reform movements."

Reflecting on that insight, Susan had an epiphany—"the grand idea of pecuniary independence. Woman must have a purse of her own." To do that, she realized, women had to have equal property rights. Fired up, she organized an extensive petition campaign to secure married women the right to their own wages and equal guardianship of their children. For months, she and sixty women canvassed the state getting signatures. Her plan was to present the petitions to the New York State Legislature when it was in session in Albany in February 1854. In addition, she scheduled a woman's rights convention in Albany, on February 14 and 15. Determined to spur Elizabeth into action, Susan presented her plan to her and insisted that she give an address on the legal disabilities of women to both the convention and a joint session of the judiciary committees of the Legislature.

"I find there is no use saying 'no' to you," Elizabeth responded and asked Susan to find a sympathetic lawyer who would identify eight of the "most atrocious" laws affecting women. Elizabeth could, she told Susan, "generalize and philosophize by myself but I have not time to look up statistics . . . surrounded by my children, washing dishes, baking, sewing, baking."

"Because I Am a Woman"

Susan's friend Judge William Hay sent Elizabeth thirteen laws and added his agreement that she was admirably suited to write the address. Echoing Hay, Reverend William Ellery Channing, a reform-minded minister in Rochester, wrote to Elizabeth that no one could tell the "story of woman's wrongs as strongly, clearly, tersely, eloquently" as she could.

This speech, Elizabeth later wrote, was "a great event" in her life and she felt very "nervous." Susan suggested she go to Rochester and confer with Reverend Channing. That she did, while Susan stayed with her children. Channing enthusiastically endorsed her speech. Her father was another matter.

Judge Cady had read an announcement about Elizabeth's

upcoming speech in the newspaper. There are two versions of what happened next. More than forty years later in her autobiography, Elizabeth portrayed a positive, even tender, encounter that included "tears filling" Judge Cady's eyes as he listened to her speech. He offered some suggestions and said he could find her even "more cruel laws" to quote. Then they "kissed each other good-night." In the other version, Judge Cady strenuously objected, offered her bribes, and threatened to disinherit her.

The later version is perhaps more plausible because of a letter she wrote to Susan several months after her speech: "I passed through a terrible scourging when last at my father's. I cannot tell you how deeply the iron entered my soul. I never felt more keenly the degradation of my sex. To think that all in me of which my father would have felt proper pride had I been a man is deeply mortifying to him because I am a woman."

What was her mother's reaction? For that time period, there is no record. But she most likely supported Elizabeth based on her actions after her husband's death when she tended to her grandchildren, thus freeing Elizabeth to travel; donated money; welcomed reformers in her home; and signed a suffrage petition.

"Heads About the Size of an Apple"

Elizabeth gave a stirring speech. Proclaiming women as "daughters of the revolutionary heroes of '76," she demanded "a new code of laws." She described the "position of woman" from four perspectives: "woman as woman," "woman as wife," "woman as widow," and "woman as mother." She debunked the frequently cited argument that only "a few sour, disappointed old maids and childless women" demanded equal rights with a series of rhetorical questions, including "Think you that the woman who has worked hard all her days in helping her husband to accumulate a large property consents to the law that places this wholly at his disposal?"

Elizabeth's speech was generally well received. Susan had had fifty thousand copies of the speech printed in pamphlet form. Each legislator got a copy; the rest Susan sold to earn money to cover the printing cost. The press coverage ranged from favorable to hostile. Negative articles did not bother Elizabeth; she dismissed them as accounts from the pens of reporters whose heads "were about the size of an apple." As for a group of women who accused her of abandoning her children to give the speech, she calmly replied that hers were nearby in a hotel with their nurse. Where, she asked the women, were their children?

Despite Elizabeth's persuasive speech and petitions signed by thousands of people, the legislators refused to change laws that discriminated against married women. Doing that, most of them believed, would "unsex every female in the land" and overthrow the divinely ordained institution of marriage in which man was the head.

"It Is Not Wise"

For this great event, Susan had worn her bloomers. Elizabeth, however, had recently stopped wearing hers; instead she wore a black silk dress with a white lace collar and a diamond pin. She had loved wearing bloomers, a style she had copied from her cousin Libby, who is credited with being the first to wear them. "Like a captive set free from his ball and chain," she recalled, "I was always ready for a brisk walk through sleet and snow and rain, to climb a mountain, jump over a fence, work in the garden, and, in fact, for any necessary locomotion." But "the physical freedom," she later explained "did not compensate for the persistent persecution and petty annoyances suffered at every turn."

Gangs of boys jeered and threw stones at women wearing bloomers. Crowds of men accosted them. Friends and family members expressed disapproval and embarrassment. The press derided their appearance. After one of Elizabeth's speeches, she was described as "resembling a man in her dress, having on boots like a man, dickey like a man, vest like a man." Two years of that had exhausted her patience.

Susan had had it too, but she stubbornly refused to give in to public pressure. Finally, however, in early 1854, she heeded Elizabeth's admonition to "let down a dress and petticoat. The cup of ridicule is greater than you can bear. It is not wise, Susan, to use up so much energy that way."

"Brilliant Conversation at the Table"

After the New York State Legislature refused to heed their petitions, Elizabeth once again curtailed her involvement in the woman's rights movement. "My whole soul is in the work," she told Susan, "but my hands belong to my family." Henry continued to be away for months at a time conducting legal business, attending meetings for various causes, and immersing himself in the politics of the new Republican Party. He wrote many more letters to Elizabeth than she did to him, perhaps because he was not encumbered with managing a household of lively children.

In a letter addressed to "Margaret Livingston Stanton" (Maggie, who was four years old at the time), Henry wrote

My dear daughter

*I want your mother to write me a letter. I have
told her so several times; yet she does not write.
Now, my daughter, if she does not write to me
immediately, I want you to take a pen & sit down &
tell me all the news.... Tell your Mother that I
have seen a throng of handsome ladies, but I had
rather see her than the whole of them; but, I intend
to cut her acquaintance unless she writes me a
letter. Kiss the baby & the boys for me.*

Your affectionate father Henry B. Stanton

When Henry was home, he played with the children and
worked in the garden and orchard. In the evening, he insisted
on uninterrupted time to read the evening paper. Afterward,
they might all play games, one of Elizabeth's favorite activities.
"She always played to win," her children later recalled, "and was
sorely disappointed when she did not succeed."

The annual National Woman's Rights Convention was meeting in Philadelphia, Pennsylvania. Lucretia requested Elizabeth's
presence: "Cant thou take thy baby, & come to our Woman's
Convention? We shall need thee and all other <u>true</u> women."
No, she couldn't, Elizabeth replied. Susan, however, planned to
attend, and accepted Lucretia's invitation to stay with them:

*It will give us pleasure to have thy company at 338
Arch street, where we hope thou wilt make thy home.
We shall of course be crowded, but we expect thee
and shall prepare accordingly. We think such as
thyself, devoted to good causes, should not have to
seek a home.*

Twenty-four people stayed with the Motts. During meals, Lucretia sat Susan at her left hand; William Lloyd Garrison was at her right. Afterward, a little cedar tub filled with hot sudsy water was placed in front of Lucretia. She washed the silver, glass, and fine china. Susan dried them on "the whitest of towels, while the brilliant conversation at the table went on uninterrupted."

11

"WHERE ARE YOU?"

CHALLENGING TIMES
1854–1859

O N CHRISTMAS DAY, SUSAN EMBARKED on a mission to get support for the woman's rights petition. She planned to canvass fifty-four counties in New York. Wendell Phillips loaned her fifty dollars. Elizabeth continued to write letters and articles for newspapers, but as for doing more than that, she warned Susan, "As soon as you all begin to ask too much of me, I shall have a baby. Now be careful; do not provoke me to that step."

Susan's family helped her get ready to undertake her mission. During the coldest and snowiest winter in ten years, she planned to travel for five months, to small towns and villages where most people had never seen a woman speaker. There was so much to do: handbills advertising her meeting, along with a letter from her requesting it be displayed two weeks before her arrival, needed to be folded, addressed, and mailed to local sheriffs and postmasters. Sheaves of woman's rights literature and copies of the petitions had to be packed in her carpetbag. Then there were her clothes—a shawl, a bonnet, a simple black silk dress with a basque waist (a waistline that dipped to a V in the front), and shoes.

The diary and records she always meticulously kept included details of her adventures: "the day very cold, snowy, sleighing very poor . . . could not [get] a church, school house or academy [to] speak in—held meeting in a dining room of landlord." A newspaper reporter described her as having "pleasing rather than pretty features, decidedly expressive countenance, rich brown hair very effectively and not all elaborately arranged, neither too tall nor too short, too plump nor too thin."

After she spoke in Albany, a gentleman in her audience joined her for the stage ride to Lake George. A solicitous companion, he provided a heated plank on which she could warm her feet. After her meeting, he took her in his sleigh filled with robes and drawn by two spirited gray horses to his house to meet his sister and spend the day. For the next several days, he drove her to meetings and tended to her needs; then he proposed. She was not tempted by the well-cared-for life he offered her; instead it prompted her to "strongly continue in her chosen work."

"Struggle in Deep Water"

Although Elizabeth stayed close to home, she continued spreading the woman's rights message through her letters and articles. A prolific writer, she wrote for the women's papers, the *Lily* and the *Una*. Her articles regularly appeared in the national newspaper the *New York Tribune*. At first, she asked for Henry's opinion before submitting her pieces, but not for long. "Husbands are too critical," she wrote to Susan.

In March she wrote to Lucretia about her plan to write a book about the history of the woman's movement. "This is the right work for thee, dear Elizh.," Lucretia replied. "Do thyself justice. Remember the first Convention originated with thee." The book did not get written, at least, not then; it was too big a project, and Henry was pressuring her to give up her woman's rights work.

In a letter that she asked Susan to keep "strictly confidential," Elizabeth wished she "were as free" as Susan. Then she "would stump the State in a twinkling." But, she confessed, she could not because Henry objected to "all that is dearest" to her. He was "not willing that I should write even on the woman question. . . . Sometimes, Susan, I struggle in deep water." Ever optimistic, Elizabeth ended her letter, "However, a good time is coming and my future is always bright and beautiful. Good night."

In her letter to Elizabeth, Lucretia had noted the recent "rapid progress" of the woman's rights movement and the number of talented women leaders "already in the field." That number significantly decreased in 1855 when both Lucy Stone and Antoinette Brown got married. (Best friends in college, they married the Blackwell brothers. Lucy married Henry, but kept her own name, a scandalous act in those days. Antoinette married Samuel.) Susan felt "great regret." Of course, both Lucy and Antoinette reassured her that they would continue to work for woman's rights, but she had seen one effective leader after another get overwhelmed by the demands of marriage and then children. The prime example was her dear friend Elizabeth, who, once again, was pregnant.

"The Life Is a Very Good One"

Susan herself was struggling to keep up her pace. Her arduous speaking tour throughout New York had left her with back pain. She managed to attend two conventions: the annual teachers' convention and the annual state woman's rights convention. But no more; worried that the pain would eventually prevent her from continuing with her "life work," she entered the Worcester Hydropathic Institute, run by her cousin Dr. Seth Rogers, a supporter of woman's rights and a practitioner of the "water cure," a four-to-six-week regime of rest and outdoor exercise that included a limited diet, no alcohol or tobacco, and copious amounts of water used for washing, bathing, soaking, and drinking.

Gradually Susan improved, although she complained that her day was "so cut up with four baths, four dressings and undressings, four exercisings, one drive and three eatings," that she did not have time "to put two thoughts together." She did, however, manage a trip to Boston, the city where Elizabeth had been so stimulated. Susan was too. In a letter to her family, she described the sights: Mount Auburn Cemetery, the Bunker Hill Monument, and the library of sixteen thousand books belonging to Theodore Parker, the reform-minded minister Elizabeth had heard preach when she lived in Boston.

When Susan returned to Rochester, she took out a life insurance policy that required a medical certificate. On December 18, the doctor recorded this information about her at the age of thirty-five: "Height, 5 ft. 5 in.; figure, full; chest measure 38 in.; weight, 156 lbs.; complexion, fair; habits, healthy. . . . The life is a very good one."

"Do Get All on Fire"

Elizabeth gave birth to another white-flag baby, Harriot Eaton Stanton, known as Hattie, in 1856. She was, she wrote to Susan, "very happy, that the terrible ordeal is passed & that the result is another daughter." Hattie was a month old when Elizabeth vented her frustration in another letter to Susan: "Imagine me, day in and day out, watching, bathing, dressing, nursing and promenading the precious contents of the little crib. . . . I pace up and down these two chambers of mine like a caged lioness longing to bring nursing and housekeeping cares to a close." Susan could not wait for that day to come; she had urgent work for Elizabeth to do.

The next state teachers' convention was fast approaching, and Susan was unable to write the speech she had been asked to give. Writing to Elizabeth, she pleaded for help, "So for the love of me, & for the saving of the <u>reputation of womenhood,</u> I beg you with one baby on your knee & another at your feet & four boys whistling buzzing hullooing <u>Ma Ma</u> set your self about the work. . . . <u>don't</u> say <u>no</u>, nor <u>don't delay</u> it a moment, for I must have it done. . . . Now will <u>you load my gun</u>, leaving me to pull the trigger & let fly the powder & ball . . . do get all on fire."

"Come here," Elizabeth replied, "and I will do what I can." Together they juggled household and writing tasks and produced another bold speech that called for coeducation because girls and boys were equal in intelligence. It also castigated women teachers for passively accepting salaries below what men received.

At the convention, many of the women rejected the call for equal pay because that would be unfeminine. "What an infernal set of fools these school-marms must be!! Well, if in order to please men they wish to live on air, let them. The sooner the present generation of women die out the better. We have jackasses enough in the world now without such women propagating any more," Elizabeth wrote to Susan.

"To Do Battle Alone"

While Elizabeth was tending to her children, Susan accepted an offer from the American Anti-Slavery Society to be an agent for ten dollars a week, as long as she could continue her work for the woman's rights movement. She fretted that Lucy (who was pregnant) and Antoinette (who had had a baby and was pregnant again) had abandoned the movement and left "poor brainless me to do battle alone." Elizabeth counseled her, "You, too, must rest, Susan, let the world alone awhile."

That was impossible. The country was tearing itself apart over the issue of slavery. Congress had passed two bills that inflamed and divided public sentiments—the Fugitive Slave Act in 1850, which included steep penalties for anyone who helped a slave escape, and the Kansas-Nebraska Act in 1854, which opened up land to slavery where it had been prohibited by the Missouri Compromise of 1820. In 1857, the U.S. Supreme Court ruled in the Dred Scott case that slaves were property, not people, and that Congress did not have the right to prohibit slavery.

Susan hired white and black antislavery speakers; together they went on lecture tours. But she outlasted all of them as each one succumbed to the hardships: miserable weather, taxing transportation, hostile crowds, illness, and unpalatable food. "O, the crimes that are committed in the kitchens of this land!" she complained.

In March she went to Maine to speak on woman's rights for

the unprecedented fee of fifty dollars. Arriving at the snowy, slushy, muddy time of year, she spoke in Bangor and surrounding villages. "Many a woman, and man too," one newspaper reporter wrote, "went home that night with the germ of more active ideas in their heads."

"I Will Do Anything to Help You"

Before Susan's next annual appearance at the state teachers' convention, she and Elizabeth wrote resolutions that denounced the exclusion of "colored youth from our public schools," protested the firing of a woman teacher when it "was discovered that colored blood coursed in her veins," and denounced the fact that "teachers and pupils of the colored schools of New York City were denied access to free concerts."

Susan first introduced these resolutions, then she threw "another bomb" and put forth this demand: "That it is the duty of all our schools, colleges and universities to open their doors to woman and to give her equal and identical educational advantages side by side with her brother man."

That would be "a vast social evil," declared Charles Davies, president of the state teachers' association. The resolutions were soundly defeated.

Elizabeth was delighted by Susan's performance. "I did indeed see by the papers that you had once more stirred that pool of intellectual stagnation, the educational convention. . . . I glory in your perseverance," she wrote to her. "Oh! Susan, I will do anything to help you on. . . . You and I have a prospect of a good long life. We shall not be in our prime before fifty, & after that we shall be good for twenty years at least."

Earlier that year she had promised Susan that "in two or

three years I shall be able to have some hours of each day to myself. My two older boys will then be in college or business and my three younger children will be in school." (Susan undoubtedly noticed when she read this that Elizabeth forgot to count her baby Hattie.)

"I Do Long to Be with You"

Susan needed Elizabeth's reassurance. She was discouraged and disheartened by the struggle to recruit people to speak at the next annual national woman's rights convention. "How I do long to be with you this very minute," she wrote to Elizabeth, "to have one look into your very soul, & one sound of your soul stirring voice. . . . I have very weak moments. . . . [H]ow my soul longs to see [you] in the great Battlefield. . . . If you come not to the rescue, who shall?"

Elizabeth had announced that Hattie was her last baby, but, at the age of forty-two, she was once again pregnant. Susan expressed her feelings in a letter to Antoinette, "[A]h me!!! alas!! alas!!!! Mrs. Stanton!! . . . For a moment's pleasure to herself or her husband, she should thus increase the load of cares under which she already groans."

Her last red-flag baby, Robert Livingston Stanton, known as Bob, was born in 1859. "You need expect nothing from me for some time," she wrote to Susan. "I have no vitality of body or soul. . . . You have no idea how weak I am & I have to keep my mind in the most quiet state in order to sleep." Undoubtedly unwilling to lose her connection with Susan, she wrote, "I am always glad to hear from you & hope to see you."

Elizabeth soon bounced back. "I am full of fresh thoughts and courage and feel all enthusiasm about our work," she wrote to Susan. "I hope to grind out half a dozen good tracts during the summer. . . . The children are all well. The house is cleaned. The summer's sewing all done and I see nothing now to trouble me much if all keep well." Six weeks later, however, her servants quit, her older boys came home from school, and Susan needed the tracts. Although Elizabeth said she was no longer in a "situation to think or write," she agreed to exert herself. "When you come I shall try," she wrote to Susan, to "grind out what you say must be done. I expect to get my inspiration facts & thoughts from you."

"I Have Looked for You"

In the fall of 1859, shock waves reverberated throughout the country with the news of John Brown's bloody guerrilla raid on the federal armory in Harpers Ferry, Virginia. Brown's plan to incite a general slave uprising failed, but his attempt convinced Southerners that abolitionists would stop at nothing to end slavery, an institution that they believed was protected under the Constitution and that benefited Northern businesses and consumers. Many Northerners, including Elizabeth and Susan, heralded John Brown, who was captured, tried, and executed, as a martyr. Public opinion was aflame with fiery rhetoric; the country was on the cusp of dissolution and civil war.

Gerrit Smith was one of the Secret Six who had funded Brown's raid. Distraught over John Brown's fate and the fact that he might face legal charges, Gerrit committed himself to an insane asylum. Within weeks of these calamitous events, Elizabeth's father died, compounding the emotional turmoil she already felt. Christmas was approaching, and, as usual, Henry would be away. But Susan had promised to come. On December 23, Elizabeth wrote to her: "Where are you? Since a week ago last Monday, I have looked for you every day . . . but lo!

you did not come. . . . The death of my father, the worse than death of my dear Cousin Gerrit, the martyrdom of . . . John Brown—all this conspires to make me regret more than ever my dwarfed womanhood. In times like these, everyone should do the work of a full-grown man."

Susan arrived in time for Christmas, and, as always, she fired up Elizabeth to continue to fight for the freedom she coveted.

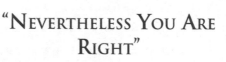

12

"Nevertheless You Are Right"

CONTROVERSY
1860

S USAN WAS IN ALBANY LOBBYING the legislators when the chairman of the judiciary committee, Anson Bingham, told her that "Mrs. Stanton must come" because it appeared that legislators might approve the bill extending woman's rights that had been defeated in 1854. Afraid to leave and relax her constant lobbying efforts, Susan asked Martha Wright to go to Seneca Falls and persuade Elizabeth to write a speech. The women of New York, Susan wrote, depend "upon her bending all her powers to move the hearts of our law-givers at this time."

Evoking the name of the famous French general, Elizabeth replied, "If Napoleon says cross the Alps, they are crossed." However, she insisted that Susan come to Seneca Falls to help her. "In thought and sympathy we were one," Elizabeth later recalled, "and in the division of labor we exactly complemented each other. . . . She supplied the facts and statistics, I the philosophy and rhetoric." Their method, Susan later told her biographer, was to "sit up far into the night arranging material and planning their work."

The next day, Elizabeth would "seek the quietest spot in the house and begin writing." Susan "would give the children their breakfast, start the older ones to school, make the dessert for dinner and trundle the babies up and down the walk, rushing in occasionally to help the writer out of a vortex."

By the time Elizabeth arrived in Albany, the Married Women's Property Act of 1860 had passed. A momentous achievement, due to the relentless efforts of Susan and other activists, the bill gave a married woman in New York the right to own property, collect her own wages, engage in her own business, enter into contracts, and sue and be sued. She would have the same "powers, rights and duties in regard" to her children as her husband had; upon the death of her husband she would inherit the same property rights that he would have inherited upon her death. Elizabeth devoted her speech before a joint session of the judiciary committees to demanding the "sacred right" of woman suffrage.

"He Had No More Right to Whine"

The Tenth National Woman's Rights Convention convened in May at Cooper Institute in New York City. On the first day, Susan was lauded for her arduous petition campaigns and lobbying efforts that culminated in the recent passage of legislation for married woman's rights—except for the man who yelled out, "She'd a great deal better have been home taking care of her husband and children." The next day Elizabeth "set the convention on fire" with a speech in support of resolutions in favor of liberalizing divorce laws to allow women to divorce husbands who were violent or habitually drunk, or who abandoned them.

Wendell Phillips, a longtime friend and ally, was outraged.

The issue of divorce, he said, had nothing to do with woman's rights because the laws of divorce did not rest unequally upon women. He made a motion not only to defeat Elizabeth's resolutions but also to expunge any mention of them from the written record of the convention proceedings. Stunned by Wendell's disapproval, Elizabeth later wrote that her "face was scarlet" and she "trembled with mingled feelings of doubt and fear." Noting her distress, the Reverend Samuel Longfellow (brother of the famous poet Henry Wadsworth Longfellow), who was sitting beside her, leaned over and whispered in her ear, "Nevertheless you are right, and the convention will sustain you."

Wendell's motion was defeated, but the controversy over liberalizing divorce laws raged on in the press and from the pulpit. Elizabeth and Susan stood their ground. Elizabeth wrote letters to hostile newspaper editors. Susan dealt with Reverend A. D. Mayo, an abolitionist, who told her, "You are not married, you have no business to be discussing marriage."

"Well, Mr. Mayo," she replied, "you are not a slave, suppose you quit lecturing on slavery."

During the controversy, a few longtime allies supported Elizabeth and Susan. Lucretia wrote that she had the "fullest confidence" in their "united judgment." In response to Amy Post's encouragement, Elizabeth replied that she was glad she had not anticipated Wendell's disapproval because, she wrote, "The desire to please those we admire and respect often cripples conscience."

When Elizabeth heard that Wendell was continuing to criticize her for bringing up the issue of divorce, she wrote to Susan, "He has no more right to whine than I would have if I had been defeated. The fact is he over-rated his personal power, and was mortified to find it so little." Susan attributed his position to the fact that "he is a man and can not put himself in the position of a wife; can not feel what she does under the present marriage code."

Elizabeth agreed. "The men know we have struck a blow at their greatest stronghold."

The divorce controversy prompted a group of women to hold another convention with a ban on controversial topics, such as divorce. How, Elizabeth wondered in an article she wrote about that convention, "can an earnest soul, in search of truth, set bounds to its investigation?"

The convention was a dud, and the energy for follow-up gatherings fizzled out. That did not surprise Susan, who wrote, "Cautious, careful people, always casting about to preserve their reputation and social standing, never can bring about a reform. Those who are really in earnest must be willing to be anything or nothing in the world's estimation, and publicly and privately, in season and out, avow their sympathy with despised and persecuted ideas and their advocates, and bear the consequences."

For now, the disagreement did not rupture the relationship between the factions. Wendell sent money from the Hovey Fund (money left by Charles Hovey, a Boston businessman, to promote antislavery and other causes) that Susan requested to publish the proceedings of the convention, including Elizabeth's speech and resolutions. Elizabeth invited him to visit during the winter. William Lloyd Garrison, who had sided with Wendell, agreed to publish Elizabeth's speech in his abolitionist newspaper the *Liberator*.

The tensions resurfaced in December when Susan came to the aid of a desperate woman whose face was shrouded by layers of veils.

"Legally You Are Wrong, but Morally You Are Right"

The woman was Phoebe Harris Phelps, the author of several children's books and the former principal of a girls' academy in Albany. Now, with her thirteen-year-old daughter, she was in hiding from her brother, Ira Harris, and her husband, Charles Abner Phelps, both very prominent men. Her troubles had started when she confronted her husband, a member of the Massachusetts legislature, about an affair he was having with another woman. Infuriated, he threw her down a flight of stairs. He continued to abuse her and finally had her committed to an insane asylum, an easy and all too common thing for husbands to do in those days. Finally after a year and a half, her brother, a member of the U.S. Senate and a lawyer, got her released and brought her to his house.

After Phoebe pleaded to see her children, her husband allowed her son to visit her for a few weeks, then her daughter. She asked to extend her time with her daughter, but her husband refused. Her brother would not intervene; instead he said, "The child belongs by law to the father and it is your place to submit. If you make any more trouble about it we'll send you back to the asylum." With that threat, she fled with her daughter.

Finding refuge with a Quaker family in Albany, Phoebe and her daughter stayed there until her husband found out where they were. That is when she sought out Susan, who was staying with her friend and coworker Lydia Mott. They discreetly checked with people who confirmed the woman's story, but added that they were too afraid of the brother and husband to get involved. Unafraid of anyone, Susan and Lydia decided that Susan should find a hiding place for the woman and her daughter in New York City. Disguised as an old woman wearing a tattered shawl and green goggles with her shabbily dressed daughter, Phoebe boarded the train on Christmas afternoon. Susan boarded shortly after they did, only to find Phoebe traumatized from having seen her brother, who was sending his son back to boarding school. Fortunately her disguise fooled her brother.

They were turned away from one hotel after another in New York City because they were unaccompanied by a man. After hours of trudging through slush and snow, Susan told a hotel clerk that they would spend the night in the lobby. He threatened to call the police. She called his bluff and said, "Very well, we will sit here till they come and take us to the station." With that, the clerk rented them an unheated room. The next day, after an exhausting search, Susan found someone who would shelter the mother and her child.

Satisfied that she had done all she could, Susan returned to Albany. The woman's family soon figured out Susan's role in the affair and began to badger her about revealing the hiding place. They publicly said that she had "abducted a man's child and must surrender it." They threatened to have her arrested. Worried that her involvement would taint the antislavery cause, Wendell sent her a telegraph with the message "Let us urge you at once to advise and insist upon this woman's returning to her relatives."

At an antislavery convention, William Lloyd Garrison confronted Susan. "Don't you know the law of Massachusetts gives the father the entire guardianship and control of the children?"

"Yes, I know it," she replied, "and does not the law of the United States give the slaveholder the ownership of the slave? And don't you break it every time you help a slave to Canada?"

"Yes, I do."

"Well, the law which gives the father the sole ownership of the children is just as wicked and I'll break it just as quickly. You would die before you would deliver a slave to his master, and I will die before I give up that child to its father."

Susan felt betrayed by "the two men whom I adore and reverence." Her father was the only important man in her life who stood by her. "My child," he wrote, "I think you have done absolutely right, but don't put a word on paper or make a statement to any one that you are not prepared to face in court. Legally you are wrong, but morally you are right, and I will stand by you."

Phoebe and her daughter were safe for a year. Then, on a Sunday morning, as the girl walked to church, her husband's men abducted her. The girl and her mother never saw each other again.

"I Think You Risk Your Lives"

Abolitionists were worried about the newly elected president of the United States, Abraham Lincoln. Instead of embracing their single-minded commitment to immediate emancipation as the way to end slavery, Lincoln articulated a mix of positions: He opposed the extension of slavery, but he promised to enforce the odious Fugitive Slave Act that allowed for the return of escaped slaves; he said he believed that slavery was wrong, but he also said that the government should not interfere with people who thought slavery was right.

Slaveholders were not reassured by what Lincoln said. To them, his election and the ascendance of the Republican Party, a party formed in 1854 to oppose the expansion of slavery, left them no choice but to break away from the United States. In January 1861, four slaveholding states seceded: South Carolina,

Mississippi, Florida, and Alabama. Georgia, Louisiana, and Texas joined them on February 1.

Worried that Lincoln might make compromises to lure the slaveholding states back, abolitionists launched a campaign in January under the slogan "No Compromise with Slaveholders! Immediate and Unconditional Emancipation!" Susan put together a team of lecturers to tour New York that included Samuel J. May, a staunch abolitionist and woman's rights advocate, and Elizabeth, who finally felt free to go. Her older children were away at school. Amelia Willard, her live-in housekeeper, was more than capable of running the house and caring for the younger children. Henry was in Washington, DC, covering the tumultuous events as a newspaper correspondent.

Hissing, hooting, yelling, bellowing mobs of boys and men met them at every stop from Buffalo across the state to Albany. In Syracuse, ruffians threw rotten eggs, broke benches, and brandished knives and pistols. Obscene effigies of Susan and Samuel were dragged through the street and burned in the public square. Mayors and police refused to protect them. Alarmed by the newspaper reports, Henry wrote to Elizabeth, "I think you risk your lives. . . . The mobocrats would as soon kill you as not."

Undeterred, Elizabeth shifted her emphasis in her speeches from abolition to the right of free speech. In Albany, they finally met a mayor who was, in Elizabeth's words, "a man of courage and conscience, who said the right of free speech should never be trodden under foot." To protect that right, he sat on the platform with a revolver across his knee and dispatched police officers throughout the audience with orders to arrest any troublemakers.

In the spring of 1861, Wendell, perhaps in a gesture of reconciliation, offered to use the Hovey Fund to send Elizabeth on a three-month speaking tour to Europe. She longed to go; the trip would give her "new life and inspiration." Susan offered to stay with the children, and Elizabeth replied that she would leave them with her "without the least hesitation." But in the end she refused; war was imminent. Her older boys—Neil, age nineteen; Kit, age seventeen; and Gat, age sixteen—were drilling with a military regiment in Seneca Falls. From his vantage point as a reporter in Washington, Henry was writing letters describing the rising war fever.

Elizabeth embraced the idea of a war to end slavery. She also agreed to a request from Wendell and other abolitionists to suspend the campaign for woman's rights and focus on the war effort. Not Susan. She held fast to her principles as a pacifist. She also insisted that they must not suspend the fight for woman's rights. But when Elizabeth and the other speakers pulled out of the Eleventh National Woman's Rights Convention, Susan was forced to cancel the event. "I have not yet seen one good reason for the abandonment of all our meetings," she exclaimed in a letter to Martha Wright, "and am . . . more and more ashamed and sad."

13

"PUT ON YOUR ARMOR AND GO FORTH!"

WOMEN RALLY
1861–1866

ELIZABETH AND SUSAN WERE AT LOGGERHEADS. Each one argued for her point of view, neither one bending. Elizabeth believed that if women worked for the war effort, they would be rewarded with suffrage. Susan knew better, perhaps because she had spent ten years in the trenches trudging door to door with petitions, lecturing in remote places to people who came to gawk at a woman who dared to speak in public, struggling to raise money to rent halls, print tracts, and provide for her travel, meager food, and primitive lodging.

Whatever differences Elizabeth and Susan had about motives, goals, strategies, or tactics, they resolved them in private. "We have indulged freely in criticism of each other when alone, and hotly contended whenever we have differed," Elizabeth later recalled. "To the world we always seem to agree and uniformly reflect each other. Like husband and wife, each has the feeling that we must have no differences in public."

"I Long for Action"

The Civil War began in April 1861. Elizabeth was in Seneca Falls tending to her children with the help of Amelia. Neil, Kit, and Gat continued to drill. Susan had returned to the farm in Rochester. While she was there to tend the farm and her invalid mother, her father left to visit his sons who lived in Kansas. Susan's diary reveals both the hard work she had undertaken and her restlessness with her life: "Tried to interest myself in a sewing society; but little intelligence among them. . . . The teachers' convention was small and dull. . . . Washed every window in the house today. Quilted all day . . . stained and varnished the library bookcase today. . . . The last load of hay is in the barn. . . . Fitted out a fugitive slave for Canada with the help of Harriet Tubman. . . . To forever blot out slavery is the only possible compensation for this merciless war."

Susan and Elizabeth were avid readers of newspapers, magazines, tracts, nonfiction books, poetry, and novels. During this time, Susan noted in her diary that she was reading the forty-four love sonnets, *Sonnets from the Portuguese,* by Elizabeth Barrett Browning, a renowned poet then and now. She also read *Adam Bede,* the first novel by the acclaimed writer George Eliot (the pen name of Mary Ann Evans). Hetty Sorrel, a beautiful young woman; Captain Arthur Donnithorne, a dashing squire; and Adam Bede, a handsome carpenter, are the love triangle at the heart of the story. The plot involves an out-of-wedlock pregnancy, infanticide, a murder trial, a last-minute reprieve, and ends with the marriage of Adam and Dinah Morris, Hetty's cousin and a Methodist lay preacher.

"I finished *Adam Bede* yesterday noon," Susan wrote to Elizabeth. "I can not throw off the palsied oppression of its finale to poor, poor Hetty—and Arthur almost equally commands my sympathy. . . . It will not do for me to read romances; they are too real to shake off."

"You speak of the effect of *Adam Bede* on you," Elizabeth replied. "It moved me deeply. . . . O, Susan, are you ever coming to visit me again? It would be like a new life to spend a day with you. How I shudder when I think of our awful experience with those mobs last winter, and yet even now I long for action."

"I Am Sick at Heart"

In January 1862, Susan attended a state antislavery convention in Albany, but she was not able to generate any support for a woman's rights convention. Worried that she was settling into the routine of her life on the farm and losing her passion for "public work," Susan left Rochester to give antislavery lectures.

While Susan was traveling, Elizabeth was getting ready to move to New York City. Henry had a new job as a deputy collector for the Custom House Office. In April, Susan arrived at Seneca Falls to help with the packing. Then she went on ahead with four of the boys and took care of them until the rest of the family arrived. When Elizabeth hired a private teacher to educate her children at home, Susan castigated her: "Any and every private education is a blunder, it seems to me." Yes, she agreed that public schools had "short-comings," but they were outweighed by the benefit of learning "side by side with the very multitude with whom they must mingle as soon as school days are over."

On April 10, 1862, the New York legislature repealed parts of the bill that had passed in 1860, including giving mothers the same rights as fathers to make decisions regarding their children. Susan felt that the legislators had been emboldened by the cessation of the campaign for woman's rights. "While the old guard sleep, the young 'devils' are wide-awake, and we deserve to suffer for our confidence in 'man's sense of Justice,'" she wrote to Lydia Mott. "I am sick at heart."

That summer Susan attended her last state teachers' convention, satisfied at what she had accomplished for women teachers. In the fall, she continued to give antislavery speeches on the topic "Emancipation: The Duty of the Government." Then, on November 25, 1862, she suffered the worst blow of her life—the unexpected death of her beloved and supportive father. For a time, Susan felt "stunned and helpless," but fueled by the belief that her father would want her to carry on, "her old strength came slowly back."

"A War of Ideas"

The war wore on. For two years, President Lincoln had refused to oppose slavery because he did not want to antagonize the border states that remained in the Union—Kentucky, Missouri, Maryland, and Delaware—where slavery was legal. The war was being fought, he said, to restore the seceding states to the Union. In a Fourth of July speech, Susan had denounced Lincoln. The war, she said, was "not simply a question of national existence, but of the value of man."

Finally, on January 1, 1863, President Lincoln issued the Emancipation Proclamation, which freed the slaves in all the Southern states fighting against the Union. He did not free slaves in border states or in Southern states under Union control on the grounds that these areas were not waging war. Slaves themselves had pressured Lincoln to issue the Emancipation Proclamation by "self-emancipating" themselves in large numbers and fleeing to Union forces. Under the proclamation, the freed slaves could join the

Union army, and hundreds of thousands did. Although abolitionists welcomed the Emancipation Proclamation, they knew that it
did not apply after the war ended and that slavery would still be
protected by the Constitution. They were not even confident
that the Union would win the war. The army had suffered a series of setbacks. Casualty rates were appallingly high. An increasingly vocal group of Northern politicians were promoting a
peace movement that would allow slavery. They called themselves Peace Democrats; abolitionists labeled them Copperheads,
likening them to the venomous copperhead snake. Confusion
over the purpose of the war was undermining support for it
among civilians and soldiers, who were deserting at the rate of
two hundred men a day.

In mid-January, Susan received a letter from Henry Stanton,
who was still in Washington, DC, working as a journalist. "The
country is rapidly going to destruction," he wrote. If the Union
lost, slavery would endure. "Here then is work for you," he wrote.
"Susan, put on your armor and go forth!"

By February, Susan had moved into Elizabeth's home in
New York City. Together they formed a new organization—the
Women's Loyal National League. Women were already raising
money, knitting socks, sending foodstuff, tending to wounded,
sick and dying soldiers, working on farms and in factories, spying
on the enemy, and disguising themselves as men and fighting on
the battlefield. Now Elizabeth and Susan planned to enlist women
in a "war of ideas"—emancipation for all slaves.

They sent out a "Call for a Meeting of the Loyal Women
of the Nation" to be held in New York City. Women from all
over the North attended. Elizabeth spoke. The Hutchinson family sang rousing freedom songs. Susan boldly stated, "Shame on
us if we do not make it a war to establish the Negro in freedom."

A series of resolutions were introduced, including one in favor of extending "civil and political rights to all citizens of African descent and all women." Including "all women" was going too far, some participants angrily objected. Not so, Susan pointed out. "It is the simple assertion of the great fundamental truth of democracy that was proclaimed by our Revolutionary fathers." The resolutions passed, and the women pledged to "give support to the government in so far as it makes a war for freedom."

From an office at the Cooper Institute, Susan spearheaded a massive campaign to collect millions of signatures on petitions for a law abolishing slavery. Scores of volunteers were exhorted to "go to the rich, the poor, the high, the low, the soldier, the civilian, the white, the black—gather up the names of all who hate slavery, all who love liberty, and would have it the law of the land, and lay them at the feet of Congress."

They worked throughout a miserably hot and humid summer. As the petitions were returned, Elizabeth enlisted her three younger sons to roll up each one and mark the number of signatures on the outside. Susan ran the day-to-day operation, which included raising money to pay rent, printing costs, postage, and other expenses. Her salary was a meager twelve dollars a week. She saved money by staying at Elizabeth's at a reduced rate. Every day for lunch she spent thirteen cents at a restaurant for a dish of strawberries with two tea-rusks (a hard, dry biscuit) and a glass of milk.

"Terrible Times"

On July 13, 1863, mayhem broke out in New York City as violent mobs protested a new draft law that created a lottery to select male citizens for military duty. Black men were exempt because they were not citizens. Wealthy white men could avoid serving by paying the government three hundred dollars or by hiring a substitute. The law infuriated white workers in New York City, many of whom were proslavery because they feared competition for jobs from an influx of freed slaves. The rampage lasted for a week. Murderous rioters attacked black people, threatened abolitionists, and burned down buildings, including the Colored Orphan Asylum, one block from Elizabeth's house.

Elizabeth's son Neil was standing outside her house when the ruffians stampeded down the street. They seized him, while shouting, "Here's one of those three-hundred-dollar fellows!" Recounting the incident in a letter to her cousin Nancy Smith, Elizabeth described how Neil, quick-witted, steered the leaders to a saloon where he treated them to drinks and joined them in giving three cheers for "Jeff Davis," the president of the Confederacy.

"Thus," Elizabeth wrote, "he undoubtedly saved his life by deception, though it would have been far nobler to have died in defiance of the tyranny of mob law. . . . You may imagine what I suffered in seeing him dragged off." Taking her other children and servant to the top floor, she opened the skylight and left them with instructions in case of an attack to run out on the roof into a neighboring house. Then she "prepared a speech, determined, if necessary, to go down at once, open the door and make an appeal to them as Americans and citizens of the republic."

When a squad of police and two companies of soldiers arrived, Elizabeth gathered up her children and servants and fled to the safety of her mother's home in Johnstown. As for Susan, she was on her way to work when she discovered that the mob had shut down all the means of transportation. Making her way by ferry across the East River, she sought refuge at her cousin's house in Flushing, Queens, only to discover that there was trouble there too. "These are terrible times," she wrote home. "We all arose and dressed in the middle of the night, but it was finally gotten under control."

"We Will Have a Room Ready for You"

Susan and Elizabeth soon returned to work circulating petitions. The first batch was presented to Congress in February 1864. Two free black men carried the large bundle of rolled-up petitions into the Senate, where Senator Charles Sumner presented them to his colleagues. "These petitions are signed by 100,000 men and women, who . . . ask nothing less than universal emancipation," he said. Repeatedly he requested additional petitions with signatures to show his colleagues that there was enormous public support for passage of the amendment abolishing slavery. By August 1864, the league had sent petitions with over three hundred thousand signatures, two-thirds of them from women. It was the first grassroots campaign in America on behalf of a constitutional amendment.

The Civil War ended in April 1865 with a Union victory. That same year the Thirteenth Amendment, which abolished slavery, was added to the Constitution. The Women's Loyal National League was widely praised for its contributions. Although satisfied with her efforts, Susan still believed it had been a disastrous mistake to suspend the campaign for woman's rights during the long war. Elizabeth still believed that women would be rewarded for their work and granted suffrage.

With the work of the Loyal League finished, Susan accepted her brother Daniel's invitation to visit him and his new wife,

Anna, in Leavenworth, Kansas. During Susan's absence, Elizabeth moved her family into a new house in New York City. "We will have a room ready for you," she wrote to Susan. "I long to put my arms about you once more and hear you scold me for all my sins and shortcomings. . . . Oh, Susan, you are very dear to me. I should miss you more than any other living being on this earth. You are entwined with much of my happy and eventful past, and all my future plans are based on you as coadjutor. Yes, our work is one, we are one in aim and sympathy, and should be together. Come home."

Susan was not inclined to leave Kansas. The change had refreshed her, although she worried about being seduced by the pleasures of long carriage rides in the prairies with Anna. She did, however, miss Elizabeth. "How I wish you were here & free with me to travel & see & be seen," she wrote to her.

"Woman's Cause Is in Deep Water"

The post–Civil War period, known as Reconstruction, was tumultuous. The assassination of President Lincoln five days after the Union victory left a tragic vacuum of political leadership. Congress was controlled by the Republican Party, which was controlled by former abolitionists known as Radical Republicans. Determined to stay in power, the Radical Republicans wanted to secure the votes of former male slaves by enfranchising them. They did not, however, intend to fight for woman suffrage. That issue, they said, was too controversial. It would split the Republican Party and jeopardize the chance of winning black male suffrage. The question was how to enfranchise black men without opening the door to black or white women.

The answer lay in the wording of the proposed Fourteenth Amendment to the Constitution, which was intended to make freed slaves citizens. The first section established that anyone "born or naturalized in the United States" is a citizen. The second section defined a citizen as "male," thus for the first time interjecting gender into the Constitution. When Elizabeth heard about the amendment, she was outraged. "If that word 'male' be inserted as now proposed . . . it will take us a century at least to get it out again," she wrote to Gerrit Smith. "Oh! my cousin! Heal my bleeding heart with one trumpet note of manly indignation."

He refused. As did Wendell Phillips, the newly elected president of the American Anti-Slavery Society (AASS), who declared it was now "the Negro's hour," a phrase he coined for the agenda of first enfranchising black men. In a letter to Elizabeth, he wrote, "I think such a mixture would lose for the Negro far more than we should gain for the woman."

"My question is this," she fired back. "Do you believe the African race is composed entirely of males?"

In a letter to Susan, she wrote, "Woman's cause is in deep water. . . . Come back and help. . . . I seem to stand alone."

After eight months in Kansas, Susan returned and moved into a room in Elizabeth's house. Henry was there now too, plus all seven children, who ranged in age from twenty-three to six, and Amelia Willard. Henry practiced law. Neil helped him. Kit and Gat attended Columbia University Law School; Theo attended the College of New York City; Maggie and Hattie went to a boarding school; and Bob attended a public school. Elizabeth's sister Tryphena and her husband, Edward Bayard, lived nearby. Her sister Harriet, who was a widow, lived with them. The youngest sister, Catharine, lived on Long Island but frequently stayed at Tryphena's house.

Stout and rotund, Elizabeth was fifty years old. Her hair was now an eye-catching brilliant white color that she carefully arranged in a crown of curls. Tall and lean, Susan was a few months shy of forty-six years old. Her straight dark-brown hair was parted in the middle, sides swept over her ears, and gathered in a bun on the back of her head. Together the seasoned warriors revived the fight for woman suffrage.

To their old friends and allies, Elizabeth wrote letters and articles. Susan traveled to their homes. They started a petition campaign for a woman suffrage amendment to the Constitution. When petitions with ten thousand signatures were presented to Congress, a senator warned his colleagues that Elizabeth and Susan "have their banner flung out to the winds. They are after you; and their cry is for justice."

"The Gate Is Shut"

On May 10, 1866, Susan and Elizabeth convened the Eleventh National Woman's Rights Convention in New York City, the first woman's rights convention to be held after the Civil War. A resolution was passed to create a new organization—the American Equal Rights Association (AERA)—to demand universal suffrage. "We can no longer   work in two separate movements," Susan declared, "to get the ballot for the two disfranchised classes—the negro and woman—since to do so must be at double cost of time, energy and money." Robert Purvis, who was of mixed race and had helped many slaves escape during the 1850s, supported universal suffrage. He said, according to Susan, that he and his son should not be enfranchised before his daughter because she "bore the double disability of sex and color." Although Wendell gave an eloquent speech at the convention, Elizabeth and Susan noted how he adroitly skirted the issue of woman suffrage.

Before long it became clear that other friends and allies were aligning themselves with the effort to first enfranchise black men. Elizabeth's letters to the *National Anti-Slavery Standard*, the official paper of the AASS, were no longer being published. Susan was informed that she would now have to pay "full advertising rates" to publish notices of woman's rights meetings. "The gate is shut, wholly," she said.

Undeterred, Susan and Elizabeth persevered. They wrote articles and letters, distributed tracts, organized meetings, and circulated petitions asking Congress to "extend the right of suffrage to woman." In response to a woman who refused to sign a petition, Elizabeth replied that her action "would have been a wet blanket to Susan and me were we not sure that we are right. . . . When your granddaughters hear that . . . you made no protest, they will blush for their ancestry."

Lucretia and James Mott initially refused to sign the petition because they felt it was "emphatically the negro's hour." Elizabeth changed their minds by persuasively putting forth her reasons—Congress was still debating the Fourteenth Amendment, the New York State Constitution was going to be revised, and the "negro's hour was decidedly the fitting time for woman to slip in." Explaining their change of mind in a letter to Wendell, Lucretia asked him to support woman suffrage in this "perilous hour."

He refused.

"It Was a Blunder"

In August 1866, Elizabeth made a bold decision. She put herself on the ballot as a candidate to represent the Eighth Congressional District in New York City; the Constitution, she said, did not prevent women from being elected to an office.

Running as an independent, she proclaimed, "I would gladly have a voice and vote in . . . Congress to demand universal suffrage. . . . On no principle of justice or safety can the women of the nation be ignored."

In October, her cousin Libby invited her to Peterboro, New York, for a visit. Elizabeth reluctantly refused because, she pointed out, in addition to campaigning, she "must buy butter and meat, hear youngsters spell and multiply . . . Then comes Susan, with the nation on her soul, asking for speeches, resolutions, calls, attendance at conventions. So you now see why I cannot accept your invitation."

Twenty-four people cast their vote for Elizabeth in the November election. Having proven her point that even though women were denied the right to vote, they could still run for a political office, her only regret was that she had not gotten photographs of her "two dozen unknown friends."

By the end of 1866, Congress had passed the Fourteenth Amendment, in which the word *male* appears three times. (Two years later, it was ratified by the states and added to the Constitution.) Clearly disabused of her belief that women would be rewarded for focusing on the war effort, Elizabeth conceded that it had been a mistake to suspend the fight for woman's rights during the Civil War.

"I was convinced at the time that it was the true policy," she reflected in her autobiography, "I am now equally sure it was a blunder."

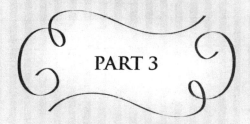

PART 3

14

"KEEP THE THING STIRRING"

TWO CAMPAIGNS
1867

Eʟɪᴢᴀʙᴇᴛʜ ᴀɴᴅ Sᴜsᴀɴ ᴛʜʀᴇᴡ ᴛʜᴇᴍsᴇʟᴠᴇs into two state battles for woman suffrage in 1867; both fights were over whether or not to take the words *white* and *male* as qualification for voting out of the state constitution. In New York the issue was before a constitutional convention, which would issue a report in June. In Kansas the voters would decide in a referendum in November.

Elizabeth fired the first salvo in January when she argued before a committee of New York State legislators that women should be appointed delegates to the constitutional convention. Although she reported that Susan approved of her speech, the committee appointed only men. Undaunted, she and Susan and their band of coworkers resolutely lobbied committee members, circulated petitions, and held meetings to rally public support.

In the spring, a request arrived from Samuel Wood, a Kansas state senator, urging Susan to send her strongest speakers to canvass the state in support of the woman suffrage referendum. Unwilling to remove either herself or Elizabeth from the New York campaign, Susan asked Lucy Stone, who had returned to the fight after a twelve-year hiatus to tend to her family, and her husband, Henry Blackwell, to go.

"There Is a Great Stir"

In May, Elizabeth and Susan attended the American Equal Rights Association meeting in New York City. Sojourner Truth, who was Elizabeth's house guest, spoke. Once a slave named Isabella Baumfree, she had renamed herself and become an outspoken abolitionist and woman's rights advocate. "There is a great stir about colored men getting their rights, but not a word about the colored women theirs, you see the colored men will be masters over the women," Sojourner proclaimed. "I suppose I am about the only colored woman that goes about to speak for the rights of colored women. I want to keep the thing stirring, now that the ice is cracked."

A resolution for universal suffrage was unanimously passed that declared "Women and colored men are loyal, liberty-loving citizens, and we can not believe that sex or complexion should be any grounds for civil or political degradation." From Kansas, Sam Wood sent a telegram with a message that heartened the audience: "With the help of God and Lucy Stone, we shall carry Kansas!"

Lucy, however, was not as confident, as she sensed the lack of support for woman suffrage from Republicans, the dominant political party in Kansas. She was also alarmed by the lack of support in the widely read, highly influential newspaper, the *New York Tribune*, edited by Horace Greeley, a longtime friend and ally. "I could not sleep the other night, just thinking about it," she wrote to Susan.

Lucy and Henry left Kansas after two months; their coworker Olympia Brown and the popular Hutchinson Family Singers went in their stead. Upon her return, Lucy went to New York City to confront Horace. After teasing her about crying over his lack of support, he agreed to give her "a finger's length" of space in his newspaper to write anything she liked. He also wrote a semipositive editorial about the Kansas campaign for woman suffrage.

"Tabooed in the Future"

On June 27, Elizabeth and Susan testified in Albany before the committee that would recommend whether or not to strike the word *male* out of the New York State Constitution. The chairman was Horace Greeley, who now appeared to favor enfranchising black men before women. "The best women I know," he repeatedly said, "do not want the vote."

He asked Susan, "Miss Anthony, you know the ballot and the bullet go together. If you vote are you ready to fight?"

"Yes, Mr. Greeley, just as you fought in the late war—at the point of a goose-quill!" Susan's quip elicited laughter at Horace's expense.

He was infuriated by what happened next. Because there were no women delegates, Susan and Elizabeth had asked a sympathetic male delegate to present the woman suffrage petitions with 28,000 signatures. Horace did not know that Elizabeth and Susan had asked his wife to sign and circulate a petition. He found out when the man stood up and said, "Mr. Chairman, I hold in my hand a petition signed by Mrs. Horace Greeley and 300 other women of Westchester asking that the word 'male' be stricken from the constitution."

In retaliation, Horace successfully pressured delegates to make it possible for black men to vote, but not women. Several weeks after the convention, Elizabeth and Susan encountered Horace at a social event. Confronting them, he denounced them as the "most maneuvering politicians in the State of New York." Then he informed them that he had "given strict orders at the *Tribune* office that you and your cause are to be tabooed in the future." Furthermore, if mention of Elizabeth in a news item was unavoidable, she would be referred to as "Mrs. Henry B. Stanton."

In recounting the incident in a letter to a friend, Elizabeth wrote, "Of course this will not deter me from speaking my mind in the future as in the past, though I am sorry for our cause. . . . This may do something to retard our final triumph, but it will take more than Horace Greeley and the *New York Tribune* to prevent the success of the movement. . . . So, more valiant than ever, I am as always, Your old friend and co-worker, 'Mrs. Henry B. Stanton!'"

After the defeat in New York, Susan and Elizabeth were free to campaign in Kansas. But first Susan had to raise money. She solicited funds from supporters, and at the height of a hot, sticky summer in New York City, she trekked along Broadway selling advertisements for suffrage publications. In a letter to Martha Wright, Susan expressed her feelings of desperation about "so much waiting to be done, and not a penny but in hope and trust." But she soldiered on because "we must not lose Kansas now, at least not from lack of work done according to our best ability."

"We Have Not Slept a Wink"

On August 28, Elizabeth and Susan boarded the train for Kansas; the fifteen-hundred-mile trip would require them to change trains several times.

Kansas was frontier country. The state capitol was still being built in Topeka (construction took thirty-seven years). There were sporadic conflicts between federal troops and Native American tribes. White settlers lived in primitive cabins in sparsely settled areas. Roads were faintly outlined tracks across prairies. Telegraph and postal service was unreliable. Towns were likely to have more saloons than stores, more cowboys than farmers, more outlaws than teachers.

Helen Ekin Starrett, who was awaiting their arrival, later wrote, "All were prepared beforehand to do Mrs. Stanton homage for her talents and fame." However, many people were prejudiced against Susan. Elizabeth's appearance— her short roly-poly shape, sparkling blue eyes, rosy cheeks, and clouds of the whitest of white hair carefully arranged around her head— disarmed many people. Her quick wit, sunny personality, and the fact that she had raised seven children made her very appealing.

That was not the case for Susan, with her tall, lean shape, angular features, slightly askew eye, and stern demeanor. Her reputation also suffered because she bore the brunt of hostile remarks in unfriendly newspapers. Getting to personally know Susan, however, converted most people, as it did Helen Starrett, who was charmed by her "genial manner and frank, kindly face" and soon considered her a "beloved and helpful friend."

Susan and Elizabeth arrived in Atchison, Kansas, in early September and spent the first two weeks campaigning with Sam Wood under rugged conditions. The worst were the infestations of insects, including chinch bugs. "We have not slept a wink for several nights, but even in broad daylight our tormentors are so active that it is impossible," Susan reported in a letter home. "We find them in our bonnets, and this morning I think we picked a thousand out of the ruffles of our dresses. I can assure you that my avoirdupois [weight] is rapidly reduced."

Shortly after their arrival, the Republican Party met in Lawrence, Kansas, and passed a resolution that they were "unqualifiedly opposed to the dogma of 'Female Suffrage.'" An Anti-Female Suffrage Committee was appointed to ensure defeat in November. In light of this alarming development, Susan and Elizabeth decided that they should divide their duties. Susan set up headquarters in Lawrence, where she could distribute suffrage tracts and coordinate the activities of local women who supported suffrage.

Elizabeth resolutely set off on a speaking tour accompanied by Charles Robinson, an antislavery man who had founded Lawrence in 1854 and had been elected the first governor of Kansas. Two mules pulled the ex-governor's open carriage, packed with a "bushel of tracts, two valises, a pail for watering the mules, and a basket of apples," as well as other food that they bought along the way: dried herring and slippery elm, pieces of dried inner bark from the slippery elm tree, which they could chew or use to make gruel, tea, or a poultice.

In her autobiography, Elizabeth described how they went to the "very verge of civilization." They spoke in the morning and afternoon, and at night by candlelight. They found themselves in small log cabins; in large mills and barns; in unfinished schoolhouses, churches, and hotels; and in the open air. Along the way, they were often lost. To find their way on moonless nights, Charles walked ahead with his coat off so Elizabeth could see his white shirt and drive slowly behind him. For food, she recalled, "We frequently sat down at a table with bacon floating in grease, coffee without milk sweetened with sorghum, and bread or hot biscuit, green with soda, while vegetables and fruit were seldom seen."

One night to escape from bedbugs, Elizabeth decided to sleep outside in the carriage. She had just fallen asleep when "a chorus of pronounced grunts and a spasmodic shaking of the carriage" jarred her awake to discover that the carriage was surrounded by long-nosed, black, flea-infested pigs who were using the iron steps of the carriage as scratching posts. "I had a sad night of it," she recalled, "and never tried the carriage again, though I had many equally miserable experiences within four walls." That included the night she felt a mouse scamper across her face and discovered a mouse nest in her bed. "Fortunately," she wrote, "I was very tired and soon fell asleep. What the mice did the remainder of the night I never knew, so deep were my slumbers. But, as my features were intact, and my facial expression as benign as usual the next morning, I inferred that their gambols had been most innocently and decorously conducted."

Elizabeth never regretted the discomforts of the campaign. "I was glad of the experience," she wrote. "It gave me added self-respect to know that I could endure such hardships and fatigue with a great degree of cheerfulness."

"To Be Sure Our Friends, on All Sides, Fell Off"

In October, Susan and Elizabeth made a fateful decision. They accepted George Francis Train's offer to campaign for woman suffrage. A wealthy, flamboyant entrepreneur, he was a crowd-pleasing speaker who had a gift for mimicry and repartee. Because he was a Copperhead, or a proslavery Democrat, they had been reluctant to associate with him. But as Republicans and abolitionists abandoned woman suffrage, Elizabeth and Susan, along with Sam Wood, Charles Robinson, and two local women, sent a telegram to George, who was in Omaha, Nebraska, that read "Come to Kansas and stump the State for equal rights and female suffrage."

When Lucy found out, she was appalled. George Train, she wrote, was "a lunatic, wild and ranting." In defending their decision, Elizabeth pointed out that Republicans and abolitionists did not "shut out all persons opposed to woman suffrage." Therefore she asked why should they not "accept all in favor of woman suffrage . . . even though they be rabid proslavery Democrats?"

He arrived in time to campaign with Susan for the last two and a half weeks before the vote. Their speaking tour took them throughout Kansas from Lawrence to Olathe, Paola, Ottawa, Mound City, Fort Scott, Humboldt, LeRoy, Burlington, Emporia, Junction City, Manhattan, Wyandotte, Topeka, and back to Leavenworth. On election day, Susan, Elizabeth, and the Hutchinson Family Singers rode in an open carriage to all the polling places in Leavenworth, where they gave speeches and the Hutchinson family sang suffrage songs, including one John had written, titled "Kansas Suffrage Song," with the verse:

> *We frankly say to fathers, brothers,*
> *Husbands, too, and several others,*
> *We're bound to win our right of voting.*
> *Don't you hear the music floating?*

Both referendums were overwhelmingly defeated. Out of thirty thousand votes, 10,502 white men voted for black male suffrage, 9,091 voted for woman suffrage. Elizabeth later wrote that she believed both propositions would have passed except for the Republicans' "narrow policy, playing off one against the other." Susan heralded the 9,070 votes as the "first ever cast in the United States for the enfranchisement of women."

George offered two more opportunities to Elizabeth and Susan, one irresistible, the other a dream come true. The first was a woman suffrage lecture tour for the three of them that he would finance. The second was his promise to underwrite their own weekly woman suffrage newspaper to be called the *Revolution*. Elizabeth initially wavered because of their friends' protests, but then sided with Susan: "I take my beloved Susan's judgment against the world," she once wrote. "After we discuss any point and fully agree, our faith in our united judgment is immovable, and no amount of ridicule and opposition has the slightest influence."

The lecture tour was a luxurious experience for Susan and Elizabeth—the best rooms in the best hotels, fine food, flowers—and it garnered a great deal of publicity. "The agitation was widespread, and of great value," Elizabeth later recalled. "To be sure our friends, on all sides, fell off, and those especially who wished us to be silent on the question of woman's rights, declared 'the cause too sacred to be advocated by such a charlatan as George Francis Train.' We thought otherwise." She and Susan had "solemnly vowed that there should never be another season of silence until woman had the same rights everywhere on this green earth, as man."

15

"MALE VERSUS FEMALE"

DIVISION IN THE RANKS
1868–1870

TRUE TO HIS WORD, GEORGE FRANCIS TRAIN provided the money to start publishing the *Revolution*. Susan was the business manager. Elizabeth and Parker Pillsbury, a social reformer, orator, and writer, were the editors. The first edition was published on January 8, 1868. In an editorial, Elizabeth wrote that it would be "charged to the muzzle with literary nitro-glycerine." Week after week, it was, as Elizabeth published uncensored articles and editorials on anything and everything that pertained to women— divorce reform, child rearing, unfair working conditions, equal education, and woman suffrage. Parker covered political events. Together, Susan said, Elizabeth and Parker "can make the pages burn and freeze—laugh and cry."

Their old friends were beside themselves. In a letter to Susan, William Lloyd Garrison, the pioneering abolitionist, condemned George as a "crack-brained harlequin." The public response was mixed. An editorial in the *Cincinnati Enquirer* declared it "spicy, readable and revolutionary." It was "plucky, keen, and wide awake," pronounced the *Home Journal*, a society newspaper. The editor of the *New York Sunday Times*, however, expressed the opinion that Elizabeth should tend to her "domestic duties" and that Susan needed a "good husband and a pretty baby."

As for Elizabeth and Susan, the *Revolution* was a powerful mouthpiece for spreading their ideas and mobilizing supporters. To cover operating expenses, Susan hustled after subscribers from the president of the United States to supporters in California. She solicited advertisers, but only for products that she and Elizabeth considered reputable.

Adept in writing satire, sarcasm, and ridicule, Elizabeth employed them in her articles and editorials. She spared no one— not her cousin Gerrit when he refused to sign one of their petitions or Wendell for refusing to back universal suffrage. Although Gerrit took her attack in stride, Wendell did not. In a letter to a friend, Elizabeth recounted an unpleasant encounter with him at an event in Boston: "In quite a large circle of my friends, [he] refused to shake hands with me, rebuffing my advance with the rather surly remark, 'Mrs. Stanton is no friend of mine.'" Concluding that he could not stand her satire of him, although he did not hesitate to use it himself, she wrote, "Seeing that he feels it, I will give him some more!"

The breach with their friends and allies widened as Elizabeth, with Susan's support, insisted on tackling taboo subjects such as liberalizing divorce laws and dress reform. Having given up on bloomers, she now proposed that women wear men's clothing for three reasons: convenience, freedom from lewd remarks, and equal wages for women who were dressed like men who were doing the same job.

Elizabeth and Susan also took on controversial causes that their old friends feared would sully the woman's movement, such as the case of twenty-year-old Hester Vaughn. Abandoned by her husband, Hester was working as a servant when she was impregnated and deserted by another man. On her own in the middle of the winter, she found refuge in an unheated room, where she gave birth. By the time they were discovered, the baby was dead and Hester nearly dead. The *Revolution* and the Working Woman's Association, a group Susan formed of typesetters and clerks, rallied support to her side. They sent Dr. Clemence Lozier, a staunch woman's rights activist, to investigate, published demands for a new trial, and held a huge meeting in New York City.

In speeches and articles, Elizabeth railed against the unequal moral code that found Hester guilty of infanticide, but not her seducer and the legal system that prevented women from serving as lawyers, judges, and members of the jury. Elizabeth and her cousin Libby visited Hester in prison. Then they personally presented their plea for clemency to the governor of Pennsylvania, who finally agreed to release Hester.

"Propulsive Force"

After the Fourteenth Amendment, which defined a citizen as "male," was ratified in July 1868, Elizabeth and Susan issued a call for a National Woman Suffrage Convention, the first to be held in Washington, DC, in order to lobby legislators. On January 19 and 20, 1869, people from twenty states gathered together, a sign of the growth of the woman's movement. A number of senators and representatives spoke, raising the hope that perhaps Congress would pass a woman suffrage amendment.

A prominent journalist, Grace Greenwood, the pseudonym of Sara Jane Lippincott, covered the convention. She described

Susan as giving a speech in "her usual pungent, vehement style, hitting the nail on the head every time, and driving it in up to the head." Elizabeth's speeches were "models of composition— clear, compact, elegant, and logical. . . . There is no denying or dodging her conclusions." Elizabeth, Grace concluded, was the "swift, keen intelligence" of the movement, and Susan "its propulsive force," while Lucretia Mott was its "soul."

"It Will Be Male Versus Female, the Land Over"

In the wake of losing the Civil War, Southern legislatures passed Black Codes, or laws that limited the freedom of black people and undermined the Fourteenth Amendment. The Klu Klux Klan, a terrorist group, was organized by former Confederate soldiers who were committed to perpetuating white supremacy. Concealing themselves in white—robes, masks, and tall, cone-shaped hats—the Klan terrorized and murdered former slaves, in particular black men who voted for candidates who were Republicans, the political party that had passed the Thirteenth Amendment prohibiting slavery.

In an effort to protect black male voters, the Republican-led Congress passed the Fifteenth Amendment in February 1869, which prohibited the government of the United States or of any individual state from denying a citizen the right to vote "on account of race, color, or previous condition of servitude." Noting that the word *sex* was omitted, Elizabeth and Susan were outraged. "Woman will then know with what power she has to contend. It will be male versus female, the land over," Elizabeth wrote in the *Revolution*. She railed against establishing an "aristocracy of sex." Her rhetoric became increasingly anti-immigrant and black men. Susan protested that the amendment would "put two million more men in position of tyrants."

Lucy Stone, who was already at odds with Elizabeth and Susan over their alliance with George Train and the *Revolution*, vehemently disagreed with them about the Fifteenth Amendment. "There are two great oceans [of wrongs]," she said, and she would be thankful if *"any* body can get out of the terrible pit. . . . I thank God for the Fifteenth Amendment." In Boston, Massachusetts, where she lived, Lucy threw herself into organizing suffrage workers to wrest control of the movement from Elizabeth and Susan.

Fired up, Elizabeth and Susan headed west to rally supporters in Ohio, Illinois, Indiana, Missouri, and Wisconsin. They traveled from Chicago to St. Louis on a train with the new Pullman sleeper cars. Delightedly, Elizabeth described the experience as "like magic to eat, sleep, read the morning papers, and talk with one's friends in bedroom, dining room, and parlor, dashing over the prairies at the rate of thirty miles an hour."

"Division in the Ranks"

In the midst of the fight over the Fifteenth Amendment, Representative George Washington Julian introduced a joint resolution in Congress proposing the Sixteenth Amendment, a woman suffrage amendment. Elated, Elizabeth wrote in the *Revolution* that March 15, 1869, the day he introduced the resolution, "will be held memorable in all coming time." Hoping to recruit allies to work for passage of the amendment, she and Susan prepared for the next meeting of the American Equal Rights Association (AERA). Adopting a conciliatory tone to smooth hurt feelings and repair the breach, they sent out hundreds of letters. "I wish so much all petty jealousies could be laid aside, for all that our cause needs now for a speedy success is union and magnanimity," Elizabeth wrote to one former ally. In the May issue of the

Revolution, they announced the dissolution of their relationship with George Francis Train. In her editorial, Elizabeth explained, "Feeling that he has been a source of grief to our numerous friends . . . he magnanimously retires."

The well-attended AERA meeting opened on May 12, 1869, in Steinway Hall in New York City, with Elizabeth presiding. All went well until a debate broke out over whether or not Elizabeth and Susan should resign from the association because of their position on the Fifteenth Amendment. Although they remained, it was clear that there would be no reconciliation.

In response to the contentious meeting, Elizabeth and Susan invited a select group of women to a reception at the office of the *Revolution.* There they formed a new organization—the National Woman Suffrage Association (NWSA). Elizabeth was elected president. This news prompted Lucy to put out a feeler for forming a separate national organization for people "who cannot use the methods, and means, which Mrs. Stanton and Susan use." Newspapers began to speculate about "division in the ranks of the strong-minded" women. Addressing an editorial to the "Boston malcontents," Elizabeth offered to resign as president of the NWSA if that would reunite them.

Then Isabella Beecher Hooker entered the fray. The half sister of Henry Ward Beecher, the prominent preacher, and Harriet Beecher Stowe, the best-selling author of *Uncle Tom's Cabin,* Isabella had been prejudiced against Elizabeth and Susan until they spent time together and she was smitten by them. Attempting to broker a rapprochement, she organized a reconciliation convention and sent out a list of instructions on how to dress and behave.

"I did my best to obey orders," Elizabeth later recalled, "and appeared in a black velvet dress with real lace, and the most inoffensive speech I could produce; all those passages that would shock the most conservative were ruled out, while pathetic and aesthetic passages were substituted in their place. From what my friends said, I believed I succeeded in charming everyone but myself and Susan who said it was the weakest speech I ever made. I told her that was what it was intended to be."

Despite Isabella's efforts, the tension continued unabated. Lucretia tried to ameliorate the situation; she traveled to New York and Boston to plead with both sides to "merge their interest in one common cause." But to no avail.

On November 24, 1869, Lucy and her allies gathered in Cleveland, Ohio, to form the American Woman Suffrage Association (AWSA). Elizabeth did not attend. Having recently signed up as a speaker with the New York Lyceum Bureau, she was on a lecture tour. Susan, however, was there. Henry Ward Beecher was elected the president. The establishment of a new newspaper, the *Woman's Journal*, was announced. The primary purpose of the organization was stated: to conduct state-by-state campaigns, contrary to NWSA's focus on passage of the Sixteenth Amendment, with which every state would have to comply. A letter from William Lloyd Garrison was read that included a thinly veiled attack on Susan and Elizabeth.

Finally Susan asked to speak. The new organization, she said, was a sign of the growing strength of the woman's movement. "So, I say to you to-night: don't be scared. Our situation is most hopeful and promising. These independent and separate movements show that we are alive." Criticizing the Fifteenth Amendment, not because it enfranchised black men, but because it ignored women, she urged everyone to work for passage of the Sixteenth Amendment. Reading newspaper accounts of Susan's speech, Elizabeth applauded her spunk and fortitude for boldly speaking up at their former friends' rival convention. In the *Revolution*, she wrote that they "deplored" the division in their ranks. The "personal bickerings" distracted the old friends from the real enemy of woman's rights: "prejudice, custom, unjust laws, and false public sentiment."

"No Power in Heaven, Hell or Earth"

The years of attacks by their enemies and friends had taken a toll on Elizabeth and Susan. In a letter to Susan dated December 28, 1869, Elizabeth wrote, "You and I know the conflict of the last twenty years; the ridicule, persecution, denunciation, detraction, the unmixed bitterness of our cup for the past two, when even friends have crucified us." Elizabeth, who was on her lecture tour in St. Louis, Missouri, also expressed her opinion about two looming issues in their relationship: the fate of the *Revolution* and her increasing reluctance to attend conventions.

Financially, the *Revolution* was in trouble. Although it had attracted three thousand paying subscribers, not enough businesses were willing to spend money on advertisements. Susan appealed to her friends and family. "My paper must not, shall not go down," she wrote to her cousin Anson Lapham. "I know you will save me from giving the world a chance to say, 'There is a woman's rights failure; even the best of women can't manage business.'" He sent money, as did her sister Mary. A friend sent five hundred dollars.

Isabella persuaded her half sister Harriet to serialize her forthcoming novel in the *Revolution*, a surefire way to attract subscribers and advertisers. They, however, had a condition: Susan and Elizabeth must change the name of the *Revolution* to "The True Republic, or something equally satisfactory to us." Susan sought Elizabeth's opinion

"My Dear Susan," Elizabeth replied, "As to changing the name of the *Revolution*, I should consider it a great mistake. . . . Establishing woman on her rightful throne is the greatest revolution the world has ever known or ever will know. To bring it about is no child's play. . . . A journal called the *Rosebud* might answer for those who come with kid gloves and perfumes . . . but for us . . . there is no name like the *Revolution*." Susan agreed. Isabella and Harriet withdrew their offer. Susan continued her increasingly futile search for money to save the *Revolution*.

As for Susan's insistence that Elizabeth preside over the next annual convention, Elizabeth reminded her that she hated conventions because she did not like to "manage other people" or to have other people "manage" her. Besides, she wrote, she would do more good on her lecture tour talking to Western women than to Washington politicians. She offered to pay someone else to take her place at the convention. "But of course," she added, "I stand by you to the end. I would not see you crushed by rivals even if to prevent it required my being cut into inch bits. . . . No power in heaven, hell or earth can separate us, for our hearts are eternally wedded together. Ever yours, and here I mean *ever*."

Would Elizabeth's declaration of loyalty include presiding over one more convention? For now, it did.

"Already Free"

The second annual National Woman Suffrage Convention in Washington, DC, opened on January 19, 1870. It was scheduled to last for two days, but the enthusiastic participants continued meeting for a third day. Letters from prominent people were read. Politicians, judges, ministers, and suffrage workers gave speeches. At a follow-up meeting before a joint congressional committee, Elizabeth boldly argued that women already had the vote under the recently ratified Fourteenth Amendment, a new legal theory that had been first articulated by Francis Minor, a lawyer in St. Louis, and his wife, Virginia, president of the Woman Suffrage Association of Missouri. Since the amendment established that "All persons . . . are citizens of the United States," the Minors reasoned that women are persons, therefore they are citizens, and the right to vote is inherent in citizenship.

The Minors' proposition, which became known as the New Departure, seemed like a promising path to securing the vote. Susan and Elizabeth enthusiastically promoted it, along with the stirring refrain "Already Free."

16

"The Crowning Insult"

ANOTHER BATTLE
1870–1871

For several months, a sensational trial had been going on in New York City. Throughout America, people were devouring every shocking and scandalous detail. Daniel McFarland, an alcoholic and abusive man, had been married to Abby Sage. Together they had two sons. A successful actor, Abby had financially supported the family. Finally she divorced Daniel and entered into a new relationship with Albert D. Richardson, a prominent reporter for Horace Greeley's *New York Tribune*. One day, Daniel walked into Albert's office and shot him. As Albert lay dying, he and Abby were married in a ceremony performed by Henry Ward Beecher and attended by Horace and other prominent people.

Upon Albert's death, Daniel was arrested. During his trial, the press coverage portrayed Abby as a wanton woman and Daniel as a sympathetic figure. In mid-May, he was acquitted on the grounds of insanity, set free, and given custody of one of his and Abby's sons. Many people,

particularly women, were outraged. Seizing on the verdict as a "golden opportunity" to educate women about their situation under the law, Susan and Elizabeth took a bold step—they arranged two women-only meetings to protest the verdict, the press treatment of Abby, and the law that gave custody of a child to a man who was a murderer. Thousands of indignant women attended each meeting and enthusiastically applauded for Susan and Elizabeth.

First, Susan spoke, then she introduced Elizabeth, who was "robed in quiet black, with an elegant lace shawl over her shoulders and her beautiful white hair ornamented with a ribbon." In her speech, Elizabeth critiqued the double moral standard, the all-male justice system, biased laws, and biased press coverage. As usual, Elizabeth and Susan were attacked by the press for discussing such unladylike subjects. They had expected that response; what they had not expected was the outpouring of similar stories from so many women.

"My Own Death-Warrant"

On May 18, Susan finally accepted the inevitable—she could no longer pay for the *Revolution*. In fact, there was a debt of ten thousand dollars. Four days later, she formally transferred her beloved newspaper to Laura Curtis Bullard for the sum of one dollar. "It was like signing my own death-warrant," she wrote in her diary.

"Our *Revolution* no more!" Elizabeth wrote to her. "There is a sadness, though relief in the fact." Susan, who was the business manager, however, felt only sadness, but she determinedly set out on a lecture tour to earn money and pay off the debt. Elizabeth felt no responsibility to help her financially, perhaps

because she had worked as an unpaid editor or because she was helping support two households, one in New York City, where Henry spent most of his time, and the other a spacious house she had recently bought in Tenafly, New Jersey, a town not far from New York City. She also paid school and college tuitions for her children. Whatever Elizabeth's reasons, Susan shouldered the debt and eventually paid back every cent.

Susan spent the summer on a lecture tour in the West. Elizabeth stayed in Tenafly, reading, writing, and tending to her family. "I never want to go to another convention," she wrote Isabella. If she did, it would be only because she was worried about "outside influences" or if Susan made her. "No other mortal," she wrote, "has the faculty of pulling me out of my retreat."

The current state of the suffrage movement, Susan wrote to a friend in England, was "at a dead-lock." The Republicans—a "purse-proud, corrupt, cowardly party: not that I expect from the Democrats anything better"—who controlled Congress were afraid to support the Sixteenth Amendment, lest they be voted out of office in the presidential election of 1872. Even worse, she continued, was Elizabeth's reluctance to attend conventions and the loss of the *Revolution*. "We, E.C.S. and S.B.A.," she wrote, "have let slip from our hands all control of organizations and newspapers." It would take "some terrific shock to startle the women of this nation into a self-respect . . . [and] force them to break their yoke of bondage."

Clearly concerned about Susan's spirits, Elizabeth sent her a letter dated June 27, 1870: "Dearest Susan, Do not feel depressed, my dear friend. What is good in us is immortal. . . . We shall not have suffered in vain. How I long to see my blessed Susan!"

"Between Two Fires"

In late September, Susan interrupted her lecture tour in response to Elizabeth's pleas for her to help Paulina Wright Davis plan a convention in New York City to mark the twentieth anniversary of the first national woman's rights convention that had been held in 1850 in Worcester, Massachusetts. Although Paulina had ably planned the first one, she was struggling to finalize the arrangements for this one.

On October 1, Susan arrived in Tenafly on the four P.M. train. "Met Mrs. S & Hattie driving out," she wrote in her diary, "got in & rode an hour with them—Henry," she noted, had "gone to Washington." (The seven children now ranged in age from twenty-eight to eleven years old. Neil lived in Louisiana, Kit practiced law and lived with his father in New York City, Gat lived on a farm in Iowa, Maggie and Theo were away at school, and Hattie and Bob lived in Tenafly.)

For three weeks, Susan traveled back and forth between Tenafly and New York City by train and ferry to plan the convention. Some days she stayed in Tenafly and worked with Elizabeth: "Took walk at dusk—the day perfectly charming. . . . Wrote all day on the government branch of true republic took ride at dusk Bob & Hattie drivers—I leavy rain all night. . . . Writing writing beautiful day. . . . Mrs S & self wrote & worked up to 3 P.M. then dinner & she started for Washington at 5 P.M [to give a speech on the next day]. . . . Hattie & self took a walk—then went to my room & to bed—perfectly tired out."

The convention was a grand success. Lucretia, Sarah Pugh, Elizabeth, Olympia Brown, and more than two hundred people attended, including Sarah J. Smith Tompkins, the first black woman to be appointed a school principal in New York

City. Shortly afterward, both Elizabeth and Susan left on their lecture tours.

From Chicago, Elizabeth wrote a letter to Amelia Willard, her longtime housekeeper. "I send you a splendid recipe for corn muffins. Try it so that you can give me some when I return. I hope to see you in two weeks." She described her tour in Iowa; her son Gat, who lived there, traveled with her. "What times we have had," she wrote, "what detestable tea, coffee, what forlorn rooms and dirty beds." Finally they arrived in Chicago and reveled in their stay at the elegant Sherman House, where they had "nice room, clean beds and something good to eat."

Susan, who was at a woman suffrage convention in Detroit, Michigan, received a telegram that her nephew Thomas, Guelma's son, was dying, just five years after his sister Ann Eliza had died at the age of twenty-three. "I loved her merry laugh," Susan wrote at the time, "her bright, joyous presence." Now, twenty-one-year-old Thomas was dying; she hastened to his bedside. Once again she was reminded of "the brittleness of life's threads."

In December, Isabella wrote to Elizabeth and Susan and proposed taking charge of the annual National Woman Suffrage Convention in Washington, DC. She would make all the arrangements, pay all the expenses, and preside. The convention would focus on the Sixteenth Amendment; no controversial issue would be discussed, such as divorce or the rights of working women. Given her distaste for conventions, Elizabeth was agreeable, but she was annoyed when Isabella asked her to stay away. In a letter to Martha Wright, she wrote, "I think her letter quite blunt and egotistic and somehow it hurts my self-respect."

Susan, however, "declined to be snubbed, subdued or displaced" and was furious with Elizabeth. Isabella was a newcomer to the woman's movement, while Elizabeth was a pioneer. Therefore, Susan wrote, it was "suicidal" for Elizabeth to drop out: "O, how I have agonized over my utter failure to make you feel and see the importance of standing fast and holding the helm of our good ship to the end of the storm. . . . How you can excuse yourself, is more than I can understand."

Elizabeth sent Susan's letter to Martha with this comment, "You see I am between two fires, all the time. Some, determined to throw me overboard, & Susan equally determined that I shall stand at the mast head, no matter how pitiless the storm."

Organizing the convention proved too much for Isabella, and she begged for help. Elizabeth refused (she sent one hundred dollars and a letter to be read at the event), but Susan responded in person. Shortly after she arrived in Washington, she read a surprising announcement in a newspaper: Victoria Woodhull, a brand-new advocate for woman suffrage, was going to address a joint congressional committee on the day the convention was scheduled to begin.

Brazen and controversial, Victoria and her sister Tennessee Claflin, who had grown up in poverty, had recently become the first women stockbrokers on Wall Street. Skilled at enlisting the help of powerful men, they had made a fortune that they used to start *Woodhull and Claflin's Weekly*, a newspaper in which they promulgated shocking ideas: sex education, spiritualism (the belief that living people can communicate with the spirits of the dead), legalized prostitution (allegedly Tennessee was a prostitute), women serving in the military, vegetarianism, free love, and woman suffrage.

Victoria had persuaded a representative to Congress to

present a written memorial asking for passage of a declaratory act that would enforce woman's right to vote under the Fourteenth Amendment. Her memorial had been referred to the joint committee that she was scheduled to address. Susan and Elizabeth knew of her and about her memorial, but they had not met her. Clearly the time had come. Susan, Isabella, and Albert Gallatin Riddle, a strong woman suffrage advocate (and the male escort they needed to gain entrance to the meeting room), went to hear her.

Unlike her flamboyant reputation, Victoria appeared to be modest and serious. She echoed the Minors' argument, known as the New Departure, that women had the right to vote under the Fourteenth Amendment because they were citizens. The Fifteenth Amendment, Victoria also argued, which included the clause that the right to vote could not be denied "on account of race," also gave women the right to vote, because "women, black and white, belong to races." After she spoke, Susan told the committee members to listen to this "new, fresh" voice and "grant our appeal, so I can lay off my armor, for I am tired of fighting." She invited Victoria to the woman suffrage convention that was opening that afternoon.

Victoria came with her sister Tennessee. "Two New York ᵗnsations . . . ," a newspaper reporter described them, "both in ʳk dresses, with blue neckties, short, curly brown hair, and ᵇby Alpine hats, the very picture of the advanced ideas ᵃre advocating." Repeating her woman suffrage speech, ᵃ was well received. However, word of her appearance firestorm of protests by people who insisted that her ᵗ as an advocate of "free love" would taint the woman ᵛement.

Following the events in the newspapers, Elizabeth had two responses: In a letter to Susan, she warned her, "Do not have another Train affair with Mrs. Woodhull." In response to men who objected to Victoria's presence on the convention platform, she wrote, "When men who make laws for us in Washington can stand forth and declare themselves pure and unspotted . . . then we will demand that every woman who makes a constitutional argument on our platform shall be as chaste."

"We Will Win the Battle Yet"

It appeared that Congress would soon pass the declaratory act that would enable women to vote. Although a small group of women had recently presented an antisuffrage petition to the Senate, more than 80,000 women signed a prosuffrage statement. Women who were connected to prominent men expressed their support, including Julia Dent Grant, the wife of President Ulysses Grant. Some newspaper editors endorsed the idea. Republican politicians who controlled Congress now seemed to support it, as did influential constitutional lawyers.

"I feel new life," Susan wrote to an advocate, "now hope that our battle is to be short, sharp & decisive under this 14th & 15th amendment claim—it is unanswerable."

The next crucial step was for the joint judiciary committee to make a favorable report to Congress. But on January 30, 1871, the committee issued a negative report: Congress did not have the power to act because women were not citizens, they were only "members of the state." Therefore it was up to each state to decide whether or not to enfranchise women.

That report, Elizabeth wrote to Susan, was "the crowning

insult." She reminded Susan of the speech she had given decrying the "aristocracy of sex" that the Fifteenth Amendment had established. "That night in Washington when you said you had never before seen me so on the rampage," she wrote, "I had a vivid intuition of the dark clouds hanging over us; and now they are breaking."

Outraged by the "open declaration" that women were "not citizens," Elizabeth exhorted Susan into action: "So go ahead and 'deal damnation round the land with a high hand,' as the *Tribune* says you do; only don't run in debt in order to do it." Then perhaps recognizing that she, too, needed to return to the fray, she used a plural pronoun in her last sentence: "We will win this battle yet, Susan!" and signed it "With love unchanged, undimmed by time and friction."

In May, Elizabeth joined Susan at the annual state woman suffrage convention in New York City. Lucretia came, she explained in a letter to her sister Martha, despite her "feeble health, to identify" herself with the New York branch of the suffrage movement. The Boston group had offended her sensibilities by recently passing resolutions that unfairly linked the New York group with "the doctrine of Free Love."

Seeking to bolster Victoria's standing, Elizabeth seated her between herself and the venerable Lucretia. That did not stop the press, in particular Horace Greeley, from trumpeting her notoriety in their newspapers and dubbing the convention "The Woodhull Convention." Victoria gave a defiant speech: "We mean treason, we mean secession. We are plotting revolution; we will overthrow this bogus republic and plant a government of righteousness in its stead."

Thrilled by Victoria's fiery rhetoric, Elizabeth declared that she was "a grand, brave woman, radical alike in political, religious, and social principles." Susan, however, was becoming wary of Victoria. She suspected that Victoria had attached herself to the suffrage movement in order to advance a personal ambition that she had recently revealed—to run for president of the United States.

17

"I HAVE BEEN &
GONE & DONE IT!"

TAKING A STAND
1871–1872

D ESPITE THEIR SIMMERING DISAGREEMENT over Victoria
Woodhull, Susan and Elizabeth decided to do a
joint lecture tour that would take them across the country
to California. They traveled in style on the new transcon-
tinental railroad. "We have a drawing-room all to ourselves," Susan wrote in a letter to her sisters, "and here we
are just as cozy and happy as lovers." The sight out their
window of slow-moving prairie schooners carrying pioneers westward or a "lone cabin-light on the endless prairie" prompted Elizabeth to reflect that there is "real bliss, if
only the two are perfect equals, two loving people, neither
assuming to control the other." Susan agreed: "Yes, after
all, life is about one and the same things, whether in a prairie schooner and sod cabin, or the Fifth Avenue palace.
Love for and faith in each other. . . . It is not the outside
things which make life, but the inner, the spirit of love."

Along the way, they stopped to give suffrage speeches,
including one to "women alone." The idea of addressing
women separately was hers, Elizabeth explained in a

letter to her cousin Libby. "What radical thoughts I then and there put into their heads . . . these thoughts are permanently lodged there! That is all I ask."

In Denver, Colorado, the governor and his wife welcomed them. Large audiences heard them speak. The press was uncharacteristically positive. A reporter for the *Denver News* acknowledged that the "press sneers at Miss Anthony, men tell her she is out of her proper sphere, people call her a scold, good women call her masculine, a monstrosity in petticoats." But after hearing her speak, he concluded that "if one-half of her sex possessed one-half of her acquirements, her intellectual culture, her self-reliance and independence of character, the world would be the better for it."

They were invited to speak at a newly established colony in Colorado named Greeley, after Horace Greeley, who had provided the money for the founder Nathan Cook Meeker, a former reporter for Horace's newspaper. Nathan's son Ralph described their visit in a letter to the *Tribune*: "Mrs. Stanton and Miss Anthony were the guests of my father and mother here in our rough adobe house. They melted into the family life like sunshine, and soon seemed like friends who had lived here for years." Although most of the residents, he noted, had adopted Horace's antisuffrage stance, they were receptive to what Elizabeth and Susan had to say.

Their arrival in San Francisco, during the dry and dusty season in mid-July, prompted great fanfare. A suite for them in the elegant Grand Hotel was filled with flowers and food. They were taken on sailing excursions in the harbor and for drives to the seashore and along the coast. Elizabeth noted the windmills for pumping water that were everywhere, "a very pretty feature in the landscape." Huge audiences of admirers,

143 ∽

detractors, curiosity seekers, and suffrage advocates, whom Elizabeth dubbed their "suffrage children," flocked to their lectures.

Soon, however, they ran afoul of public opinion by getting involved in the case of Laura D. Fair who had murdered her lover, A. P. Crittenden, a prominent judge with a wife and children, after he dropped her. Laura had been tried and sentenced to be hanged. Wanting to hear Laura's side of the story, Elizabeth and Susan visited her in jail, an act for which they were soundly criticized in local newspapers. The attacks escalated after Susan gave a speech in which she appeared to sympathize with Laura's plight because a married man had apparently used her and then jilted her. Other newspapers across America picked up the story. Although Elizabeth received some of the vitriol, Susan bore the brunt. "Never in all my hard experience," she wrote in her diary, "have I been under such fire." In another entry, she wrote, "I never before was so cut down."

Faced with such a furor, Susan and Elizabeth took a break. By train and private carriage, the intrepid companions traveled to see the wonders of California—the geysers and mountain ranges, which Elizabeth described as "piled one above another, until they seemed to make a giant pathway from earth to heaven." Their trip included a visit to Yosemite Valley, a remote, rugged area of spectacular natural beauty. A long, steep, narrow trail led down the mountain into the valley.

Wearing linen bloomers for the descent on horseback, Elizabeth and Susan met their guides on a very hot and dusty day. Susan mounted her horse. But Elizabeth set off on foot. (Their accounts of why she walked differ: Susan wrote that Elizabeth was too "fat" to get into the saddle; Elizabeth reported that the horse's back was so broad she could not reach the stirrups, thus as the horse started the descent, she felt as if she was going to pitch forward out of the saddle over the horse's head.)

Elizabeth slowly made her way down, alternating between walking and sliding, catching hold of rocks and twigs to steady herself, while she and her guide, who was leading her horse, argued about whether it was better to "trust one's own legs, or, the horse." Four hours later, she arrived in the valley "covered with dust, dripping with perspiration," her clothes in "tatters." After dispatching the guide to find their host, Mr. Hutchins, and tell him "to send a wheelbarrow, or four men with a blanket to transport" her to the hotel, she lay down on the grass and "fell asleep, perfectly exhausted."

Fortunately the first carriage had just been delivered to the valley that day, and finally Elizabeth arrived at the hotel. Susan, Elizabeth recalled, met her on the steps of the hotel and "laughed immoderately at my helpless plight." Elizabeth, Susan later recalled, appeared to be "pretty nearly jelly."

A hot bath and long night's sleep restored Elizabeth, and she and Susan spent several days exploring the "glory and grandeur" of Yosemite. They spent a day at the nearby Calaveras Grove, a stand of giant sequoia trees. Many of the trees had been given the names of distinguished men. As for unnamed trees, Elizabeth and Susan tacked on cards (with their guide's permission) with the names of distinguished women, including Lucretia Mott and Lucy Stone.

On August 22, 1871, Elizabeth boarded the train headed East. She stopped in Johnstown, New York, to visit her mother, who was eighty-six years old and ailing. A week later her mother died, and Elizabeth returned for the funeral. Her mother, she said, was a "grand brave woman."

"Want to Tell You"

Since Susan was not welcome to lecture in California, she accepted an invitation from Abigail Scott Duniway, a suffrage advocate and editor of a weekly newspaper, the *New Northwest*, to speak in Oregon and Washington Territory. Boarding a ship in San Francisco bound for Portland, Susan endured seven miserable days of stormy seas. On the second day, she noted in her diary, "Strong gale and rough seas. Tried to dress—no use— back to my berth and there I lay all day. Everybody groaning, babies crying, mothers scolding, the men making quite as much fuss as the women." Finally, on the seventh day, she wrote, "I felt well enough to discuss the woman question with several of the passengers. Arrived at Portland at 10 P.M., glad indeed to touch foot on land again."

Still shaken by the fury unleashed against her in San Francisco, Susan was apprehensive the first time she spoke in Portland. But it went well. "The first fire is passed. . . . The wet blanket is now somewhat off," she wrote to Elizabeth. "I want to tell you," she continued, "that with my gray silk I wore a pink bow at my throat and a narrow pink ribbon in my hair!" She spent the rest of the year lecturing in the Northwest. "I miss Mrs. Stanton," she wrote in a letter to her family in Rochester. "Still I can not but enjoy the feeling that the people call on me." She welcomed the opportunity to answer questions and "sharpen her wit," instead of sitting silently and listening to Mrs. Stanton's "brilliant scintillations as they emanate from her never-exhausted magazine. . . . Whoever goes into a parlor or before an audience with that woman does it at the cost of a fearful overshadowing." She had "cheerfully" paid that price because she "felt that our cause was most profited by her being seen and heard, and my best work was making the way clear for her."

Everywhere she went, Susan promulgated the New Departure, the argument that women already had the right to vote under the Fourteenth and Fifteenth amendments. She exhorted women to "seize their rights to go to the polls and vote" in the upcoming presidential election. Determined to continue holding annual National Woman Suffrage Conventions in Washington, DC, but aware of Elizabeth's antipathy for conventions, Susan wrote to her, "Remember that you—E.C.S. are President . . . and that is <u>your immediate duty as such</u>—to <u>issue the call forthwith, at once</u>—<u>without delay</u> . . . [a] good, strong, singing bugle blast—inviting every earnest worker & speaker to come."

Her intent, Susan wrote, was to "fire your soul to the importance of seizing the helm of our ship again . . . & keep the ship from running on shoals and quicksand."

In her last diary entry for 1871, Susan wrote, "Thus closes 1871, a year full of hard work, six months east, six months west of the Rocky Mountains; 171 lectures, 13,000 miles of travel; gross receipts, $4,318, paid on debts $2,271. Nothing ahead but to plod on."

Elizabeth wrote the call, and Susan returned in time to join her at the convention in Washington. A resolution was adopted demanding that Congress pass a declaratory act to clearly state that women had the right to vote under the Fourteenth and Fifteenth amendments. Another resolution urged women to act as if they had the right to and go to the polls on election day. Once again Elizabeth and Susan addressed a congressional committee. Once again the committee issued a negative report on the question of woman's right to vote. Susan returned to the lecture tour. Elizabeth canceled her engagement and stayed in Tenafly to tend to Hattie, who was ill.

While at home, Elizabeth packed up a big bundle of colorful rags and clothing her children had outgrown and sent them to Lucretia, who loved to make rag carpets. A delighted Lucretia replied with a description of her pleasure at "looking over each piece, opening every pinned up bundle, amazed that thou had collected so much."

"A Sad Day for Me"

In the spring, Elizabeth got embroiled in Victoria Woodhull's scheme to launch a new political party. A presidential election would be held in November, and Victoria, who had announced herself as a candidate, needed a party to nominate her. Susan was adamantly opposed to the idea of forming a new party. "All our time and words in that direction are simply thrown away," she wrote to Elizabeth. Furthermore, she warned her, "my name must not be used to call any such meeting." Nevertheless, in April, Susan's name appeared on a call published in *Woodhull and Claflin's Weekly* to form a new party at the annual May meeting of the National Woman Suffrage Association (NWSA), at Steinway Hall in New York City. Elizabeth's name was there too, along with Isabella's and Matilda Joslyn Gage's.

It was by chance that Susan saw the announcement; a gentleman had handed her a copy of a newspaper to read while she was waiting in a small train station in Illinois. Furious, she sent a telegraph with instructions to remove her name and headed back East. Arriving at Elizabeth's home, she had it out with her but could not shake Elizabeth's enthusiasm for Victoria and a new party.

Calling Susan "narrow, bigoted and headstrong," Elizabeth refused to serve as president of the NWSA; instead, Susan was elected. In the evening of the first day of the annual meeting,

Victoria appeared and started to speak. Susan declared the meeting adjourned and ordered the janitor to turn off the gas lights.

The next day, thwarted in her attempt to appropriate the NWSA, Victoria and her supporters met at Apollo Hall. During a raucous meeting, she was nominated for president of the United States. Frederick Douglass, who was not there, was nominated for vice president. (He refused the nomination.)

Abandoned by Elizabeth, Susan presided over the last day of the convention. Demoralized but relieved that she had kept NWSA out of Victoria's clutches, Susan wrote in her diary, "A sad day for me; all came near being lost. Our ship was so nearly stranded by leaving the helm to others, that we rescued it only by hair's breadth. . . . I never was so hurt by the folly of Stanton."

In the aftermath, Elizabeth distanced herself from Victoria, although she continued to admire her outspokenness. Susan forgave her "oldest and longest tried woman friend, ECS."

"Never So Blue in My Life"

That summer, political parties met to nominate presidential candidates. President Ulysses Grant's corrupt administration had split the Republican Party. One faction, called the liberal Republicans, met in Cincinnati, Ohio, and nominated Horace Greeley. The regular Republican Party met in Philadelphia and nominated Grant for a second term. The Democrats met in Baltimore and also nominated Greeley. Susan and Isabella lobbied all three parties to recognize woman suffrage in their platform.

Only the regular Republicans included a statement in their platform affirming that women's demand for "equal rights should be treated with respectful consideration." Susan was triumphant; finally a major political party had acknowledged women in its official party platform. Admittedly she recognized the "meagerness" of the statement and "the timidity of politicians"; nevertheless, she promised to work for the Republican Party.

Elizabeth was not elated; the statement was but "a splinter." Feeling "intensely bitter," she wrote to Susan, "I do not feel jubilant over the situation; in fact I never was so blue in my life. . . . Dear friend, you ask me what I see. I am under a cloud and see nothing." Despite her gloomy mood, Elizabeth joined Susan at some campaign events, but only because she could not abide the thought of Horace Greeley winning the election.

Shortly after losing the election to Grant, Horace died. Writing to Susan, Elizabeth remarked that she was "dreadfully shocked" but noted that he was "one of woman's worst enemies." His departure, she prophesized, would smooth the path to enfranchisement. "Here, as in many other cases," she wrote, "you and I have made enemies of old friends because we stood up first and always for woman's cause and would not agree to have it take second place. Expediency does not belong to our vocabulary."

"Register Now!"

For several years, scores of women had gone to local polling places to assert what they believed was their constitutional right to vote. Mary Ann Shadd Cary, a black journalist, had been allowed to register in Washington, DC, but not to vote. Sojourner Truth had tried to vote in Battle Creek, Michigan. Through a blizzard and past a crowd of jeering men in New Hyde Park, New York, Sarah Grimké and her sister Angelina had led forty women to dispose of ballots in a special box. In

Vineland, New Jersey, activists had set up a box at the polling place in which 172 women, both black and white, had placed their ballots. In 1871, Nanette Gardner's vote for a state official was actually counted in Detroit, Michigan.

Susan had wanted to vote too, but she was never at her home in Rochester, New York, long enough to meet the requirement that voters had to be in residence for thirty days before the election. Finally, in the fall of 1872, she was, but first she needed to register.

Four days before the election, she read a notice in the newspaper:

> **Now register! Today and tomorrow are the only**
> **remaining opportunities. If you were not permitted to**
> **vote, you would fight for the right, undergo all priva-**
> **tions for it, face death for it. . . . Register now!**

Taking the notice at face value, Susan and her three sisters— Guelma, Hannah, and Mary—went to the registry office in the eighth ward, located in a barber shop. The inspectors reluctantly entered their names as voters, but only after Susan read aloud the Fourteenth Amendment. At Susan's request, more women showed up and were registered in the eighth ward. By the next day, many more women had registered in other wards in the city. Two of the three local newspapers noted the event, but refrained from editorializing. The third newspaper condemned the action and insisted that any inspector who accepts a woman's vote on election day "should be prosecuted to the full extent of the law."

Before taking the next step—voting on November 5, 1872— Susan sought legal advice. Numerous lawyers turned her away. Finally, Henry R. Selden, a prominent lawyer and former judge,

agreed to study the documents she had compiled that supported the argument that women had a constitutional right to
vote. Convinced, after a thorough review, that her claim was
valid, he told her, "I will protect you in that right to the best of
my ability."

On election day, Susan, her sisters Guelma, Hannah, and
Mary, and several other women, who lived in the eighth ward
in Rochester, voted. (The women who had registered in other
wards stayed home, apparently intimidated by the threat of
being arrested.) "Well," she wrote to Elizabeth, "I have been &
gone & done it!! Positively voted." Newspapers across the country carried the story, most of them calling for punishment of the
women, especially of Susan. Two weeks later, she was arrested.

The United States deputy marshal refused Susan's suggestion
that he handcuff her. He did, however, allow her to change her
dress before escorting her to court to be arraigned on the criminal charge of voting "without having a lawful right to vote."
After a series of hearings, her trial was scheduled for June 17,
1873.

18

"OUR FRIENDSHIP IS
TOO LONG STANDING"

GAINS AND LOSSES
1873–1879

SUSAN'S UPCOMING TRIAL ATTRACTED a great deal of attention. The pros and cons were discussed in the pages of private letters and newspapers and wherever people met. Susan undertook an exhausting tour throughout Monroe County, where her trial would be held, to lecture on the question "Is it a Crime for a Citizen of the United States to Vote?" She buttressed her argument with quotations from the Declaration of Independence, the Constitution, Supreme Court decisions, and the writings of James Madison and Thomas Paine. Acknowledging the effectiveness of her persuasive speech, the U.S. District Attorney concluded he could "hardly find twelve men so ignorant on the citizen's rights—as to agree on a verdict of Guilty." Therefore, he asked Judge Ward Hunt, a recently appointed judge who would preside over the trial, to move it to the village of Canandaigua, the county seat in Ontario County.

The trial was a sham. Judge Hunt was, in Susan's words, "a small-brained, pale-faced, prim-looking man, enveloped in a faultless black suit and a snowy white tie." He refused to allow her to testify because she was "not a competent witness." He preempted the jurors' role by ordering them to "find a verdict of guilty." That night in her diary, Susan fumed against "the greatest judicial outrage history has ever recorded!" The next day she returned to court to be sentenced.

"Has the prisoner anything to say why sentence shall not be pronounced?" Judge Hunt asked.

"Yes, your honor," she replied, rising to her feet. "I have many things to say; for in your ordered verdict of guilty, you have trampled under foot every vital principle of our government. My natural rights, my civil rights, my political rights, my judicial rights, are all alike ignored. Robbed of the fundamental privilege of citizenship, I am degraded from the status of a citizen to that of a subject; and not only myself individually, but all of my sex, are, by your honor's verdict, doomed to political subjection under this, so-called, form of government."

The judge tried to silence her, but Susan was unstoppable. He tried again and again, six times in all. Finally, she sat down. Ordering her to rise to be sentenced, the judge fined her one hundred dollars and court costs.

Stating that she would never pay a dollar of the "unjust penalty," Susan declared that she would continue to "educate all women to do precisely as I have done, rebel against your manmade, unjust, unconstitutional forms of law, that tax, fine, imprison and hang women, while they deny them the right of representation in the government." To that end, she had thousands of copies of the trial proceedings printed and distributed.

Under the law, the judge should have sent Susan to jail until she paid her fine. Then she would have had the right to appeal to a higher court. Determined to forestall that, he announced, "Madam, the Court will not order you committed until the fine is paid."

The judge's conduct was thoroughly denounced even in antisuffrage newspapers. Public opinion was mixed; Susan was cast as a hero, a martyr, a criminal, a threat to an orderly society. Matilda Joslyn Gage, who had attended the trial, was outraged. Elizabeth was not. In explaining her lack of indignation to Matilda, she wrote, "My continuous wrath against the whole dynasty of tyrants has not left one stagnant drop of blood in my veins to rouse for any single act of insult." She did, however, publish an article about the case in the *New York Times*. "It is as you say," she wrote to Susan, "terribly humiliating to be asking these supercilious boys to consider our right" and signed it "Your rebellious friend, E.C.S."

Although the judge had thwarted Susan's plan to appeal to a higher court, another important case—*Minor v. Happersett*—would make its way to the Supreme Court of the United States. Like Susan, Virginia Minor went to vote in St. Louis, in 1872. (She and her husband, Francis, had introduced the New Departure, the legal argument that the Fourteenth Amendment gave women the right to vote.) But when Reese Happersett, the registrar, refused to register her, she filed a lawsuit against him. In 1875, the Supreme Court ruled against her in a unanimous opinion that although women were citizens, the "Constitution of the United States does not confer the right of suffrage upon anyone." The power to determine who could vote belonged to the states, the justices asserted, thus pronouncing a death sentence on the New Departure strategy. Resolute in the face of defeat, Susan and Elizabeth and their coworkers redoubled their efforts in support of a Sixteenth

Amendment to the Constitution that would prohibit states from denying women the right to vote.

But then Victoria Woodhull detonated a powder keg that set off what Elizabeth later described as a "great social earthquake." In the pages of her newspaper, Victoria published an exposé of an affair between Henry Ward Beecher, a powerful clergyman, and Elizabeth "Lib" Tilton, a member of his congregation and the wife of Theodore Tilton, who was also a member. Beecher had been president of AWSA, the rival woman suffrage organization established by Lucy Stone. Victoria named Elizabeth as one of her sources for the scandalous story.

Lib had confided in Susan, who told Elizabeth, expecting her to remain silent. However, the story spread—Lib's mother publicized it to defend Lib against Henry Beecher's claim that she had seduced him. Theodore (who had just ended his own dalliance with another woman) told his version to Elizabeth, and they both told Victoria. Victoria published the graphic details to expose Henry's hypocrisy because he had been publicly criticizing her for her advocacy of "free love." Shortly after she published the scandalous story, Victoria was arrested and sent to jail under a federal law that made it illegal to send obscene material through the United States Postal Service.

Then a reporter wrote a newspaper article in which Elizabeth denied Victoria's version. Susan accused Elizabeth of abandoning a woman to save a man's reputation. Indignant that Susan would believe a reporter rather than trust her, "a friend of twenty years' knowledge," Elizabeth explained, "I simply said I never used the language Victoria put in my mouth." The words she used were "clothed in refined language at least however disgusting the subject."

Theodore filed a lawsuit against Henry; a sensational trial

ensued that lasted three months and ended in a hung jury. In the aftermath, Theodore divorced Lib and went to live in Paris. Lib disappeared from public scrutiny. Victoria moved to England, where she married a wealthy man and renounced free love. Henry, backed by powerful and rich members of his church, maintained his prominent position.

The press had a heyday. Susan was hounded to reveal what she knew. Reporters stalked her. Passengers on trains queried her. She kept silent; to speak, she believed, would incriminate Lib. Elizabeth agreed but felt compelled to protest the hypocrisy and injustice in her speeches and articles, especially since part of Henry's strategy was to intimidate and discredit anyone who might testify against him. To that end, he and his lawyers spewed vitriol against Lib, Victoria, Elizabeth, Susan, and Isabella Beecher Hooker, his half sister, who had urged him to confess. He smeared woman suffrage activists as "insane" and "human hyenas" and "free lovers."

Susan supported Elizabeth's outspokenness, until she repeated information to a reporter that Susan had warned her to keep confidential. Infuriated, Susan wrote her a scathing letter. "Offended, Susan," Elizabeth responded, "come right down and pull my ears. I shall not attempt a defense." But, she explained, she could not keep silent in the face of the "terrible onslaught on the suffrage movement. . . . We must not let the cause of woman go down."

"We Ask Justice"

The United States celebrated its centennial in 1876. Patriotic events were scheduled to run from January through June, culminating with a gala event on the Fourth of July in Philadelphia. Noting that the Centennial Celebration committee neglected to plan events that honored women's contributions, or even to include women participants at the gala celebration, the National Woman Suffrage Association (NWSA) passed a resolution pointing out that "one-half of the citizens of this nation, after a century of boasted liberty, are still political slaves," and demanding "justice for the women of this land."

In late May, Susan and Matilda set up the NWSA's Centennial headquarters near Independence Square in Philadelphia. Elizabeth "found them pleasantly situated" when she arrived in mid-June after finishing her lecture tour. Writing in her diary, Susan noted that she was "glad enough to see her & feel her strength."

Together Elizabeth, Susan, and Matilda wrote a "Woman's Declaration of Rights" that would be read during the main event. But they were refused a seat on the platform; finally they managed to secure five tickets in the audience. July 4 was recorded as one of the most oppressively hot days in an already extremely hot summer. Waiting until the Declaration of Independence had been read, Susan and the others then rose to their feet, walked to the platform, and presented their Declaration to Thomas W. Ferry, the vice president of the United States.

Then they went to a platform in front of Independence Hall, where Lucretia Mott presided over a five-hour-long ceremony. Elizabeth and other women spoke. The Hutchinsons sang. Susan read the Woman's Declaration aloud while Matilda held an umbrella over her head to protect her from the broiling sun. People applauded as Susan ended with the words: "We ask justice, we ask equality, we ask that all the civil and political rights that belong to citizens of the United States, be guaranteed to us and our daughters forever."

"I Am Immersed to My Ears"

Ever since the mid-1850s, Elizabeth had planned to write a history of the woman's movement. Lucretia had encouraged her, but she had never found the time to focus on it. Now together, she and Susan, undoubtedly fired up by the invisibility of women in the hoopla over the Centennial, decided the time had come. Their idea was to solicit material from advocates throughout America, including firsthand accounts, speeches, letters, biographical sketches, reports from conventions, portraits, newspaper articles, and legal documents. They enlisted Matilda to help them compile, edit, and write the *History of Woman Suffrage*.

For years, Susan had filled trunks and boxes with letters, documents, articles, tracts, books, posters, cartoons, advertisements, petitions, resolutions, diaries. Some were pasted in scrapbooks that her father had urged her to make. Others were loose. She had everything shipped to Elizabeth's house. Optimistically they thought they could finish the book in four months and blocked out four months of working time—August through November. Writing to a friend, Susan reported that they were "working for dear life" in Elizabeth's "delightfully quiet & pleasant home" in Tenafly, New Jersey.

They kept at it for months, interspersed with the comings and goings of Elizabeth's college-age children—Theo, Maggie, Hattie, and Bob. (Neil, Kit, and Gat lived elsewhere.) Occasionally Henry would come to Tenafly, but he spent most of his time in New York City, where he practiced law. Amelia Willard was still a mainstay in the household. They had a horse, named Jule after George Julian, the prosuffrage representative in Congress; chickens; and Bruno, an immense Saint Bernard dog who, according to Elizabeth, had a "wonderful head" and a "beautiful coat of long hair." Around his neck he wore a "bright brass collar."

Susan and Elizabeth had met when Theo was several months old, and Susan was like another parent to him and his younger siblings. Writing to Susan about the children or forwarding their letters, Elizabeth typically referred to them as "*our* children." In one letter, Elizabeth wrote, "There is no doubt you have had a part in making them what they are. There is a depth and earnestness in these younger ones and a love for you that delight my heart."

Elizabeth's daughter Maggie later described how they sat across from each other at a large desk "with innumerable drawers and doors" that stood in the center of a sunny room with a large bay window, hardwood floors, and a fireplace. They each had an "ink stand, bottle of mucilage, and array of pens, pencils, knives, brushes, etc."

They were "fresh and amiable" in the mornings, Maggie recalled. "They write page after page with alacrity, they laugh and talk, poke the fire by turn, and admire the flowers on their desk . . . suddenly . . . from the adjoining room I hear a hot dispute about something. . . . Sometimes these disputes run so high that down go the pens, one sails out of one door and one out the other, walking in opposite directions around the estate, and just as I have made up my mind that this beautiful friendship . . . has at last terminated, I see them walking down the hill, arm in arm. . . . When they return they go straight to work. . . . They never explain, nor apologize, nor shed tears, nor make up, as other people do."

The project turned out to be bigger than either of them imagined. Soon the mass of material overwhelmed them. "I am immersed to my ears and feel almost discouraged," Susan wrote in her diary. "The prospect of ever getting out a satisfactory history grows less each day."

"I Should Feel Desolate Indeed"

In late January 1877, Susan and Elizabeth left for their separate lecture tours. Susan's lasted nine months and took her to Iowa, Wisconsin, Kansas, Nebraska, and Missouri. She went to Colorado when she heard that there was going to be a woman suffrage referendum there in October. Throughout the sparsely settled state, she traveled by stagecoaches and wagons over high mountains, through deep canyons, and across arid plains. Occasionally she found a clean place to sleep and eatable food. Writing to her, Elizabeth cautioned, "Do be careful, dear Susan, you can not stand what you once did. I should feel desolate indeed with you gone." On election day, the male voters rejected woman suffrage.

Elizabeth spent five months on the circuit. "I sit today in a forlorn old hotel, poor bed and worse fare, and yet I am comfortable. These trips have taught me one thing in regard to myself and that is that I can be happy under most conditions," she wrote to Hattie, a senior at Vassar College. In a letter to Maggie she wrote, "You would laugh to see how everywhere the girls flock round me for a kiss, a curl, an autograph." She admitted to being lonely and fatigued, but it was worth it because she was "doing an immense amount of good in rousing women to thought and inspiring them with new hope and self-respect."

At the end of the 1870s, Susan and Elizabeth could count gains and losses. Many states had changed laws that discriminated against women. Schools, colleges, universities, and trade schools were opening their doors. Women were filling jobs in government, factories, and businesses. In the early 1830s, Harriet Martineau, a prominent English journalist, had toured America and found women employed in seven occupations: milliner, dressmaker, tailoress, seamstress, factory worker, teacher of young children, and domestic servant. In 1880, the census found women engaged in 350 occupations.

Women had won the right to vote in municipal elections, or local affairs, known as partial suffrage in Kansas, school suffrage in Massachusetts, and full suffrage in the territories of Wyoming and Utah. A resolution to pass a woman suffrage amendment to the Constitution had been introduced. Although most newspapers were antisuffrage, some press coverage was respectful, even laudatory. Of course, there were many mudslinging reporters who described advocates as "withered beldames" (or ugly old women) or "cats on the back roof" and advised them to "go home."

A network of suffrage organizations existed across the country; new recruits joined in record numbers. A woman in St. Paul, Minnesota, confessed to Susan that for ten years she had swallowed the "newspaper ridicule" of her. However, she wrote in a letter, "Your lecture tonight has been a revelation to me. I wanted to come and touch your hand, but I felt too guilty. Henceforth I am the avowed defender of woman suffrage."

Their losses included the demise of the *Revolution*; failure to secure full woman suffrage in Kansas and New York, or passage of the Sixteenth Amendment to the Constitution; breaches with some of their friends and allies; the deaths of others, including Gerrit Smith and Martha Wright; and setbacks dealt by the courts in the *United States v. Susan B. Anthony* and *Minor v. Happersett*.

At times, their relationship had been tested. But, as Elizabeth once wrote, "Our friendship is of too long standing and has too deep roots to be easily shattered. . . . Nothing that Susan could say or do could break my friendship with her; and I know nothing could uproot her affection for me."

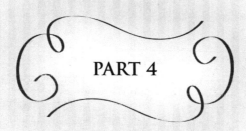

PART 4

19

"WE STOOD APPALLED"

MONUMENTAL PROJECT
1880–1883

ELIZABETH ENDED HER LECTURE TOUR on the verge of pneumonia. While she recuperated at home, Susan continued her peripatetic lifestyle. It was a presidential election year, and she envisioned a multipronged campaign—thousands of women attending mass meetings, signing petitions, and sending postal cards (a new product that sold for a penny)—to force the political parties to endorse the Sixteenth Amendment. She outlined her plans to Sara Spencer, the secretary of the National Woman Suffrage Association (NWSA, the organization Susan and Elizabeth founded in 1869), including "the rousingest rally cry ever put on paper." Susan asked Sara to write to Elizabeth and "fire her soul and brain, and get her to work on resolutions, platform and address." Since Elizabeth "has been to the dinner-table," Susan assured Sara, "I infer she is well enough to begin to work up the thunder and lightning."

Elizabeth and thousands of women vigorously executed Susan's plan. But their efforts "had not the slightest influence" on either major political party; the Republican and Democratic platforms "contained not the slightest reference to the claims of women or, in fact, to their existence." Refusing to campaign for politicians who stood with "their heel on the neck of woman," Susan and Elizabeth returned to their monumental project—the *History of Woman Suffrage.* Elizabeth later described how they had turned the "large room with a bay-window" into a "literary workshop" where the sun poured in on them from all sides. A "bright wood fire" burned in the fireplace; a "bouquet of nasturtiums" stood on the table with a dish of grapes and pears. Day in and day out, she wrote, they worked, "laughing, talking squabbling."

On election day, November 2, the Republican carriage, decorated with flags and evergreens, stopped at Elizabeth's house to take male voters to the polls. She announced that she would "go down and do the voting." She owned the house and paid the taxes—besides, none of the males were at home. Accompanied by Susan, she boarded the carriage and was driven to the polling place. "The inspectors were thunderstruck," she wrote in her autobiography. Apparently afraid that she was going to seize the ballot box, the inspector grasped it, covering the opening with one hand. "Oh, no, madam!" he sputtered. "Men only are allowed to vote. . . . I cannot accept your ballot." Placing her ballot on his hand, Elizabeth replied that she "had the same right to vote that any man present had."

November 12, a "bright sunny day," was Elizabeth's sixty-fifth birthday. Susan was away for several days, and her family was scattered—Hattie in France; Theo in Germany; Maggie, Gat, and Neil in Iowa; Bob away at college in New York. Kit and Henry were in New York City. It was the day she began keeping a diary: "My philosophy," she noted, "is to live one day at a time, neither to waste my force in apprehension of evils to come, nor regrets for the blunders of the past." The next day, she read in the newspaper that her "much loved friend Lucretia Mott" had died. Remembering Lucretia's "repose, self-control, and beautiful spirit," Elizabeth "vowed," as she had many times before, to "try to imitate her noble example."

On November 20, Elizabeth noted in her diary that Susan and Matilda had arrived to work on volume one of the *History of Woman Suffrage*. Although they "stood appalled before the mass of material," they worked steadily, often until midnight, all through the winter. Periodically Matilda returned to her home in Fayetteville, New York. Susan complained in a letter to a friend, "I am just sick to death of it. I had rather . . . *make* history than write it." But Elizabeth happily immersed herself in the work. "We are getting on finely with our *History*," she noted in her diary.

Friends pitched in to help. Although she was bedridden and over seventy years old, Clarina Howard Nichols wrote some reports and sent them to Elizabeth. Finally, in early spring, the book was finished. "I welcomed it with the same feeling of love and tenderness as I did for my firstborn," Elizabeth confided in her diary. Heartened by excellent reviews, they started on volume two.

Susan and Elizabeth interspersed their work with attending a series of conventions in the New England states, starting in Boston, the headquarters of the American Woman Suffrage Association (AWSA), their rival organization. A new recruit, Rachel Foster, made all the arrangements. Writing to her, Susan confessed, "It is such a relief to roll off part of the burden on stronger, younger shoulders."

They were welcomed by the governor of Massachusetts and

the mayor of Boston. Although Lucy Stone wrote positively about their arrival in the *Woman's Journal*, there was no effort toward reconciling the two factions. Indeed, Susan enlisted Harriet Robinson, who had recently split with Lucy, to secretly recruit AWSA members to the NWSA. She advised her on "a little stratagem. . . . "Keep cool—keep quiet—as military men say—'lay low—and work on'—move on to the taking of the fort."

Elizabeth, however, felt that "union of the suffrage forces would be a move in the right direction." Regardless of what happened, she wrote to Isabella, "Our cause is too great to be hurt permanently by what any one individual or group of individuals may do." People had said that she had "injured the suffrage movement beyond redemption; but it still lives. Train killed it. Victoria Woodhull killed it, the *Revolution* killed it. . . . But every time it is stricken to earth it comes up again with fresh power."

"This Slightest Recognition"

In July, Elizabeth admonished Susan to "leave these state conventions alone . . . at least until we can finish the *History*." Susan heeded her, and soon they were back in their old routine; then Elizabeth was stricken with malaria. Her family attributed her illness to the strain of writing the book. Susan vehemently disagreed. "It is so easy to charge every ill to her labors for suffrage, while she knows and I know that it is her work for women which has kept her young and fresh and happy all these years."

During her illness, Elizabeth told Susan that she was more afraid that "she never should finish the *History* than from the thought of parting with all her friends." In October, she had recovered and Susan returned to Tenafly for several months. Her last diary entry for 1881 read, "The year closes down on a wilderness of work, a swamp of letters and papers almost hopeless."

Early in January 1882, Susan received a "most surprising letter" from Wendell Phillips. Eliza Eddy, a longtime supporter, had instructed him to make her will and divide a portion of her estate between Susan and Lucy "to use for the advancement of the woman's cause." Personally, Susan lived at a subsistence level; the money she earned by lecturing and selling tracts, or that Lucretia and others donated, or that working women squeezed out of their meager salaries to give her, she spent "for the cause." Her share of Eliza's bequest was about $24,000, more money than she had ever had. It was a timely inheritance, and Susan would use it to cover the costs of publishing the future volumes of the *History* and to widely distribute free copies.

They interrupted their work to attend the annual National Woman Suffrage Convention in Washington. After years of intense lobbying, petitioning, and speaking, they achieved a tiny victory: the Senate finally agreed to appoint seven senators to a select committee on woman suffrage. But even this small step roused the ire of politicians opposed to woman suffrage: Senator George Graham Vest of Missouri denounced the decision as "mischief to the institutions and to the society of the whole country." Senator John Tyler Morgan of Alabama predicted that the result would be "disbanded families."

Addressing the committee members, Elizabeth said that their appointment "thrilled the hearts" of their "countrywomen." They were "grateful for even this slight recognition." Susan celebrated the achievement in her diary: "If the best of worldly goods had come to me personally, I could not feel more joyous and blest." They gave each man a copy of the *History of Woman Suffrage.*

Surely, they must have thought that victory was possible in their lifetime.

"A Heavily Veiled Woman"

Hattie, who had been traveling and studying in Europe, was summoned home to help finish volume two. Elizabeth was running out of energy. Susan was restless. She chafed at her confinement. "O, how I long to be in the midst of the fray," she confided in her diary. "I shall feel like an uncaged lion when this book is off my hands."

Their work was complicated by the fact that the volume they were working on covered the period of the split into two rival organizations. Lucy Stone, who founded the AWSA, had summarily rejected Elizabeth's requests for material. She had too much to do, plus no one should write the history "while the war goes on." Hattie took on the task because she thought it would "do credit" to her mother and Susan if "they rose above the roar of battle and gave space for a record of the work of their antagonists." Elizabeth agreed, although "at no point," she said, could Hattie consult her. Susan paid Hattie one hundred dollars.

The work on volume two was done by mid-May, and Elizabeth and Hattie left on a ship bound for Europe. With them they took a box of volume one of the *History,* piles of baggage, and a baby carriage for Elizabeth Cady Stanton II, known as Lizette, the child of Theodore and his wife Marguerite Berry. After spending time with them at their home in France, Elizabeth moved with Hattie to a convent near the University of Toulouse, where Hattie attended classes. Within a few months, however, Hattie decided to marry a "tall, dark Englishman," named William Henry Blatch, Jr., known as Harry.

After Hattie's wedding in England, Elizabeth, whose reputation was well known there, attended a woman's rights meeting in Glasgow, Scotland. She spent several weeks in London, renewing friendships with leading reformers and intellectuals. On a day when "one of the blackest and most dense fogs" shrouded London, she was visited by a heavily veiled woman. When she "threw off her concealment," Elizabeth wrote in her diary, "there stood Victoria Woodhull." Now the wife of a prominent Englishman, she took Elizabeth to her "beautiful home." Victoria had endured "great suffering," Elizabeth wrote in her diary, "May the good angels watch and guard her."

"She Is Not to Be There"

During Elizabeth's absence, Susan kept up her ceaseless fight for woman suffrage. The struggle had been going on for years in Nebraska, spearheaded by Clara Bewick Colby and Lucy and Erasmus Correll. Finally in 1882, a referendum would take place in November. Susan was summoned to campaign. En route to Nebraska by train, she wrote a letter to an old friend and co-worker that reflected both her longing for Elizabeth and her awareness that she was no longer young: "Only think, I shall not have a white-haired woman on the platform with me. . . . Mrs. Stanton's presence has ever made me feel that we should get the true and brave words spoken. Now that she is not to be there, I can not quite feel certain that our younger sisters will be equal to the emergency, yet they are each and all valiant, earnest and talented, and will soon be left to manage the ship without even me."

Seven thousand people showed up to hear her speak in the

newly built Boyd's Opera House in Omaha, Nebraska. Another huge crowd listened to her in Lincoln, Nebraska. The
press coverage was generally fair, although there were the
usual nasty articles, including one with the headline "Mad Anthony's Raid." Despite a massive effort by prosuffrage forces,
male voters soundly defeated the referendum. Celebrating the
outcome, antisuffrage students at the state university conducted a mock funeral procession with an effigy of Susan
placed in the coffin. Midway into the torchlit spectacle, prosuffrage students commandeered the effigy and spirited it out
of sight.

Susan celebrated her sixty-third birthday on February 15,
1883. A reporter described her as having "an extra wrinkle in
her face, a little more silver in her hair, but her blue eyes are
just as bright . . . her step as active as when she was forty. . . .
her face is wonderfully intellectual, and she moves about like
the woman of purpose she is."

Suffrage advocates across America marked the day. Groups
and individuals sent her letters, telegrams, flowers, and gifts,
including a man who sent her one hundred dollars. Use it to
buy a shawl, he wrote in a note, adding, "I don't believe in
woman suffrage, but I do believe in Susan B. Anthony."

Susan attended an event in Philadelphia presided over by an
old friend, Robert Purvis. He read resolutions that honored
her and spoke about the "stormy periods of persecution and
outrage" that she had weathered in the fight to end slavery
and then to gain "woman's emancipation from civil and political debasement." Susan replied that she had "been only one of
many men and women who have labored side by side in this
cause." She singled out Lucretia and Elizabeth, who had led her
"to consider and accept the then new doctrine" of woman's

rights. "Alone I should have been as a mere straw in the wind," she said.

She capped off the celebrations by sailing for Europe at the end of February. Despite the cold weather, a crowd stood on the wharf to bid her farewell. Wearing a black velvet bonnet, velvet-trimmed black silk dress, and a beaver-lined black cloak, she waved farewell. Elizabeth had been urging her to come, as had her friends, who thought it was time she had a vacation. She finally agreed when Rachel Foster offered to make the arrangements and accompany her.

After twelve days at sea, they disembarked at Liverpool, England, and took the train to London, where Elizabeth was waiting on "the tiptoe of expectation." Writing to her sister, Susan reported that "Mrs. Stanton was at the station, her face beaming and her white curls as lovely as ever."

"More Worlds to Conquer"

Susan spent nine months in Europe. With Rachel she traveled throughout Italy, Switzerland, Germany, and France. She spent a great deal of time with Elizabeth in London and Basingstoke, where Hattie, who was pregnant, lived with her husband. Together they visited prominent reformers, woman suffrage activists, religious and political leaders, and attended woman suffrage meetings. In June she and Elizabeth were invited to speak on the American woman's movement. Hattie divvied up the topics: Elizabeth discussed the educational, social, and religious aspects, and Susan covered employment and the legal and political situation. "Our friends said we spoke well; but we were not at all satisfied with ourselves," Elizabeth wrote in her diary. "Well, the ordeal is over and everybody is delighted," Susan wrote in her diary. "Even the timid ones expressed great

satisfaction. Mrs. Stanton gave them the rankest radical sentiments, but all so cushioned they didn't hurt."

Hattie's baby Nora was born in September. "The first bugle
blast of the event was at dinner and in six hours all was over,"
Elizabeth wrote to her cousin Libby. A week later, she wrote in
her diary, "As I sit beside Hattie with the baby in my arms, and
realize that three generations of us are together, I appreciate
more than ever what each generation can do for the next one,
by making the most of itself."

Elizabeth had been abroad for a year and a half. Now Susan
convinced her that they had "more worlds to conquer." It was
time for her to return; together they would plan an international meeting of women in Washington. "I prefer a tyrant of
my own sex," Elizabeth once wrote, "so I shall not deny the
patent fact of my subjection; for I do believe that I have developed into much more of a woman under her jurisdiction . . .
than if left to myself reading novels in an easy chair, lost in
sweet reveries of the golden age to come without any effort of
my own."

Her last day with Hattie and Nora was her birthday, November 12. "When Hattie and I parted," she wrote in her diary,
"we stood mute, without a tear, hand in hand, gazing into each
other's eyes. My legs trembled so that I could scarcely walk to
the carriage. The blessed baby was sleeping, one little arm over
her head."

While they were at sea, the governor of the Territory of
Washington signed a bill granting women in the Territory the
right to hold office and vote.

20

"Brace Up and Get Ready"

SETBACKS
1884–1889

Years of intractable resistance to their cause finally impelled Susan to curb Elizabeth's penchant for getting involved in tangential issues, such as Frederick Douglass's recent marriage to Helen Pitts, a white woman. Their "amalgamation of different races," as it was called at the time, set off a firestorm of criticism. When Elizabeth had heard the news, she proposed that they write a letter of congratulations to Frederick and Helen and send it to the press. Also, they should invite their old friend Frederick to speak at the upcoming convention. No, Susan, replied. As leaders of the movement, neither she nor Elizabeth had the right to "complicate or compromise" their arduous battle to enfranchise women. The "question of intermarriage of the races," she pointed out, affected "women and men alike"; therefore, opposition to intermarriage was not an example of "invidious discrimination" against women, which, of course, they would protest. "Your sympathy has run away with your judgment," Susan wrote in a letter that she closed with "Lovingly and fearfully yours." She

prevailed; Elizabeth limited her actions to writing a private letter to Frederick and Helen.

"Keep the Pot Aboiling"

In early spring, Elizabeth rented out the Tenafly house, perhaps
to generate income. She returned to Johnstown, New York, and
lived with her sisters in their old family home. Susan arrived to
resume work on volume three of the *History of Woman Suffrage*
and rented a sunny room, called the "Parlor Chamber" in Mrs.
Henry's Boarding House, a block away from Elizabeth.

They worked all day sorting through the "number of appall-
ing boxes of papers"—reports, clippings, personal accounts, and
autobiographical sketches that they had requested from activists. In the evening, Elizabeth noted in her diary, they would
"take a walk, then chat for a while, look over the daily [news]
papers, drink a glass of lemonade or eat an orange, and then we
part for the night." Susan went to bed early, while Elizabeth
stayed up for a couple more hours, "reading and thinking about
the great world."

Since it had always been their rule "to keep the pot aboil-
ing," Susan and Elizabeth took time away from the *History* to
hold a convention in the old courthouse, where Elizabeth's
father had argued many cases. Their agenda was "stirring the
women up to vote" in the upcoming school election, the right
they had recently won in New York. On election day, they
went to the polls and voted. In Johnstown, one woman was
elected to the school board. Two women were elected in nearby
Gloversville. The results delighted Elizabeth and Susan, although their pleasure was tempered by the defeat of a woman
suffrage referendum in Oregon.

In the spring, Elizabeth returned to Tenafly. In July, Susan came to continue the work on volume three of the *History*. "I really think of you with pity these hot midsummer days," a friend wrote to Elizabeth, "under the lash of blessed Susan's relentless energy." But, she acknowledged, Susan was just as hard on herself.

Deciphering illegible accounts and reports from coworkers "was enough to destroy our old eyes," Elizabeth complained, but they kept at it. As always, they shared pleasurable times. "Susan and I take moonlight walks now and then," Elizabeth wrote in her diary. "When weary, we sit on the benches which I have had scattered along the hillside road, and we gaze at the moon, which I enjoy more than walking." Occasionally they rode in the phaeton, a low-slung carriage, a gift from her son Neil. Having sold her reliable horse, Jule, they had to depend on whatever horse the livery had in the stable. It took both of them to keep the horse moving—Susan using the whip, and Elizabeth jerking the reins and calling out "get up." Invariably, they would become engrossed in a conversation and forget the horse, who would "soon come to a dead standstill."

Elizabeth celebrated her seventieth birthday on November 12 and was showered with telegrams and letters from across America; cablegrams from England, France, and Germany; express packages with gifts of books, pictures, silverware, mosaics, and Indian blankets; and baskets of fruit and bouquets of flowers. That day she and Susan attended a large reception at Dr. Clemence Lozier's home, where Elizabeth had been asked to speak on "The Pleasures of Old Age." It took her a "week to think up all of the pleasures," she noted in her diary. A letter from Hattie was read aloud: "Kiss dear Susan and let her kiss you for me. . . . I throw up my cap and cry hurrah for you two grand old warriors!"

On December 31, Elizabeth wrote in her diary, "We have finally penned the last page" of the *History of Woman Suffrage*. It was a monumental accomplishment—ten years of "arduous toil," three volumes, more than three thousand pages illustrated with fine steel engravings of many coworkers. Their reward for their "arduous toil" was their certainty that present and future women would be inspired to action by reading it. "Lifting woman into her proper place in the scale of being," Elizabeth wrote, "is the mightiest revolution the world has yet known, and it may be that more than half a century is needed to accomplish this."

"When the News Comes"

With the *History* finished, Elizabeth decided to return to England. First, however, she attempted to mend the breach with Lucy Stone by asking Antoinette Brown Blackwell, her friend and Lucy's sister-in-law, to arrange a meeting with the four of them—Antoinette, Lucy, Susan, and Elizabeth.

"As to meeting with Mrs. Stanton," Lucy replied, "it is out of the question with me" because she had heard that Elizabeth had written a letter in which she characterized Lucy as "the biggest liar and hypocrite she had ever seen." Susan had already complicated the situation by recently rejecting Lucy's invitation to get together during one of Susan's trips to Boston. All in all, Lucy replied that she was "too busy with the work that remains, to take time to mend broken cisterns."

In late October, Elizabeth left for England. One morning in January 1887, she was eating breakfast in her room at her daughter's home in Basingstoke, England, when Hattie entered and handed her a cablegram from New York with the news that Henry Stanton had died. "Death!" she wrote in her diary. "We all think we are prepared to hear of the passing away of the aged. But when the news comes, the heart and pulses all seem to stand still." After forty-six years of marriage, Henry, she wrote, now "leads the way to another sphere." What that was, no one knew, she and Hattie "sat together and talked all day long of the mysteries of life and death, speculating on what lies beyond."

Some years earlier, Elizabeth had sought to reassure Isabella Beecher Hooker about her marriage because, she wrote, "I fear from our conversation you may imagine my domestic relations not altogether happy." They are, she asserted, "far more so than 99/100 of married people. . . . Mr. Stanton . . . is a very cheerful sunny genial man, hence we can laugh together. . . . He loves music so do I, he loves oratory so do I . . . but," she acknowledged, "our theology is as wide apart as the north and south pole. . . . My views trouble him. I accept his philosophically. . . . If he could do the same we should be nearer and dearer I have no doubt."

A few days later in Washington, DC, Susan presided over the Nineteenth National Woman Suffrage Convention. A resolution was passed extending sympathy to "our beloved president, in the recent death of her husband, Henry B. Stanton." Susan read Elizabeth's annual letter: "For half a century we have tried appeals, petitions, arguments. . . . Be assured that the next generation will not argue the question of woman's rights with the infinite patience we have had for half a century."

On the second day came word that finally the full Senate had voted on the Sixteenth Amendment, which read, "The right of citizens of the United States to vote shall not be denied or abridged by any State on account of sex." Many women observed the debate from the Senate gallery. (Susan remained to preside at the convention.) One senator presented a prosuffrage petition from the Woman's Christian Temperance Union, an organization of 200,000 members. Another introduced an antisuffrage document from two hundred men, including the president of Harvard University. That document and the claim that granting woman suffrage would "unsex our mothers, wives, and sisters" prevailed; the amendment was defeated.

Noting, however, that sixteen of the senators had voted for the amendment, convention delegates passed a resolution: "That we rejoice in this evidence that our demand is forcing itself upon the attention and action of Congress, and that when a new Congress shall have assembled, with new men and new ideas, we may hope to change this minority into a majority."

But soon all-male courts, legislators, and voters delivered a series of setbacks to the cause. In February, the Territorial Supreme Court of Washington repealed the woman suffrage that had been won four years earlier. In March, the U.S. Congress passed a bill outlawing polygamy and disenfranchising women, who had been voting since 1870, in the Territory of Utah. In April, male voters in Rhode Island resoundingly rejected a woman suffrage referendum.

In the wake of these defeats, Susan turned her attention to planning for the upcoming eight-day meeting of the International Council of Women (ICW) that she and Elizabeth had set in motion during their time together in Europe. It was a massive undertaking. "Oh dear—how I wish I had Mrs. Stanton here—and I could galvanize her to make beautiful my crude glimmering of ideas," she wrote to her niece. She sent a draft of the sixteen-page program to Elizabeth, who deemed it too verbose. "Put every sentence through your metaphysical, rhetorical & common sense tweezer," she exhorted Susan.

"Full of Fight and Fire"

Elizabeth reveled in her time abroad. She read voraciously—books by British thinker John Stuart Mill, German novelist Jean Paul Richter, and Russian novelist Leo Tolstoy, and essays by the English writer George Eliot—and commented on them in her diary. She did not like Tolstoy's *Anna Karenina* because "all the women are disappointed and unhappy; and well they may be, as they are made to look to men, and not to themselves, for their chief joy."

She corresponded regularly with Susan, who was juggling attending state conventions and planning the upcoming ICW meeting. In January 1888, Elizabeth wrote to Susan, "We have jogged along pretty well for forty years or more. Perhaps mid the wreck of thrones and the undoing of so many friendships, sects, parties and families, you and I deserve some credit for sticking together through all adverse winds, with so few ripples on the surface. When I get back to America I intend to cling to you closer than ever. I am thoroughly rested now and full of fight and fire, ready to travel and speak from Maine to Florida. Tell our suffrage daughters to brace up and get ready for a long pull, a strong pull, and a pull all together when I come back."

Every day, she noted in her diary, she received letters from "the faithful," perhaps writing at Susan's behest, urging her to return for the ICW and the celebration of the fortieth anniversary of the Seneca Falls convention that she had initiated. Elizabeth did not like ocean travel in the stormy winter weather, "but for blessed Susan's sake," she wrote in her diary, "I suppose I must go." Then she changed her mind.

Susan was outraged when she received Elizabeth's letter. "I am ablaze and dare not write tonight," she wrote in her diary.

The next day, she sent Elizabeth a fierce letter that "will start every white hair on her head." The "terrible" charges she leveled against Elizabeth in her letter made Susan's "own heart ache all night, awake or asleep." Ten days passed; then, finally, a cablegram from Elizabeth arrived with three words—"I am coming." Susan was "so relieved" she felt like she was "treading on air."

Although Susan was glad to see Elizabeth, she was not pleased that she came unprepared to speak and told her she had to produce two speeches—one for the congressional suffrage committees, the other for the opening of the ICW. To that end, Susan later recalled, she "shut" Elizabeth in a room with "pen and pencil, kept a guard at the door, permitted no one to see her" until she produced her "usual magnificent address." Elizabeth's recollection of the incident was more benign: Yes, Susan had "ordered" her "to remain conscientiously" in her room and write the speeches. However, she was "permitted" to take carriage rides for an hour or two every day. And there was no guard at her door.

"We the People"

The ICW opened on March 25, 1888, in the Albaugh's Opera House, a spacious and elegant auditorium decorated with evergreens and flowers. A large portrait of Lucretia Mott surrounded by smilax and lilies of the valley stood on the platform where Susan, Elizabeth, and other dignitaries sat on elegant sofas and chairs. Soft music played while the hall filled with delegates from every state and territory in the United States and from seven countries—England, France, Norway, Denmark, Finland, India, and Canada. Fifty-three different women's organizations, from religious to literary to political, sent representatives. For eight days, women and men packed the hall in what Elizabeth called a "splendid agitation." Susan presided. When she introduced Elizabeth to deliver her keynote speech, the audience stood, clapping, cheering, and waving their handkerchiefs, a gesture of affection and respect.

Susan was in high spirits; reporters described her as "gay-hearted, good-natured." Audiences loved her for her "brightness and wit." The press appreciated her "frank, plain, open, business-like way of doing everything connected with the council." If a speaker went on too long, Susan gave them a series of warnings. First she said, "Your time's about up, my dear." Next it was, "I guess you'll have to stop now; it's more than ten minutes." Then she tugged on the speaker's skirt; finally, she would rise and go stand beside the speaker, an action that inevitably got results.

The event culminated in hearings before the congressional committees on woman suffrage where Elizabeth masterfully articulated how denying woman suffrage violated the Constitution that the legislators had sworn to uphold. "Even the preamble of the Constitution is an argument for self-government—'We, the people,'" she pointed out. There is a provision—Article 1, Section 9, Clause 9—that prohibited the United States from granting titles of nobility, yet, Elizabeth charged, "You have granted titles of nobility to every male voter, making all men rulers . . . over all women." If the legislators did not "settle this question by wise legislation," Elizabeth predicted that "it will eventually be settled by violence."

After the convention, Elizabeth, who was homeless because she had sold her house in Tenafly, set off to visit her family and friends. She spent her seventy-third birthday with her son Gat and his wife, who lived on a farm in Iowa. That winter she spent at Maggie's home in Omaha, Nebraska, where she

185 ~

delighted in taking a daily ride on a cable car that ran for nine miles "up hill and down" for a fare of fifteen cents. Neil, who also lived in Omaha, escorted her. Regardless of the weather, Elizabeth took an outside seat; Neil always sat inside with passengers who commented on the "queer old lady who rode outside in all kinds of wintry weather."

In late spring, Elizabeth relocated herself to Hempstead, Long Island, at the home of Gat and his wife, who had recently moved there from Iowa. Because she considered it her "mission to 'stir up'" conventional ideas, she agreed to speak to a group of literary and musical women who were staying at an elegant hotel in Coney Island, a nearby summer resort. "I said a good many radical things," she wrote in her diary, "but being well sugar-coated their deglutition was easy." While there, she attended several concerts. "And such music!" she wrote. "I was in the seventh heaven."

Susan, who had been lecturing and attending state suffrage conventions, came to speak to the club in August, and she and Elizabeth spent several days together. Before parting, they wrote the call for the upcoming convention of the National American Woman Suffrage Association (NAWSA), the new organization formed by the merger of the old rivals, the NWSA and AWSA. After years apart and two years of intense negotiations, the breach had finally been closed.

21

"UNDER YOUR THUMB"

A MOUNTAIN OF WORK
1890–1895

ELIZABETH WAS OVERWHELMED BY THE DEMANDS facing her in early 1890: appearances before congressional committees, Susan's seventieth birthday celebration, and the first convention of the NAWSA, the united suffrage association. She was "tempted to escape from all the excitement" and go with her daughter Hattie, who was returning in February to England, after having spent several months in the United States. That idea prompted a "stormy correspondence" with Susan. Finally, Elizabeth capitulated. In a diary entry dated January 2, she wrote, "Susan commands me to come, and so I have finally written her: 'You will have me under your thumb the first of February."

Susan made good use of the time; on February 8, Elizabeth appeared before a congressional committee. After she spoke, Senator Zebulon Vance, the chairman, asked her:

"Would women be willing to go to war if they had the ballot?"

"We would decide first whether there should be war," Elizabeth replied. "You may be sure, Senator, that the influence of women will be against armed conflicts."

She went on to say that if there were a war, women would "do their share of work"; however, they [like men who served] would be "paid for their services and pensioned at the close of the war."

A week later, on the fifteenth, Susan turned seventy. Two hundred women and men feted her at a grand banquet in Washington, DC. The dining room at the Riggs House was festooned with tropical flowers, foliage, and American flags. Gifts were piled high on a table. Seventy pink carnations were presented to her. Toasts were made. Poems, telegrams, cablegrams, and letters were read, including one from Lucy Stone signed "I am very truly your co-worker."

Elizabeth gave the main address on the friendships of women: "If there is one part of my life which gives me more intense satisfaction than another, it is my friendship . . . with Susan B. Anthony." In response, Susan said, "I never could have done my work if I had not had this woman at my right hand."

Two days later, the executive committees of the rival suffrage organizations met to formalize their union and to elect officers for the NAWSA. Lucy's proposal that she and Elizabeth and Susan refuse to be elected president had been rejected by members who rallied around Susan. In a dramatic speech, Susan implored her supporters to vote for Elizabeth. The NWSA, she said, had stood for the "utmost liberty," for the "grand principle" of welcoming "representatives of all creeds and no creeds—Jew or Christian, Protestant or Catholic, Gentile or Mormon, pagan or atheists." If you embrace that idea, she said, "vote for Mrs. Stanton." And they did.

"All Hail and Congratulations"

As the newly elected president of the NAWSA, Elizabeth gave
the opening address at the historic convention. Scheduled to
leave the next day for England, she told her audience that she
considered it a "greater honor to go to England as the president
of this association" than to go as an ambassador sent by the
government. After her speech, she introduced Hattie, who said
a few words. As they left the platform together, the audience
erupted with cheers, applause, and a flurry of waving handkerchiefs. "Needless to say," Elizabeth wrote in her diary, "I was
deeply touched by this hearty demonstration." That night
Susan wrote in her diary that Hattie "showed herself worthy of
her mother and her mother's life-long friend and co-worker. It
was a proud moment for me."

Susan reigned over the rest of the convention. "'Saint Susan,'
as her followers love to call her . . . was the life and soul of the
meeting," wrote one reporter. A month later, she sat in the gallery of the House of Representatives and witnessed legislators
debate about whether or not to admit the Territory of Wyoming into the Union as a state with woman suffrage in its constitution. Representative Joseph Washington from Tennessee
was "unalterably opposed" because woman suffrage would
"only end in unsexing and degrading the womanhood of America." After haggling for three days, the representatives voted,
and Susan finally had the "inexpressible pleasure" of seeing the
prosuffrage representatives prevail.

Next was the fight in the Senate. Senator John Reagan of
Texas warned that woman suffrage in Wyoming would "make
men of women." George Vest of Missouri declared it "a
calamity . . . an absolute crime." Nonsense, replied the Wyoming legislators, who unequivocally declared in a telegram

that they would "remain out of the Union a hundred years rather than come in without woman suffrage." That tipped the balance, and a majority of senators voted to admit Wyoming with woman suffrage intact.

By the time President William Henry Harrison signed the bill, Susan was in South Dakota campaigning in favor of an upcoming referendum on woman suffrage. She had just finished speaking when someone handed her a telegram with the news, and she read it to the crowd, who responded with mighty cheers. When the news reached Elizabeth in England, she wrote in her diary, "I cannot express the joy that this victory has brought to my soul." Forty-two years had passed since she had insisted on demanding woman suffrage at the Seneca Falls convention.

Local suffrage workers in South Dakota had pleaded for Susan to come and campaign. They were "very sanguine" for victory; she, however, was not, having had her "hopes dashed to the earth" in seven other state campaigns. Nevertheless, she went because, she said, "I shall not be cast down, even if voted down." It was a grueling experience—long rides in freight cars and in stagecoaches that creaked with every turn of the wheel over deeply rutted dirt roads, nights spent in primitive sod houses, meals that sometimes consisted of "sour bread, muddy coffee and stewed green grapes." The weather fluctuated from broiling heat to cold winds. Storms, including cyclones, were commonplace.

The referendum was defeated. When Susan returned to her sister Mary's house in Rochester, Mary remarked that it was the first time she realized that Susan was indeed seventy years old. Susan started to think that perhaps it was time to settle down and turn over some of the fieldwork to the eager young women who had joined the cause. Elizabeth supported the idea: "My advice to you, Susan, is to keep some spot you can call your own; where you can live and die in peace and be cremated in your own oven if you desire." Susan decided to move in with Mary.

For years, Mary, a retired school principal, and their mother Lucy had lived in the two-story house and kept a room for Susan, who visited when she could. After Lucy's death, Mary had rented out the first floor and lived on the second, with a room set aside for Susan. A devoted sister and suffrage worker, Mary welcomed Susan's decision; the renters moved out, and an army of carpenters, wallpaper hangers, and painters renovated the entire house. Susan's office was on the second floor, where framed photographs of her coworkers stood on her desk and hung on the wall. Elizabeth's picture was front and center. In June, when Susan officially moved in, three hundred people attended the housewarming party.

"Might Have a Home Together"

At the same time that Susan "anchored" herself to one spot, Elizabeth, after eighteen months in Europe, decided to return to America. There had been so many changes during her absence. Her son Neil had died at the age of forty-eight. Her sister Tryphena was dead. Maggie's husband had died.

She left on August 23, 1891. Her last days were "filled with sadness" as she prepared to leave "those so dear to me," especially her granddaughters. Theodore and Hattie accompanied her to the ship. "It was very hard for us to say the last farewell," she recalled in her autobiography, "but we all tried to be as brave as possible." The question was: Where would she settle when she arrived?

Susan hoped that "they might have a home together and finish their lifework." Elizabeth's children thought otherwise. Instead they insisted that their mother share an apartment with two of her offspring who lived in New York City—Maggie, now studying physical education at Teachers College, Columbia University, and Robert, a lawyer and a bachelor. That possibility, Susan wrote in a heartfelt letter to Elizabeth, set off an "inner wail" in her "soul" because it meant that she could not "carry out the dream" of her life, which was to help Elizabeth collect and "carefully dissect" all her speeches and articles and publish her "best utterances" into a single volume.

Elizabeth's children prevailed. In early September, she, along with Maggie and Robert, moved into an eight-room penthouse, which Elizabeth dubbed her "eyrie." But by the end of the month, she was in Rochester. Susan had "summoned" her to pose for Adelaide Johnson, a sculptor who had already carved marble busts of Susan and Lucretia, which were to be displayed in the Women's Building at the upcoming World's Columbian Exposition, a spectacular event to celebrate the four hundredth anniversary of the arrival of Christopher Columbus. For four to five hours a day, Elizabeth sat still while Adelaide shaped a "huge mass of clay" into her "familiar facial outlines." Because Adelaide indulged her penchant for napping, Elizabeth reciprocated by "summoning up, when awake, the most intelligent and radiant expression that I could command."

In November, Elizabeth returned to New York City and celebrated her seventy-sixth birthday with her family. Both she and Susan were ready to slow down, but in stark contrast to the days when they were reviled, they were now revered and besieged with requests to speak. "I felt that my threescore and ten and two years added ought to excuse me," Susan wrote to suffrage workers in Kansas who were begging her to attend their convention. Finally, overwhelmed by their pleas, she wrote, "I will say yes, tuck on my coat and mittens," and come. Elizabeth addressed many local groups and wrote newspaper and magazine articles. For the upcoming NAWSA convention in Washington, DC, she wrote "The Solitude of Self," a speech many people considered a masterpiece (and still do today). Elizabeth wrote that she was also inclined "to think" it the "best thing" she had ever written, at least, she added, in her "declining years."

"That Day Is Passed for Me"

The convention opened on January 16, 1892, and as the time drew near, Elizabeth informed Susan that Maggie and Robert were urging her to rest, to skip the convention; Susan would have to come and personally escort her to Washington, which is, of course, exactly what Susan did.

Elizabeth delivered her speech to the House and Senate judiciary committees and at the convention. "The point I wish plainly to bring before you on this occasion," she said, "is the individuality of each human soul. . . . Who, I ask you, can take, dare take, on himself, the rights, the duties, the responsibilities of another human soul?" The House committee had ten thousand copies of her speech printed and distributed throughout the country. Susan got a copy to give Elizabeth and wrote on it, "To Elizabeth Cady Stanton—This is pronounced the strongest and most unanswerable argument and appeal ever made by mortal pen or tongue for the full freedom and franchise of women."

It was Elizabeth's last convention. Although she was in good health, her age and her excessive weight made it difficult for her to "clamber up and down platforms, mount long staircases into halls and hotels, be squeezed in the crush at receptions, and do all the other things public life involves." In reflecting, she wrote, "That day is passed for me." Susan was elected to take her place as president of NAWSA. Anna Howard Shaw, a close ally of Susan and Elizabeth, was elected to take Susan's position as vice president at large. Elizabeth and Lucy Stone were made honorary presidents. (Lucy Stone died the following year.)

Elizabeth vowed to turn her attention to "general reading and thinking, to music, poetry, and novels." Soon, however, she found herself "wheedled into" accepting speaking engagements. Then there were Susan's demands; it was a presidential election year, and she needed speeches to deliver at the political conventions. "Susan is still on the war-path," Elizabeth noted in her diary. "All through this hot weather she has been following the political conventions. I wrote the addresses to all, and she read them." But to no avail. As they had in years past, the major political parties—Republicans and Democrats—ignored their appeals. In November, Grover Cleveland, a Democrat who was staunchly opposed to woman suffrage, was elected president.

Although the political system remained impervious to women's demands, a sea change had occurred in other arenas. Colleges and universities had opened their doors (women comprised 40 percent of the total of college graduates), and employment opportunities had expanded to include clerical jobs and professional positions as doctors and lawyers. A new image of women was emerging in the popular culture—the New Woman, who challenged the traditional notion of a "separate sphere" for a "true woman," who exemplified religious piety, sexual purity, wifely submission, and motherly domesticity. A New Woman was bold; she believed she had choices—an education, a paid position, marriage, motherhood, public service. These women and sympathetic men were enthusiastic suffrage workers. They joined organizations and attended conventions. The "whole matter" of woman's rights, Susan told a reporter in 1892, was no longer "regarded with such horror and aversion" as it once was. As for Susan and Elizabeth, they had gone from being ridiculed to being lionized, with their friendship intact.

"She Came to Stir Me Up"

A mountain of work awaited Susan in 1893, and she confided in her diary that she was "simply overwhelmed." The World's Columbian Exposition was set to open in Chicago, Illinois, where more than two hundred structures were built on the six-hundred-acre fairground. Exhibits from around the world included an eleven-ton cheese and a seventy-foot-high tower of electric lightbulbs. An amusement park featured the world's first Ferris wheel, a 250-foot-high steel structure with thirty-six cars that could hold sixty people (fully loaded, it carried 2,160 people). William "Buffalo Bill" Cody set up his Wild West show, an extravaganza with horsemen from different cultures—Turks, Gauchos, Arabs; performers such as Annie Oakley; an appearance by Sitting Bull and a band of braves; and Buffalo Bill's reenactments of his feats as a Pony Express rider.

Susan arranged for a series of congresses, or conferences, on a range of topics, to be held during the Exposition. In need of speeches, she spent a week with Elizabeth. "She came to stir me up to write papers for every Congress at the Exposition, which I did," Elizabeth noted in her diary.

They also weighed in on the controversial issue of whether or not the Fair should remain open on Sundays. Vocal religious leaders opposed the idea. Elizabeth and Susan argued it should be open for the enjoyment of people who work six days a week, as most did at that time. Elizabeth wrote articles and distributed leaflets. In a wrangle with a clergyman, Susan said she would allow a young man to go to Buffalo Bill's Wild West Show instead of church because "he'd learn more from Buffalo Bill than from listening to an intolerant sermon."

At Buffalo Bill's invitation, she attended a show. Riding his majestic horse up to her box, he swept off his cowboy hat and bowed to her while his horse reared up on its hind legs. Not to be outdone, Susan stood and bowed in return. The crowd loved it!

That fall in Colorado male voters were going to vote on a woman suffrage amendment. Carrie Chapman Catt, one of the new generation of suffrage workers, orchestrated a campaign that resulted in a resounding victory. "Now we have full suffrage in two states. My soul rejoices," Elizabeth noted in her diary. "But how slowly the world moves." Susan pronounced herself "the happiest woman in America."

In November, Susan went to New York City to celebrate Elizabeth's seventy-eighth birthday and make plans for the upcoming campaigns in two states—New York and Kansas, the same states for which they had waged hard-fought but unsuccessful campaigns in 1867. In New York, wealthy women, for the first time, actively advocated for suffrage, a development one newspaper called "an insurrection." Another first was the emergence of groups called "Remonstrants" and "Antis" comprised of women who opposed suffrage. Their claims ranged from the assertion that only an "insignificant minority" of women wanted to vote to the statement that a woman was "unfitted for the ballot because she was influenced by pity, passion and prejudice rather than by judgment."

"I seem to thrive on all this excitement," Elizabeth wrote in her diary. When Hattie arrived from England for a three-week visit in the "white heat" of the battle, she was "immediately pressed into service." By the time she left, Elizabeth noted, they had "scarcely seen each other."

But once again the "great battles" ended in failure. "I feel sad and disappointed at such contemptuous treatment," Elizabeth confided in her diary. "It is very humiliating for women . . . to have their sacred rights at the mercy of a masculine oligarchy."

California was the next battleground. A vote on a woman suffrage amendment was scheduled for the following year, and suffrage workers begged Susan to come to kick off their campaign. Before heading west, she spent a few weeks in Rochester, where she went to an antilynching lecture given by Ida B. Wells, a fearless black journalist. Ida was repeatedly and rudely interrupted by a man who identified himself as a Texan studying at the local theological seminary. Finally, he shouted, "If the negroes don't like it in the South, why don't they leave and go North?"

Jumping to her feet, Susan said, "I will tell you why; it is because they are treated no better in the North than they are in the South." Then she backed up her statement with a list of examples. After the lecture, Susan invited Ida to stay at her house. The next day, Susan instructed her stenographer to assist Ida with her correspondences. When the stenographer said she would not work for a black woman, Susan fired her.

"No Limit, if Dead"

Anna Howard Shaw accompanied Susan to California. Suffrage workers in cities along the railroad route begged her to stop and spend time with them. Leaving on April 27, 1895, Susan was heralded by admirers in Warren, Ohio; Indianapolis, Indiana; Chicago, Illinois; St. Louis, Missouri; Denver, Colorado; Cheyenne, Wyoming; Salt Lake City, Utah; Reno, Nevada. On May 20, she was led into the Golden Gate Hall in San Francisco, onto a stage decorated with bamboo, palms, and all kinds of tropical foliage. There she was seated under a canopy of roses in a chair decorated with an array of fragrant flowers—lilies, roses, carnations, sweet peas. Then woman after woman came to her with more flowers until she was "literally buried under an avalanche of the choicest blossoms." While in California, she returned to Yosemite, at the age of seventy-five, riding into the valley on the back of a mule. In the Mariposa Big Tree Grove, a park commissioner officially named one of the trees "Susan B. Anthony."

After six weeks, Susan and Anna headed home, making stops along the way. In Chicago, a reporter who had interviewed Susan when she attended the World's Fair in 1893 described her as "thinner and more spiritual-looking . . . her transparent hands grasping the arms of her chair, her thin, hatchet face and white hair, with only her keen eyes flashing light and fire. . . . She recalls facts, figures, names and dates with unerring accuracy."

In July, Susan collapsed while giving a speech in Lakeside, Ohio. Word spread that she would not survive the night. A newspaper editor in Chicago sent instructions to a reporter on the scene to write "5,000 words if still living; no limit, if dead." Louisa Southworth, a longtime close friend to her and to Elizabeth, took Susan to her summer home to recover. "I never realized how desolate the world would be to me without you until I heard of your sudden illness," Elizabeth wrote to her. "Let me urge you with all the strength I have, and all the love I bear you, to stay at home and rest and save your precious self."

Susan's diary remained blank for many days, until finally she wrote, "On the mend." In November, she went to New York City for Elizabeth's eightieth birthday party, an extravaganza staged at the Metropolitan Opera House by the National Woman's Council, an organization that represented diverse groups of women and their interests, instead of focusing only on suffrage. This disappointed some suffrage workers but delighted Susan. From the beginning, she pointed out, Elizabeth had promulgated an array of ideas and issues. "Surely," she said, "for all classes of women, liberal, orthodox, Jewish, Mormon, suffrage and anti-suffrage, native and foreign, black and white—to unite in paying a tribute of respect to the greatest woman reformer, philosopher and statesman of the century will be the realization of Mrs. Stanton's most optimistic dream."

More than three thousand people packed the opulent opera house. Elizabeth was enthroned in a large red armchair bedecked with flowers under an arch of white carnations with *Stanton* spelled out in red carnations. Susan sat beside her and opened the event by paying tribute to the "pioneers"—Lucretia Mott, Martha Wright, Frederick Douglass—and reading some of the hundreds of congratulatory messages, including an eloquent one from Theodore Tilton, who was still living in Paris. "At the present day, every woman who seeks the legal custody of

199 ∽

her children, or the legal control of her property; every woman who finds the doors of a college or a university opening to her; every woman who administers a post-office or a public library; every woman who enters upon a career of medicine, law or theology; every woman who teaches a school, or tills a farm, or keeps a shop; every one who drives a horse, rides a bicycle, skates at a rink, swims at a summer resort, plays golf or tennis in a public park, or even snaps a kodak [camera]; every such woman, I say, owes her liberty largely to yourself and to your earliest and bravest co-workers in the cause of woman's emancipation. So I send my greetings not to you alone, but also to the small remainder now living of your original bevy of noble assistants, among whom—first, last and always—has been and still continues to be your fit mate, chief counselor and executive right hand, Susan B. Anthony."

Elizabeth expressed her profound appreciation. Then telling the great audience that she was no longer "able to stand very long, nor talk loud enough," she said that she had asked Helen Potter, a young suffrage worker, to deliver her address. As always Elizabeth's intent was to stir up people. "Do all you can, *no matter what*, to get people to think," she had once written. This time she critiqued the restraints placed on women, particularly by religious institutions.

Susan had tried to get her to tone down her criticism because, she said, slowly but surely churches were adopting more liberal positions. But Elizabeth had refused to back down; it was imperative for women to question religious literature, such as the Bible, that was used to justify the elevation of men over women. However, she also made a point of acknowledging the men in the audience who "may feel that the new woman will crowd them entirely off the planet." Reassuring them, she said "they need not despair" because they will be looked after as long as they have mothers, sisters, wives, daughters, and sweethearts.

Shortly after the celebration, Elizabeth published *The Woman's Bible*, a book she had started working on while she was in England. "Church and state, priest and legislators, all political parties and religious denominations," she wrote in the introduction, "have alike taught that woman was made after man, of man, and for man, an inferior being, subject to man." She challenged this idea by scrutinizing and reinterpreting the parts in the Bible that referred to women. She had tried to enlist women to work on the project. Some initially agreed, but then backed out. Others helped her, including Clara Bewick Colby, Matilda Joslyn Gage, and the Reverend Olympia Brown. Susan refused, although she defended Elizabeth's right to write her commentaries on scriptures: "Women have just as good a right to interpret and twist the Bible to their own advantage as men have always twisted it and turned it to theirs," she told a newspaper reporter. But, as a strategy for achieving suffrage, she thought that it was foolhardy to stir up a controversy over orthodox religious beliefs.

As a Quaker, Susan belonged to a liberal religion that had always allowed women to preach and participate in governance. The Bible was a historical document, not the infallible word of God. She maintained that once women were enfranchised, conservative churches and clergymen would adopt more liberal interpretations. "Get political rights first and religious bigotry will melt like dew before the morning sun," she wrote to Elizabeth. Elizabeth vehemently disagreed. Women, she said, had to first free their minds.

22

"To Stir You and Others Up"

FREE EXPRESSION
1896–1900

A s Susan feared, *The Woman's Bible* ignited a firestorm of criticism. "I could cry a heap every time I read or think [about it]," she wrote to Clara Bewick Colby. As for Elizabeth herself, Susan admitted to Clara, "She thinks I have gone over to the enemy—so counts my judgment worth nothing more than that of any other narrow-souled body." But ever loyal, Susan concluded, "I shall love and honor her to the end—whether or not her *Bible* pleases me or not. So I hope she will do for me."

Susan's loyalty was sorely tested in January 1896 at the annual NAWSA Convention. Women who were "especially near and dear to her" introduced a resolution disavowing the "so-called Woman's Bible." Outraged, Susan expressed her indignation at their repudiation of "the right of individual opinion for every member."

Throughout the long fight for woman's rights—begun before many of the new members were born—she and Elizabeth had fought for that principle. "When our platform becomes too narrow for people of all creeds and of no creeds, I myself can not stand upon it," she declared. "You would better not begin resolving against individual action or you will find no limit. This year it is Mrs. Stanton; next year it may be I or one of yourselves, who will be the victim." She warned delegates that a vote for the resolution was a "vote of censure upon a woman who is without a peer in intellectual and statesman-like ability; one who has stood for half a century the acknowledged leader of progressive thought and demand in regard to all matters pertaining to the absolute freedom of women." By a vote of fifty-three to forty-one, the resolution passed. Susan was disconsolate.

After the convention, she visited Elizabeth, who was "thoroughly indignant over the petty action of the convention" and insistent that they both resign their positions, Susan as president and Elizabeth as honorary president. Returning home, Susan spent "three weeks of agony of soul, with scarcely a night of sleep." Her sister Mary, who had voted against the resolution, felt that for her own sake Susan should resign, however, for the good of the organization she should remain.

Still "sick at heart," Susan finally made her decision. Informing Elizabeth, she wrote, "No, my dear, instead of my resigning and leaving those half-fledged chickens without any mother, I think it my duty and the duty of yourself and all the liberals to be at the next convention and try to reverse this miserable, narrow action." Respecting Susan's reasoning, Elizabeth agreed not to resign her position. (The action was never reversed.)

Their friendship survived the trauma; their bond was indissoluble, their loyalty transcendent.

203 ∽

"Is It Not Time?"

Two states were holding elections on woman suffrage amendments in 1896—Idaho and California. "Won't it be a magnificent feather in our cap if we get both California and Idaho into the fold this year?" Susan wrote to Carrie Chapman Catt, who was working on the Idaho campaign. Susan had returned to California, having succumbed to repeated pleas from advocates to come.

"O, that I had you by my side," she wrote to Elizabeth, "what a team we would make!" Every day she sent her newspapers with reports of the campaign.

"I feel at times as if I should fly to your help," Elizabeth replied.

But, of course, she could not; her great weight limited her mobility, and she was losing her eyesight. "A great loss," she confided to her diary, "for me whose chief pleasure is reading." To compensate, she hired a young woman to read to her: "I like to sandwich the solid [nonfiction books] with the light [novels]."

Fortunately she could see enough to write. As usual, she was juggling multiple projects—an article supporting women's right to ride bicycles, the new craze; volume two of *The Woman's Bible*; and her autobiography. For the latter, she playfully asked Susan to reveal a romance from her younger days so that she could "weave a sentimental chapter entitled, for instance, 'The Romance of Susan B. Anthony's Younger Days.' How all the daily papers would jump at that!"

Victory seemed possible in California, until ten days before the election, when the Liquor Dealers' League launched a scare campaign that women voters would pass laws banning the sale of beer and whiskey. That shifted the momentum, and the amendment was defeated; the loss was tempered by the news of a victory in Idaho. Susan returned to Rochester and began planning for the upcoming NAWSA Convention to be held in Des Moines, Iowa. As always, she expected Elizabeth to produce "an argument, strong resolution, and tributes to those of our band who have died during the present year."

In her diary, Elizabeth complained, "One would think I were a machine; that all I had to do was to turn a crank and thoughts on any theme would bubble up like water." To Susan, she wrote, "Dear Susan, is it not time that some of our younger coadjutors do the bubbling? The fact is that I am tired bubbling on one subject." But, as usual, Elizabeth wrote what Susan requested for the convention.

In late January 1897, Susan boarded a train for Des Moines on a day when snow was piled high and the temperature was fifteen degrees below zero. The weather was even worse in Iowa—a heavy blizzard and twenty-four degrees below zero. Braving those conditions, sixty-three delegates from twenty states attended the convention. Susan presided. "It is not difficult for one who saw Miss Anthony for the first time to understand why she is so well beloved by her associates," a reporter wrote. She was the "most earnest worker of them all . . . their leader . . . counsellor and friend . . . [who was] not to be daunted by any obstacle."

Susan told the gathering that "the year 1896 witnessed greater successes than any" since the first convention in Seneca Falls, New York, in 1848. Utah had become a state with woman suffrage in its constitution. Male voters in Idaho had voted for a woman suffrage amendment to the state constitution. Equally important, she said, when opponents challenged that victory, the three male justices on the Idaho Supreme Court unanimously ruled in favor of the amendment. This, Susan said, was "the first time in the history of judicial decisions upon the enlargement of woman's rights, civil and political, that a court had issued a favorable ruling." To educate younger suffrage workers, Susan reviewed the long history of judicial decisions that had restricted woman's progress, including the Supreme Court ruling in *Myra Bradwell v. Illinois*, in which the court upheld a decision by the Illinois Supreme Court that denied a woman the right to practice law. In explaining his vote, Justice Joseph P. Bradley wrote that women's "natural and proper timidity and delicacy" makes them "unfit" for "many of the occupations of civil life. . . . The paramount destiny and mission of women are to fulfill the noble and benign office of wife and mother. This is the law of the Creator."

"Tired of Begging"

That spring both Susan and Elizabeth were immersed in writing projects. In Rochester, the attic in Susan's house was lined with boxes, bags, and trunks of material—reports, receipts, memorabilia, diaries, notebooks, legal papers, handbills, leaflets, petitions. Bundles of documents, newspapers, magazines, scrapbooks, and letters were stored on shelves. There, with the help of two young women, Susan and Ida Husted Harper, a journalist who was writing Susan's biography, worked together sorting through and organizing the records of Susan's extraordinary life and the fight for woman's rights.

Elizabeth could still write, but she could not read what she had written—someone else did that for her. Undaunted, she was hard at work finishing volume two of *The Woman's Bible* and her autobiography.

Periodically Susan took a break to give a speech. In late March, she reluctantly agreed to testify on behalf of a woman suffrage amendment before a committee of the New York State Legislature. Never again, she declared afterward, "would she stoop to plead her cause before one of these committees," which were now populated by the sons and grandsons of men she and Elizabeth had appealed to in previous years. She "was tired of begging for liberty from men not half her age and with not a hundredth part of her knowledge of State and national affairs."

In June, Susan and Ida went to Auburn, New York, to spend a few days with Elizabeth and Maggie, who were staying with Eliza Wright Osborne, the daughter of their old friend Martha Wright. During the day, they took long carriage rides, walked through the lovely gardens around Eliza's elegant home, and entertained friends who lived nearby. In the evening, Ida read them sections from Susan's biography. Then sitting side-by-side, Susan and Elizabeth would reminisce.

"It was a rare and sacred occasion," Ida later wrote, "and those who were present ever will cherish the memory of those two grand pioneers . . . both having given to the world fifty years of unremitting service, and yet both as strong in mind, keen in satire, as brimming with cheerfulness, as in those early days when they set about to revolutionize the prejudice and customs of the ages."

From Eliza's, Elizabeth and Maggie moved on to spend the rest of the summer with cousin Libby, who lived in Lochland, her mansion in nearby Geneva, New York. While there, Elizabeth noted in her diary that she gave several speeches. "The first one," she wrote, "at a great picnic" attended by a thousand people, where she "held forth for an hour and a half." Satisfied with reports that everyone could hear her, she wrote, "Though my eyes may be failing, my voice seems to hold its own."

"My Steadfast Friend"

That fall, Susan began reminding Elizabeth that the next convention in 1898 marked the fiftieth anniversary of the first woman's rights convention at Seneca Falls, of which she was "the prime mover and the soul, young as you were." For the occasion, Susan told her to write four papers—two for congressional committees, one for the opening of the convention, another for the closing ceremony. "Now, my dear," Susan assured her, "this is positively the last time I am ever going to put you on the rack and torture you to make the speech or speeches of your life."

"I cannot go on to Washington, as Susan urges," Elizabeth wrote in her diary. "I am really getting too old for such things— nor can I write four papers."

But she could write two. In one titled "The Significance and History of the Ballot," she proposed that Congress pass a law for "educated suffrage," the requirement that voters be able to read and write English. This was a dramatic shift from the "universal suffrage" that she and Susan had always advocated and that Susan still did. Elizabeth, however, now adopted "educated suffrage" as a tactic that would address the commonly expressed opinion that women were "too ignorant" to be allowed to vote. It would also deal with the huge influx of immigrant men, whom she viewed as uneducated and easily bribed by antisuffrage groups to vote against woman suffrage. Susan, of course, had the power to refuse to read Elizabeth's speech, but, as always committed to the free expression of ideas, she did not.

208   In her last diary entry for 1897, Elizabeth noted that both volume two of *The Woman's Bible* and her autobiography, *Eighty Years & More: Reminiscences 1815–1897*, were in print: "I am as much

relieved as if I had given birth to twins." She dedicated *Eighty Years* to Susan, "my steadfast friend for half a century." Writing to Susan, she said, "The current of our lives has run in the same channel so long it cannot be separated, and my book is as much your story, as I doubt not, yours is mine."

By the end of January 1898, Elizabeth had "practically finished" her two papers, but she was still fending off Susan, who was "urging" her to attend. "I shall not go," Elizabeth wrote in her diary, "as my eyes grow dimmer and dimmer and my legs weaker and weaker." Happily, she noted, "My brain seems as strong as ever."

A few weeks later, on her way to the convention, Susan stopped to visit Elizabeth to pick up her papers and, perhaps, personally escort her. But Elizabeth refused; Susan would have to celebrate the fiftieth anniversary of Seneca Falls without her.

The convention opened on February 13. A small, round mahogany table stood in the center of the stage. Two flags were draped over it—the American flag and the silk suffrage flag with four golden stars representing the states with full woman suffrage: Wyoming, Utah, Colorado, and Washington. It was the table at which Elizabeth had written the "Declaration of Rights and Sentiments." Originally the table had stood in Mary Ann M'Clintock's house; she passed it on to Elizabeth, who gave it to Susan as a house-warming gift when she settled down in Rochester.

It was Susan's idea to bring the historic table to the convention. She also had copies of the Declaration distributed to the delegates. "You will notice," she told them in her presidential address, "that those demands which were ridiculed and denounced from one end of the country to the other, all have now been conceded but the suffrage, and that in four States."

Susan presided over the six-day convention wearing a red shawl that had become her trademark. "Spring is not heralded in Washington by the approach of the robin red-breast but by the appearance of Miss Anthony's red shawl," a newspaper reporter noted. When she suddenly appeared at a session wearing a white shawl, reporters who were sitting at the press table sent her a note: "No red shawl, no report." Reading it out loud, she laughingly replied that she would fetch it from her hotel.

"Wake Up and Raise Your Voices"

As they had many times before, a distinguished group of women testified before two congressional committees, which received them politely but ignored their requests to recommend passage of the Sixteenth Amendment. Elizabeth's daughter Hattie was one of the women. Hattie and thirteen-year-old Nora now spent seven months of the school year in New York City. They lived with Elizabeth, Bob, and Maggie in their new spacious apartment on West Ninety-fourth Street. Nora rode the trolley to the Horace Mann School, a coeducational, experimental school, which was part of Teachers College, Columbia University. She called Elizabeth "her Queenmother" and embraced her as the "guide and philosopher" who taught her "the facts of life," including the "history of woman and of her long subjection."

Foreign affairs dominated the news in 1898 as the United States government sought to increase its influence through a policy of expansionism, a course that Elizabeth supported and Susan opposed. Before the year ended, the government had annexed Hawaii as the Territory of Hawaii. It had fought and won a short war, the Spanish-American War, and gained control over Puerto Rico, Guam, and the Philippine Islands. Cuba won its independence, although within a few years the United States gained a measure of legal control over Cuba. Ever vigilant about woman's rights, Susan and Elizabeth were outraged when Congress proposed to restrict the vote to men in these new areas. "I really believe I shall explode," Susan wrote to Clara Bewick Colby, "if some of you young women don't wake up and raise your voices in protest . . . I wonder if when I am under the sod—or cremated and floating in the air—I shall have to stir you and others up. How can you not be all on fire?"

"Her Time May Be Shorter"

In June, Susan was bound for London to attend the International Council of Women meeting, the organization she and Elizabeth had first convened in 1888. She spent several days in New York saying good-bye to Elizabeth. Earlier in the year, Elizabeth had been very ill until she had summoned Dr. Caroline Cabot, who prescribed the following regime: drink beef tea, glycerine, and whisky; inhale pine steam; take two kinds of pills throughout the day; and soak in a very hot bath. The next day, Elizabeth reported in her diary, "I am as agile as a grasshopper."

Susan returned in August and spent a week with Elizabeth and her cousin Libby in Geneva, New York. Afterward, Susan confided in a letter to Clara, "Though she may outlive me by years . . . her time may be shorter than mine."

Elizabeth was also thinking about mortality. Her sisters were in "failing health." In her diary, she quoted the words of the old hymn describing heaven as the "land of pure delight, where saints immortal reign." However, she wrote, "I must confess that I am in no hurry to go there. Life has been, and still is, very sweet to me, and there are many things I desire to do before I take final leave of this planet."

On her eighty-fourth birthday on November 12, 1899, Elizabeth noted that she received "a warm telegram from my dear Susan, and a resolution of 'respect and gratitude' from the Federation of Women's Clubs." She was in good health. Although her mobility was limited by her bulk and her sight grew dimmer, she noted that her "intellectual vision grows clearer." Recently a doctor had told her she had cataracts on both eyes. Hattie accompanied her to the doctor's office and later reported, "She accepted his diagnosis without a word. When we were seated in our carriage, I laid my hand on hers. She said, as if to herself, 'And both eyes.' She never referred to the matter again." In her diary, however, Elizabeth noted in a later entry that her friends in England had told her Queen Victoria had a cataract but refused to let surgeons remove it: "I suppose she feels just as I do—that so long as one can see fairly well, it is better to wait."

23

"Oh, This Awful Hush"

THE END
1900–1906

A T THE CLOSE OF THE NINETEENTH CENTURY, Susan decided to put the NAWSA into younger hands. She
planned to announce her resignation at the annual convention that was scheduled to meet in Washington, DC,
February 8 through 14, 1900. On the fifteenth, she would
turn eighty years old. She asked Elizabeth what she
thought "ought to be done" at the upcoming meeting.

Elizabeth's to-do list had five items: one dealt with the
male oligarchy that was established in Hawaii; two focused
on discrimination against working women. In another, she
urged a return to the principle that she and Susan held dear:
a broad-based association—"At the inauguration of our
movement," she explained, "we numbered in our Declaration of Rights eighteen grievances covering the whole range
of human experiences. On none of these did we talk with
bated breath. . . . In response to our radicalism, the bul-
warks of the enemy fell as never since. . . . But at present our
association has so narrowed its platform for reasons of policy and propriety that our conventions have ceased to point

the way." Finally, she said that annual conventions should be held in Washington in order to "examine intelligently the bills before Congress which nearly or remotely affect the women of the nation."

Susan embraced all of Elizabeth's ideas, except one; the time had passed for the association to reclaim its broad-based heritage. Most of the younger members shunned radicalism; their lives were so different from Elizabeth's and Susan's. "The hardships of the last half-century are forgotten," Susan explained. Elizabeth concurred. Many women, she observed, "seem to know nothing of the . . . progressive steps made by their own sex in the last fifty years."

The convention was fraught with emotion as Susan relinquished her role. "I am not retiring now because I feel unable, mentally or physically, to do the necessary work," she told the delegates, "but because I want to see . . . you all at work while I am alive, so I can scold you if you do not do it well." Carrie Chapman Catt, Susan's choice, was selected to succeed her. Susan was elected an honorary president, a position Elizabeth still held. "You have moved me up higher," Susan told the delegates. "I always did stand by Elizabeth Cady Stanton . . . and I am glad to be there again."

"Your Lives Have Proved"

A gala event was held to celebrate Susan's birthday. Her old friend John Hutchinson, who had been singing protest songs for fifty years, sang. Frederick Douglass's grandson Joseph played a violin solo. Coralie Franklin Cook, a professor at Howard University and founder of the Colored Women's League, spoke, as did representatives from the suffrage states. Eighty children, one by one, laid a single rose on her lap.

Elizabeth was unable to attend, but Hattie came and conveyed her mother's birthday greetings. Then she gave a tribute to Susan and Elizabeth: "The friendship of you two women will remain a precious memory in the world's history, unforgotten and unforgettable. Your lives have proved not only that women can work strenuously together without jealousy, but that they can be friends in times of sunshine and peace, of stress and storm."

Now Susan had time to undertake a project she dreaded but was determined to complete—volume four of the *History of Woman Suffrage*. She recruited Ida Husted Harper, who had written her biography, as a coeditor. Elizabeth reviewed material and wrote a steady stream of letters. "As I was wide awake last night for hours when I should have been asleep, I spent the time in thinking of you and your work," she typically wrote before going on for pages offering cogent suggestions and advice.

In September, Susan discovered that the University of Rochester was about to back out of its promise to admit female students. Two years earlier, when she and Elizabeth had raised the issue, the school finally agreed to open its doors, but for a price—$50,000 to pay for new facilities.

"Let the Girls In"

A committee of local women managed to raise $42,000, but that was it. However, they did not notify Susan about the shortfall until the evening before the deadline day. Having long dreamed of opening the doors of the university, Susan propelled herself into action. Mary planned to donate $2,000 once the school was coeducational. "Give it now," Susan insisted. "Don't wait or the girls may never be admitted."

Then she went out on a particularly hot day to canvass business owners, rich people, office workers, everyone she knew. By late afternoon, she appeared before the trustees with pledges worth $8,000, but the officials rejected one pledge of $2,000 because the man was very ill and might die before he paid. Temporarily foiled but as determined as ever, Susan pledged her life insurance to make up the difference. "They let the girls in," she wrote that night in her diary.

News of her triumph spread. The headline across two columns in the newspaper read, "Opens Its Doors to Young Women. Rochester University Henceforth a Coeducational Institution." The subheading was "Last $8,000 Needed for the $50,000 Endowment Fund Raised by Susan B. Anthony Yesterday. What Seemed a Hopeless Task Accomplished by her Energy and Courage."

Susan's heroic effort was costly. Two days later, she had a stroke. For a week, she could not speak. For a month, she needed constant care. Elizabeth wrote to Mary to keep Susan at home: "There is no necessity for her gallivanting off to the ends of the earth." Mary assured her that Susan "would stay at home & rest." That, Elizabeth replied, was "a rational idea, we all sing in chorus 'A-MEN!'"

In early October, Susan was finally able to go for a carriage ride and asked to be driven through the campus. That night, she wrote in her diary, "I thought with joy, 'These are no longer forbidden grounds to the girls of our city.'" But she worried, "Will the vows made to them be kept? Will they have an equal chance? All promises well but the fulfillment is yet to be seen."

She recovered her mental acuity and speech, but not her extraordinary stamina and resilience. That was gone, her doctor said, and warned her that she could have another stroke at any time. She should rest, get fresh air, avoid extremes in temperatures and large crowds. His advice sounded worse than death to Susan; she preferred to "die in the harness" doing her life's work. Mary understood and accepted Susan's decision to attend the Woman Suffrage Bazaar in New York City.

A huge fund-raising event at Madison Square Garden, the bazaar ran from December 3 through 8, 1900. Sale items were displayed in decorated booths—pecans from Louisana, cradles made of hundred-year-old mahogany from Maryland, and buckeye nuts from Ohio that were advertised as "a sure cure for rheumatism. Carry one in your pocket." A peace pageant was held one evening. Dressed in costumes from many countries, participants carrying olive branches marched around the hall, then laid the branches at the feet of the Goddess of Liberty, played by Alva Halstead of Brooklyn, New York.

Susan spent the week there. It was everything the doctor warned against—chilly, crowded, stuffy, overstimulating—but she appeared herself to the hundreds of people who lined up to shake her hand. Elizabeth had wanted to go, too, but Maggie and Bob had "persuaded not to do so." She spent her days "writing articles, long and short . . . in a word," she noted in her diary, "I am always busy, which is perhaps the chief reason why I am always well."

"Think of It!"

The next annual NAWSA Convention opened on May 30, 1901, in Minneapolis, Minnesota. Susan was there. As always, she had tried to get Elizabeth to come. Elizabeth replied that she thought they "had earned the right to sit in our rocking-chairs and think and write." In her diary, she added, "But it occurred to me later that that would be purgatory for Susan!" Elizabeth did, however, write an address, titled "The Duty of Church to Women at This Hour," to be read at the convention, which Susan knew would undoubtedly offend conservative delegates. Nevertheless, her loyalty to Elizabeth "was so strong . . . and the memory of her great service to the cause of woman was so faithful, that, in the face of much opposition, she had the address in full presented to the convention." Another pioneer, their old friend Olympia Brown, read it.

Susan spent the summer resting and attending a few events. In the fall, she spent several weeks with Sarah J. Eddy, whose grandfather, Francis Jackson, and mother, Eliza Jackson Eddy, had once willed generous sums of money for Susan to use for the cause. An accomplished artist, Sarah had been wanting to paint Susan's portrait. They got together at Sarah's summer home in Bristol Ferry, Rhode Island, overlooking Narragansett Bay. Susan reveled in the beauty of her surroundings—"magnificent view, ocean and islands, hills and autumn foliage." Sarah completed two paintings: a bust portrait and a full-length profile of Susan with a group of children presenting her with roses, as they had at her eightieth birthday celebration.

Elizabeth spent several months with her family at Wardenclyffe, Long Island, near where the famed inventor Nikola Tesla had just built a laboratory and transmitting tower. "He said to me the other day: 'It is possible to telegraph to all parts of the earth without wires.' Think of it! Where will the wonders of science end?" Elizabeth wrote in her diary.

"Shall I See You Again?"

The two old friends rarely saw each other, but they regularly corresponded. Elizabeth remained a prolific writer. Susan continued to attend suffrage events. In February 1902, she started out in a fierce blizzard for the annual convention of the NAWSA in Washington, DC. After waiting at the station for two hours, she boarded a train that "crept along with a snow plow in front" of it. The NAWSA was also hosting the first meeting of the International Woman Suffrage Conference. A thousand people from around the world attended—the United States, Russia, Chile, Norway, Australia, Sweden, Germany, and England. Elizabeth sent a paper on "Educated Suffrage." As always, even though she did not agree with her position, Susan insisted on having it read by Clara Bewick Colby.

In May, Susan spent a week with Elizabeth, who insisted that she stay at her apartment in a room that had been vacated by someone in the family. It was good to be there, Susan wrote in her diary, "though Mrs. Stanton does not feel quite as she used to. We have grown a little apart since not so closely associated as of old." The issue between them was Elizabeth's attitude toward religion. "She thinks the Church is now the enemy to fight," Susan wrote, "and feels worried that I stay back with children—as she says—instead of going ahead with her." In June, she spent another day with Elizabeth. Elizabeth's "wonderful brain was still strong," but her heart was not. Susan said goodbye with tears in her eyes.

"Shall I see you again?" she asked her beloved friend.

"Oh, yes," Elizabeth replied. "If not here, then in the hereafter, if there is one, and if there isn't we shall never know it."

That fall Hattie wrote to Susan urging her to come for Elizabeth's eighty-seventh birthday because she was "sure there won't be another." Susan had already planned to come, and in anticipation, she wrote a letter to Elizabeth.

It is fifty-one years since we first met and we have been busy through every one of them, stirring up the world to recognize the rights of women. . . . We little dreamed when we began this contest . . . that half a century later we would be compelled to leave the finish of the battle to another generation of women. But our hearts are filled with joy to know that they enter upon this task equipped with a college education, with business experience, with the freely admitted right to speak in public—all of which were denied to women fifty years ago. . . . These strong, courageous, capable, young women will take our place and complete our work. There is an army of them where we were but a handful.

Two weeks before Elizabeth's birthday, Hattie sent a telegram to Susan with this news: "Mother passed away at three o'clock." Susan was devastated. For hours she sat alone in her study, where Elizabeth's picture hung on the wall. In the evening, Mary coaxed her downstairs to eat some supper. A reporter was waiting to get her reaction. She spoke to him of their "unbroken friendship" and how they "never believed any talk of disloyalty of one to the other." That although they "did not agree on every point," they always agreed "on the central point of woman suffrage." The best parts of their lives together, she said, were "the days when the struggle was the hardest and the fight the thickest; when the whole world was against us and we had to stand the closer to each other; when I would go to her home and help with the children and the housekeeping through the day and then we would sit up far into the night preparing our ammunition and getting ready to move on the enemy."

Susan left the next day to attend Elizabeth's funeral. It was a private event in her apartment. "Oh, this awful hush," Susan wrote to Ida Harper. "It seems impossible that voice is stilled which I have loved to hear for fifty years. Always I have felt that I must have Mrs. Stanton's opinion of things before I knew where I stood myself. I am all at sea—but the laws of nature are still going on. . . . What a world it is, it goes on and on just the same no matter who lives or who dies!"

During the week that Elizabeth would have turned eighty-seven, Susan was in Auburn, New York, with Eliza Wright Osborne, the niece of Lucretia Mott and daughter of Martha Wright. Elizabeth's cousin Libby and a few other friends joined her to share their memories.

"Press Forward"

A few days before Elizabeth died, she had written a letter to President Theodore Roosevelt asking him to advocate for woman suffrage. Susan followed up on Elizabeth's appeal. "Dear Mr. Roosevelt, let us not watch and wait in vain." But, like all the presidents before him and most elected officials, Roosevelt did nothing. At the NAWSA Convention in 1903 in New Orleans, Louisiana, Susan repeated Elizabeth's exhortation· "The pioneers have brought you within sight of the promised land. . . . Go ahead, press forward!"

The following year, the NAWSA Convention met in Washington, DC, and, as she had since 1869, Susan testified before a congressional committee. "We have waited," she reminded them. "How long will this injustice, this outrage, continue?" In May, at the age of eighty-four, she went to Berlin, Germany, to attend the International Council of Women. In 1905, the NAWSA Convention was scheduled to be held in Portland, Oregon. Refusing to worry about her health, Susan decided to attend. "Why not this one?" she replied to a concerned friend. Mary went with her. They met up in Chicago with a hundred delegates and traveled across the country in special train cars.

In Portland, Susan was given a hotel room with a spectacular view of Mt. Hood, a sight that thrilled her. During her stay, she participated in the dedication of a bronze statue of Sacajawea. Created by Alice Cooper, it was the first statue erected of a woman "because of deeds of daring." Susan told the audience, "Let men remember the part that women" have played and vote for woman suffrage.

In 1906, the NAWSA Convention was held in Baltimore, Maryland. Susan arrived with a bad cold and struggled to attend the meetings. At the final gathering, she told the delegates, "The fight must not cease; you must see that it does not stop." A few days later, a birthday celebration was held for her in Washington, DC. When a letter was read from President Theodore Roosevelt congratulating her on her eighty-sixth birthday, she exclaimed, "I would rather have President Roosevelt say one word to Congress in favor of amending the Constitution to give women the suffrage than to praise me endlessly!"

Susan was exhausted, but she rallied to express her gratitude for the celebration. "There have been others also just as true and devoted to the cause—I wish I could name every one—but with such women consecrating their lives—failure is impossible."

Those words—"failure is impossible"—were the last words Susan B. Anthony spoke in public. On March 13, 1906, she died at home in Rochester, New York. The next day, Elizabeth's daughter Maggie wrote to Mary, "So dear Susan has gone and left you! I wonder if she and mother are walking hand in hand in the great beyond? A long time ago a sculptor here in New York made a cast of mother's and Susan's hands clasped. I got it out yesterday, threw a yellow silk kerchief over a pillow and laid the hands thereon. Then I got out numerous pictures that I have and placed them around. . . . In front of this group I stood a vase of yellow flowers. I quite felt with all these pictures and with the clasped hands that both mother's and Susan's souls were with me in my little home."

EPILOGUE

SUSAN WAS RIGHT ABOUT FAILURE BEING IMPOSSIBLE, but it took another fourteen years before a woman suffrage amendment was added to the Constitution of the United States, on August 26, 1920. By then three other amendments had been ratified, and so the Sixteenth Amendment that Elizabeth and Susan fought for ended up being the Nineteenth Amendment. It reads "The right of citizens of the United States to vote shall not be denied or abridged by the United States or by any State on account of sex."

A year later, on Susan's birthday, February 15, 1921, an unveiling ceremony was held in the United States Capitol Rotunda for the *Portrait Monument to Lucretia Mott, Elizabeth Cady Stanton, and Susan B. Anthony,* sculpted by Adelaide Johnson (the sculptor Elizabeth and Susan posed for in Rochester in the 1890s). Carved from an eight-ton block of marble from Carrara, Italy, the massive monument was quickly relegated to the Crypt, a much less visible space, where tour guides dubbed it "Three ladies in a tub." In 1997, after a passionate grassroots effort, the monument was relocated to the Rotunda.

CHRONOLOGY

1815   Elizabeth Cady is born in Johnstown, New York, November 12.

1820   Susan Brownell Anthony is born in Adams, Massachusetts, February 15.

1833   Elizabeth graduates from the Troy Female Seminary.

1839   Susan becomes a teacher in New Rochelle, New York.

1840   Elizabeth marries Henry Stanton. They travel to London, England, for the World's Anti-Slavery Convention, where she meets Lucretia Mott.

1842   Elizabeth gives birth to her first child.

1846–49 Susan teaches in Canajoharie, New York, where she joins the Daughters of Temperance.

1848   Elizabeth, along with Lucretia Mott, Martha Coffin Wright, Mary Ann M'Clintock, and Jane Hunt, organize the first woman's rights convention, which takes place on July 19–20 in Seneca Falls, New York. Elizabeth authors the Declaration of Sentiments. A second woman's rights convention is held in Rochester, New York, on August 2, which Susan's parents and sister Mary attend.

1851   Amelia Bloomer introduces Elizabeth and Susan in Seneca Falls, New York.

1852   Susan and Elizabeth found the Women's New York State Temperance Society. Elizabeth is elected the president. The following year, they leave the organization. Susan attends her first woman's rights convention.

1854   Susan campaigns for woman's rights throughout New York.
        Elizabeth gives her "Address to the Legislature of New York." Susan has fifty thousand copies printed for distribution.

1856   Susan becomes an agent of the American Anti-Slavery Society.

1859   Elizabeth gives birth to her seventh and last child. She has five sons and two daughters, all of whom live to be adults, an unusual occurrence at that time.

1860   Susan and other woman's rights activists lobby the New York Legislature, which passes the Married Women's Property Act.
        Elizabeth addresses joint committees of the New York Legislature.

1861   Susan and Elizabeth undertake a "No Compromise with Slaveholders" lecture tour.
        The Civil War begins.

1863   Elizabeth and Susan organize the Women's Loyal National League to agitate for the end of slavery.

1866   Elizabeth and Susan help found the American Equal Rights Association, which advocates for universal suffrage.
        Elizabeth is a self-nominated candidate for Congress.

1867   Elizabeth and Susan campaign for woman suffrage in New York and Kansas; both campaigns fail.

1868   Susan and Elizabeth begin publishing the *Revolution*.
        Elizabeth and Susan split with some of their friends and allies over the Fourteenth Amendment.

1869   Elizabeth and Susan found the National Woman Suffrage Association (NWSA) to fight for a woman suffrage amendment, the Sixteenth, to the United States Constitution.

Lucy Stone founds the rival American Woman Suffrage Association (AWSA) to focus on state-by-state campaigns to win woman suffrage.

Elizabeth begins crisscrossing the country on lecture tours.

Women win suffrage in the Wyoming Territory.

1870   Susan sells the *Revolution* for one dollar and joins the lecture circuit.

Women win suffrage in the Utah Territory. The right is lost in 1887 and restored in 1896.

1871   Elizabeth and Susan travel together to California on a lecture tour.

1872   Susan registers to vote on the grounds of the Fourteenth and Fifteenth amendments. She is arrested and charged with "unlawfully" voting.

1873   Susan is tried and found guilty of illegal voting.

1875   The United States Supreme Court rules in *Minor v. Happersett* that the United States Constitution does not give women the right to vote.

1880   Elizabeth and Susan retire from the lecture circuit and focus on writing their *History of Woman Suffrage*, along with Matilda Joslyn Gage.

1881   *History of Woman Suffrage*, volume I, is published. Volumes II and III will follow in 1882 and 1886.

1882   Elizabeth goes to Europe to visit two of her children and her first grandchild. While there, she connects with woman's rights advocates.

1883   Susan goes to Europe and spends time with Elizabeth. They initiate an international dialogue about woman's rights. Together, they return to the United States.

1887   The first vote on a woman suffrage amendment, the Sixteenth, is held in the United States Senate. It loses 34 to 16.

1888 Susan presides over and Elizabeth addresses the first meeting of the International Council of Women (ICW) in Washington, DC.

1890 The NWSA and the AWSA merge into the National American Woman Suffrage Association (NAWSA). Elizabeth is voted the president, after Susan's impassioned plea.
Wyoming becomes a state with woman suffrage in its constitution.
A gala celebration is held for Susan's seventieth birthday.

1891 Susan decides to settle down with her sister Mary in Rochester, New York. Elizabeth moves in with two of her children in New York City.

1892 Elizabeth gives a speech that becomes famous, "The Solitude of Self," before congressional committees and the NAWSA Convention. She resigns as president and is made an honorary president of the organization. Susan is elected president.

1893 Woman suffrage is approved in Colorado.
Marble busts of Elizabeth, Susan, and Lucretia Mott by sculptor Adelaide Johnson are on display at the World's Columbian Exposition in Chicago, Illinois.

1894 Elizabeth and Susan work on the New York woman suffrage campaign; Susan helps in the Kansas campaign; both campaigns fail.

1895 Susan campaigns for woman suffrage in California.
A gala celebration is held for Elizabeth's eightieth birthday.
Elizabeth publishes *The Woman's Bible*, volume 1.

1896 Over Susan's strenuous objections, the NAWSA votes to censor Elizabeth because of *The Woman's Bible*.
Women win the right to vote in Idaho.

1897 Ida Husted Harper works with Susan to write her biography.

1898   Volumes 1 and 2 of *The Life and Work of Susan B. Anthony* are published. Volume 3 will be published in 1908. Elizabeth publishes volume 2 of *The Woman's Bible*.

1900   Susan retires as president of the NAWSA and is made an honorary president. Carrie Chapman Catt is elected president. Susan raises the necessary money to force the University of Rochester to admit women.

1902   Elizabeth writes to President Theodore Roosevelt, asking him to advocate for woman suffrage. A few days later, on October 26, she dies, three weeks before her eighty-seventh birthday.

1903–   Susan attends NAWSA conventions in New Orleans,
1906   Louisiana; Washington, DC; Portland, Oregon; and Baltimore, Maryland. In 1904, at the age of eighty-four, she goes to the ICW meeting in Berlin, Germany.

1906   Susan dies on March 13, at the age of eighty-six.

1920   Women win the right to vote when the Nineteenth Amendment is added to the United States Constitution.

1921   The *Portrait Monument to Lucretia Mott, Elizabeth Cady Stanton, and Susan B. Anthony*, sculpted by Adelaide Johnson, is dedicated in the United States Capitol Rotunda, then placed in the Crypt, a much less visible space.

1997   The *Portrait Monument* is returned to the United States Capitol Rotunda, after a passionate grassroots lobbying and fund-raising effort.

PLACES TO VISIT

Adams, Massachusetts
- Susan B. Anthony Birthplace Museum, 67 East Road
- Quaker Meeting House, Maple Street Cemetery

Battenville, New York
- Anthonys' house from 1826 to 1839, 2835 Route 29 (a marker is on view, but the home is not currently open to the public)

Canandaigua, New York
- Bust and Painting, site of Susan B. Anthony trial, Ontario County Courthouse, 27 North Main Street

Johnstown, New York
- Plaque and Marker, site of Elizabeth Cady's birthplace, 51 West Main Street
- Fulton County Courthouse, where Elizabeth watched her father preside over trials and where, years later, she and Susan held a woman suffrage meeting, 223 West Main Street
- Marker commemorating Elizabeth Cady Stanton, Sir William Johnson Park, between Market and Williams streets
- Marker in front of Mrs. Henry's Boarding House, 9 South William Street
- Memorabilia, including Elizabeth Cady Stanton's piano, Johnstown Historical Society, 17 North William Street
- Mural with a portrait of Elizabeth Cady Stanton on the side of the Water Department building, 27 East Main Street

New York, New York
- Bust of Susan B. Anthony, The Hall of Fame for Great Americans, 2183 University Avenue (at West 181st Street), the Bronx

- Carved altar figure of Susan B. Anthony (grouped with Martin Luther King, Jr., Albert Einstein, and Mahatma Gandhi), Cathedral of St. John the Divine, 1047 Amsterdam Avenue
- Place setting representing Susan B. Anthony, *The Dinner Party* by Judy Chicago, Elizabeth A. Sackler Center for Feminist Art, Brooklyn Museum of Art, 200 Eastern Parkway, Brooklyn
- Plaque on the side of the apartment building, recently renamed the Stanton, where Elizabeth Cady Stanton died, 250 West 94th Street
- Burial site of Elizabeth Cady Stanton, Woodlawn Cemetery, Webster Avenue and East 233rd Street, the Bronx

Rochester, New York
- Plaque of Susan B. Anthony and her sister Mary, lobby, First Unitarian Church of Rochester, 220 Winton Road South
- Stained-glass window of Susan B. Anthony, Memorial African Methodist Episcopal Zion Church, 549 Clarissa Street
- The Susan B. Anthony House, 17 Madison Street, www.susan banthonyhouse.org
- Susan B. Anthony Square Park, between Madison and King streets, with *Let's Have Tea*, life-size bronze sculptures of Susan B. Anthony and Frederick Douglass by Pepsy Kettavong
- Tree and plaque honoring Susan B. Anthony, Seneca Park, 2222 St. Paul Street
- Susan B. Anthony Center for Women's Leadership, University of Rochester
- Frederick Douglass–Susan B. Anthony Memorial Bridge, Interstate 490 over the Genesee River
- Burial site of Susan B. Anthony, Mount Hope Cemetery, 1133 Mount Hope Avenue (Frederick Douglass is also buried there)

Seneca Falls, New York
- National Women's Hall of Fame, 76 Fall Street
- Women's Rights National Historical Park, vistors' center at 136 Fall Street; sites include the Wesleyan Chapel (Fall and Water streets) and the Stantons' house from 1847 to 1862 (32 Washington Street)

- Statue, *When Anthony Met Stanton,* by A. E. Ted Aub, beside Van Cleef Lake
- Seneca Falls Historical Society, 55 Cayuga Street

Tenafly, New Jersey
- Marker on Elizabeth Cady Stanton's house from 1868 to 1887, 135 Highwood Avenue (now private)

Washington, DC
- Embroidered kneeler and stained-glass window honoring Susan B. Anthony, National Cathedral
- Marble busts by Adelaide Johnson of Elizabeth Cady Stanton, Susan B. Anthony, and Lucretia Mott; Elizabeth Cady Stanton's chair; and Susan B. Anthony's desk, Sewall-Belmont House and Museum, 144 Constitution Avenue, NE; www.sewallbelmont.org
- Mahogany table on which Elizabeth Cady Stanton coauthored the Declaration of Sentiments, National Museum of American History, Smithsonian Institution, 14th Street and Constitution Avenue
- *Portrait Monument to Lucretia Mott, Elizabeth Cady, and Susan B. Anthony,* United States Capitol Rotunda

Waterloo, New York
- Hunt House, 401 East Main Street (site where first woman's rights convention was planned; part of Women's Rights National Historical Park)
- M'Clintock House, 14 East Williams Street (site where the Declaration of Sentiments was drafted; part of Women's Rights National Historical Park)

NAMESAKES

The names of Elizabeth Cady Stanton and Susan B. Anthony can be found attached to schools. Their image appeared on United States postage stamps. Susan's likeness appeared on a medallion and a United States dollar coin.

Elizabeth Cady Stanton
- The Stanton (apartment building where she died), New York, New York
- Elizabeth Cady Stanton Elementary School, Seneca Falls, New York
- Elizabeth Cady Stanton's image, along with Carrie Chapman Catt's and Lucretia Mott's, appears on a three-cent United States postage stamp titled "100 Years of Progress of Women 1848–1948," which was released in 1948

Susan B. Anthony
- Susan B. Anthony Elementary School, Daly City, California
- Susan B. Anthony Elementary School, Garden Grove, California
- Susan B. Anthony Elementary School, Westminster, California
- Susan B. Anthony School, Intermediate School 238, Hollis, New York
- Susan B. Anthony School, Minneapolis, Minnesota
- Susan B. Anthony School 27, Rochester, New York
- Susan B. Anthony School, Sacramento, California
- Susan B. Anthony Middle School for the Arts, Revere, Massachusetts
- Susan B. Anthony's image appears on a three-cent United States postage stamp titled "Suffrage for Women," which was released in 1936

- Susan B. Anthony's image appears on a fifty-cent United States postage stamp, which was released in 1955
- Susan B. Anthony's picture was featured on First Day of Issue Cover of a six-cent United States postage stamp titled "Woman Suffrage 50th Anniversary," which was released in 1970
- Susan B. Anthony's likeness appeared on a dollar coin minted from 1979 to 1981, and in 1999

Daniel Cady: Elizabeth described her father as "a man of firm character." [From Stanton, *Eighty Years and More*]

Margaret Livingston Cady: Elizabeth described her mother as "courageous, self-reliant, and at her ease under all circumstances and in all places." [From Stanton, *Eighty Years and More*]

Daniel Anthony: Susan's father encouraged her to be independent and concerned about social issues. [From Harper, *The Life and Work of Susan B. Anthony*, vol. 1]

Lucy Read Anthony: Susan never forgot her mother's "self-sacrificing devotion" to her family. [From Harper, *The Life and Work of Susan B. Anthony*, vol. 1]

Gerrit Smith was a wealthy landowner who supported many reform movements. [Courtesy of the Library of Congress]

Elizabeth Cady at age twenty. [Courtesy of the Brigham Young University Photo Archives, Rexburg, Idaho]

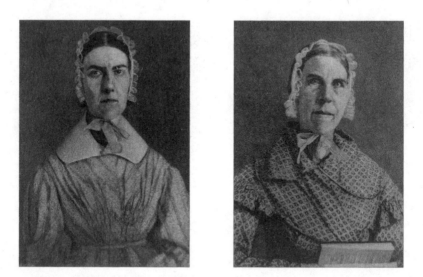

Angelina and **Sarah Grimké** were fearless abolitionists and women's rights orators and authors. [Courtesy of the Library of Congress]

The Anthonys lived in this brick house in Battenville, New York, until Daniel went bankrupt. [From Harper, *The Life and Work of Susan B. Anthony*, vol. 1]

Henry Brewster Stanton: Elizabeth included this photograph of her husband in her autobiography. [From Stanton, *Eighty Years and More*]

Lucretia Mott was one of the most prominent and widely respected people in the nineteenth century. [From Stanton, Anthony, Gage, *History of Woman Suffrage*, vol. 1]

Wendell Phillips was a notable reformer who later disagreed with Elizabeth and Susan. [Courtesy of the Library of Congress]

William Lloyd Garrison was the most reviled and revered abolitionist of the nineteenth century. [Courtesy of the Library of Congress]

Frederick Douglass escaped from slavery and became a famous lecturer and newspaper editor. [Courtesy of Wikimedia Commons]

Susan wrote to her family that her dress was made from purple, white, blue, and brown plaid muslin. [From Harper, *The Life and Work of Susan B. Anthony*, vol. 1]

In 1848, Elizabeth posed with her sons Daniel (known as Neil) and Henry (known as Kit). [Courtesy of the Library of Congress]

Martha Wright was Lucretia Mott's sister and a close friend of Elizabeth and Susan. [From Stanton, Anthony, Gage, *History of Woman Suffrage*, vol. 1]

Amy Post was a well-known reformer and proponent of radical ideas, including spiritualism.
[Courtesy of the Rochester Public Library Local History Division]

Elizabeth Smith Miller, Elizabeth's cousin Libby and close friend, is credited with introducing bloomers. [Courtesy of Coline Jenkins, Elizabeth Cady Stanton Trust]

Amelia Bloomer's name got attached to the style because she promoted it in her newspaper, including publishing this woodcut of Elizabeth in bloomers.
[Courtesy of the Library of Congress]

When Anthony Met Stanton, a memorial sculpted by Ted Aud in Seneca Falls, New York, shows (from left to right) Susan, Amelia Bloomer, and Elizabeth. [Collection of Penny Colman]

Elizabeth in 1854 with **Henry, Jr.**, known as Kit. [From Stanton, *Eighty Years and More*]

74%

Lucy Stone, once a close co-worker with Elizabeth and Susan, later formed a rival organization. [Courtesy of the Library of Congress]

24%

Susan, in 1852. [Courtesy of the Susan B. Anthony House, Rochester, New York; www.susanbanthonyhouse.org]

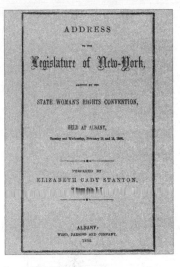

Ernestine Rose, pictured holding a rolled-up petition, was an unwavering ally of Elizabeth and Susan. [From Stanton, Anthony, Gage, *History of Woman Suffrage*, vol. 1]

Susan had fifty thousand copies of Elizabeth's speech printed in pamphlet form for distribution. [Courtesy of Coline Jenkins, Elizabeth Cady Stanton Trust]

Susan in 1856 at the age of thirty-six. [Courtesy of the Rochester Public Library Local History Division]

Elizabeth with Harriot, who was born in 1856. [From Stanton, *Eighty Years and More*]

A PETITION
for
UNIVERSAL SUFFRAGE.

A petition signed by Elizabeth, Susan, Lucy Stone, Ernestine Rose, and two of Elizabeth's sisters. [Courtesy of the National Archives, Washington, D.C.]

Sojourner Truth, a former slave and charismatic speaker, supported universal suffrage. [Courtesy of the Library of Congress]

Horace Greeley—an influential newspaper owner, editor, and writer. [Courtesy of the Library of Congress]

A sketch of the reform-minded **Hutchinson Family Singers** shows Judson, Abby, John, and Asa. [Courtesy of Wikimedia Commons]

George Train: Flamboyant and controversial, his outfits included a pair of lavender kid gloves. [Courtesy of the Library of Congress]

The *Revolution* carried the slogan "Men, their rights and nothing more: Women, their rights and nothing less." [Courtesy of the Library of Congress]

Isabella Beecher Hooker, a second-generation activist, aligned herself with Elizabeth and Susan. [From Stanton, Anthony, Gage, *History of Woman Suffrage*, vol. 2]

Elizabeth's house in Tenafly, New Jersey. [Collection of Penny Colman]

An artist's sketch of **Victoria Woodhull** giving her speech to the congressional committee in 1871.
[Courtesy of the Library of Congress]

Taken on August 19, 1870, this appears to be the first joint photograph of **Elizabeth** and **Susan**. [Courtesy of the Library of Congress]

The week before Susan's trial began, a newspaper published this cartoon titled "The Woman Who Dared." [From the New York *Daily Graphic*, June 5, 1873]

Sketches of the scandalous trio: **Elizabeth Tilton**, **Henry Ward Beecher**, and **Theodore Tilton**.
[From *Leslie's Monthly Magazine*, August 8, 1874]

Steel engravings of **Elizabeth**, **Susan**, and **Matilda Joslyn Gage** that appeared in *History of Woman Suffrage*. [From Stanton, Anthony, Gage, *History of Woman Suffrage*, vol. 1]

A sketch of **Elizabeth** advocating for the Sixteenth Amendment before a senate committee in 1878.
[From the New York *Daily Graphic*, January 16, 1887]

OPERA HOUSE, MASSILLON.

ELIZABETH CADY STANTON.
Saturday Evening, Feb'y 6, 1875.
LECTURE, "OUR GIRLS."

This poster advertised Elizabeth's speech in Massilon, Ohio.
[Courtesy of the Massilon Museum, East Massilon, Ohio]

Three generations in 1888—**Elizabeth** with **Harriot Stanton Blatch** and five-year-old **Nora**. [From Stanton, *Eighty Years and More*]

Elizabeth and **Susan** reviewing material for the *History of Woman Suffrage*.
[Courtesy of the Library of Congress]

Elizabeth and Susan organized the first International Council of Women, where they posed with women from other countries. [Courtesy of the Library of Congress]

Susan with her sister Mary, who was the first woman principal in Rochester, New York. [Courtesy of the Rochester Public Library Local History Division]

Susan and Elizabeth in front of Susan's home in Rochester. [Courtesy of the Susan B. Anthony House, Rochester, New York; www.susanbanthonyhouse.org]

Elizabeth at her eightieth birthday celebration in New York City with her son Robert and daughter Margaret. [From Stanton, *Eighty Years and More*]

The attic where **Susan** and **Ida Husted Harper** wrote her biography, which they dubbed the "bog." [From Harper, *The Life and Work of Susan B. Anthony*, vol. 2]

This picture of **Elizabeth** appeared in her autobiography. [From Stanton, *Eighty Years and More*]

In August 1899, **Elizabeth** and **Susan** vacationed with **Elizabeth Smith Miller** (Elizabeth's cousin Libby) in Geneva, New York. [Courtesy of Coline Jenkins, Elizabeth Cady Stanton Trust]

Susan at the age of 75 on a tour of Yosemite Valley with suffrage workers and guides. [Courtesy of Henry E. Huntington Library, San Marino, California]

Susan in 1897. [Courtesy of the Florida State Archives]

A Chinese newspaper in San Francisco published a sketch of Susan with an article about her campaign. [Courtesy of the Library of Congress]

Sarah Eddy's painting of children giving Susan roses at her eightieth birthday celebration. [Courtesy of the Library of Congress]

The second verse of the poem
Elizabeth wrote for Susan's eightieth
birthday. [Courtesy of the Rochester Public
Library Local History Division]

Elizabeth's flower-covered casket with a picture
of Susan at the head. [Courtesy of the Douglass Library,
Rutgers University, New Brunswick, New Jersey]

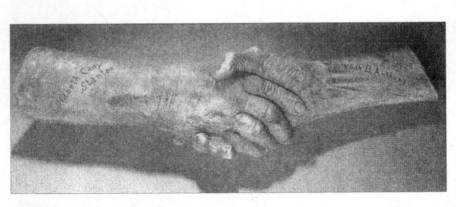

The plaster cast of Elizabeth's and Susan's clasping hands. [Courtesy of Coline Jenkins, Elizabeth Cady
Stanton Trust]

ACKNOWLEDGMENTS

As with every book I write, there are so many people who played a part. In particular, I want to thank Coline Jenkins, Elizabeth Cady Stanton's great-great-granddaughter and president of the Elizabeth Cady Stanton Trust, who continues the matriarchal lineage of "strong-minded" women, for her friendship and generosity. I am grateful for the work of scholars, including Ann D. Gordon, editor of the monumental six-volume series, *The Selected Papers of Elizabeth Cady Stanton & Susan B. Anthony*. Thanks are also due to my graduate students at Queens College, the City University of New York, who read and responded to my manuscript: Denise Gilrane, Debbie Ganeles, Marie Russell, and Christine Schachter. Over the years, I have been stimulated by conversations with my colleague Myra Zarnowski at Queens College. This is my fourth book with my terrific editor, Christy Ottaviano, and the deft designer Meredith Pratt. Thanks to them and to everyone at Henry Holt. Also thank you to Deborah J. Callery, Johnstown Public Library, Johnstown, NY; Kathy Jans-Duffy, Seneca Falls Historical Society, Seneca Falls, NY; Mary Ellen Sweeney and Claire Hawley Zarcone, Susan B. Anthony House, Rochester, NY; Dot Willsey, Gerrit Smith Estate, Peterboro, NY; and Fernanda Perrone, Rutgers University Libraries.

As always, I am forever enriched by my family, in particular my partner, Linda Hickson, who unfailingly and cheerfully supports me; no manuscript leaves my office until "every sentence" passes through her "metaphysical, rhetorical & common sense tweezer," as Elizabeth once advised Susan. While I was writing this book, my granddaughter Sophie Colman de Haën, who was three years old when I started and six when I finished, became ever more interested and engaged in the process of writing a book. She listened with interest and responded to my stories about Elizabeth and Susan, expressed her opinion about various photographs, and said she agreed it would be a good idea for me to dedicate this book to "Everyone who has fought and who is fighting and who will fight for the rights of women everywhere." Thank you, Sophie!

ELIZABETH
CADY STANTON
&
SUSAN B. ANTHONY

A friendship that
changed the world

BONUS MATERIALS

AN INTERVIEW WITH
PENNY COLMAN

What did you want to be when you grew up?

I remember wanting to be a doctor, an unusual choice for a girl growing up in the 1950s. My father, who was a doctor, thought that I should aspire to becoming a stay-at-home wife and mother—the traditional role for women at that time. To thwart my desire to be a doctor, he told me stories about medical school and how male medical students would make my life miserable. They would shun me, mess up my laboratory experiments, and leave a dead rat in my locker.

When did you realize you wanted to be a writer?

Both my parents gave me a close-up view of being a writer. I was nine years old when my mother joined the staff of a local newspaper as a journalist and photographer. Occasionally she took me with her when she went off in pursuit of a story. That same year, my father started writing a weekly column, "Everyday Psychology," for several newspapers. Two years later, I published my first article in the first edition of a newsletter I created to announce the start of our neighborhood orchestra, comprised of me, my brothers, and some of our friends.

What's your most embarrassing childhood memory?

My most embarrassing childhood memory happened when my tenth-grade English teacher held a tea party for students at her house and I showed up wearing kneesocks. All—yes, all—the other girls were wearing nylon stockings! (Remember: I grew up in the 1950s.) My impulse was to flee, until I imagined what my mother would tell me: "Pen, act like you're wearing the right thing and the others aren't!"

What's your favorite childhood memory?

My favorite childhood memory is of the farm we owned when I was in middle school. We had a goat that jumped up on the car hood; six sheep; a flock of exotic chickens (until a fox ate them); and three horses—Rusty for my dad and my oldest brother, Bucky for my two younger brothers, and Gypsy for me and my mother, which was cool because my mother didn't ride.

As a young person, who did you look up to most?

My unique artist/musician/journalist mother, an immigrant, who was born in Zagreb, Yugoslavia (now Croatia), and lived in Korycany, a small village in Czechoslovakia (now the Czech Republic). She left in 1938, the year Adolf Hitler ordered the invasion of Czechoslovakia.

What was your favorite thing about school?

At school I liked my social studies classes, especially the one taught by Mr. James Johnson, the seventh-grade teacher.

What were your hobbies as a kid? What are your hobbies now?

As a kid my hobbies included collecting things: stamps, miniature glass animals, and coins. I played the violin and piano, rode my bike, went canoeing, and played baseball with my brothers. Now you might find me walking along the Hudson River, reading, visiting a museum or historic site, working in my garden, or exploring a cemetery. I love road trips, music, kayaking, bike riding, walking, doing puzzles, playing games, and thinking and talking about ideas.

What book is on your nightstand now?

The Official Scrabble Players Dictionary, Fifth Edition and *The Secret History of Wonder Woman* by Jill Lepore.

How did you celebrate publishing your first book?

I celebrated publishing my first book by immediately starting to write another one. *Corpses, Coffins, and Crypts*, my fifteenth nonfiction book, was published a few months after my mother's death. My sister came from California and my brother came from New York to attend a book party, where I gave a speech that is posted on my website.

What inspired you to write *Elizabeth Cady Stanton and Susan B. Anthony*?

I love compelling, significant, and underreported historical stories—especially about women. These are all things I found in the unlikely friendship of two fascinating and inspiring women, Elizabeth Cady Stanton and Susan B. Anthony, who fueled the controversial nineteenth-century fight to improve the social, civil, and economic conditions of women's lives. It is a riveting story of progress and betrayal, with a host of supporting characters that range from admirable to controversial. It is an illuminating account of democracy, citizenship, voting rights, and gender equality. In short, how could I not write this book?

What was the research like?

The research was a roller-coaster ride. It started with a sinking feeling when I realized I had to read and digest an Everest-size mountain of primary source material, and evolved to a "whoopee" feeling when I took off on road trips to visit places that were part of Elizabeth Cady Stanton's and Susan B. Anthony's story, including a three-day, 880-mile trip throughout New York state.

What was the most difficult part about writing the book?

The most difficult part of writing any book is deciding what descriptions, information, incidents, quotations, anecdotes, etc., to put in or to leave out. I am constantly checking to make sure that the story I am writing is clear, coherent, and compelling. These decisions were particularly challenging with *Elizabeth Cady Stanton and Susan B. Anthony: A Friendship That Changed the World* because I was dealing with two main characters and one of the most profound social movements for equality in American history—whew!

Who was your favorite—Elizabeth Cady Stanton or Susan B. Anthony?

Both of them, but for different reasons: Elizabeth Cady Stanton because she was a scintillating thinker, prolifically influential writer, and a fearless orator. And Susan B. Anthony because she was an indefatigable doer, an organizer and planner extraordinaire, and a principled pragmatist. Both of them, for the same reasons: because of their unwavering commitment to the cause, fierce loyalty to each other, and razor-sharp wits. After reading my manuscript, my editor, Christy Ottaviano, wrote in an email that "at first [she] felt partial to Stanton, finding her ability to juggle family life with work quite impressive." As she read on, however, she "became so enamored of Anthony's strength and powerful ethical core [that Christy] ended up loving both women equally."

What do you find most inspiring about Elizabeth Cady Stanton and Susan B. Anthony?

I find many things inspiring about Elizabeth Cady Stanton and Susan B. Anthony. Mostly, however, I am inspired by their courageous perseverance. Shortly before Elizabeth Cady Stanton died in 1902, Anthony wrote to her: "It is fifty-one years since we first met, and we have been busy through every one of them, stirring up the world to recognize the rights of women." There is still a lot of stirring to do today and much inspiration to be gained from the legacy of Elizabeth Cady Stanton and Susan B. Anthony and their friendship that changed the world.

Where do you write your books?

Our 105-year-old house has four floors. I've written books on three of them. Currently my office is in the basement, where I wrote *Thanksgiving: The True Story* and *Elizabeth Cady Stanton and Susan B. Anthony: A Friendship That Changed the World*. It has ground-level windows, so it's not gloomy. (There's a short video about it on my blog.) I wrote *Where the Action Was: Women War Correspondents in World War II* in an office on the second floor, which is now used by my partner. The top floor has a bedroom and a small library. That is where I wrote *Corpses, Coffins, and Crypts: A History of Burial*. My computer was set up on a small table in a corner of the bedroom next to two side-by-side windows. The library was where I took breaks, did research, made notes, read what I had written, and revised (my favorite part of writing). I would sit on the floor under the skylight or in my favorite gray barrel chair that twirls around.

What challenges do you face in the writing process, and how do you overcome them?

I have a long list of challenges, including how to grab a readers' attention, how to keep readers turning the pages, how to write about complicated subjects in a clear, coherent, and compelling way, how to find just the right word and rhythm, how to write a satisfying, meaningful ending. To meet the challenges, I spend a lot of time thinking. I experiment with different solutions (with *Corpses, Coffins, and Crypts* I wrote twenty-three versions of the table of contents until I settled on just the right structure and chapter headings for that book).

What was your favorite book when you were a kid? Do you have a favorite book now?
As a kid I loved reading books about real people and historic events. I devoured biographies and social histories in the Signature Books series and Landmark Books series, including *The Story of Helen Keller*, and *To California by Covered Wagon*. I also loved to select a volume from our set of the *Encyclopedia Britannica* and read about whatever caught my attention, such as flowers and horses. If you mean which one of my books is my favorite? (And I do get asked that question a lot.) My answer is that they are all my favorites, although *Corpses, Coffins, Crypts* does have a special place in my heart. If you mean a favorite book by another author, I have several, including *Without Reservations: The Travels of an Independent Woman* by Alice Steinbach and *The Emerald Mile: The Epic Story of the Fastest Ride in History Through the Heart of the Grand Canyon* by Kevin Fedarko.

Do you ever get writer's block? What do you do to get back on track?
I never use the term "writer's block." It's too scary, like I've got a terminal disease. Thinking I have "writer's block" distracts me from the real issue, which is that there is a writing problem I need to solve. For example, with *Corpses, Coffins, and Crypts*, I stopped many times to think about what to put in and what to leave out. When I've got a writing problem to solve, I typically do one of two things: take a long walk or work on a jigsaw puzzle, until the solution comes to me. (I always have a puzzle underway in my office.)

What do you want readers to remember about your books?
I want readers to remember that literary nonfiction can be a great read!

What do you consider to be your greatest accomplishment?
I'm still alive, so perhaps there's more to come. But at this point, I consider my greatest accomplishment to be writing worthwhile books on important subjects that I trust make a difference in readers' lives.

What would your readers be most surprised to learn about you?

Readers would probably be surprised that once upon a time ago I hiked the almost-ten-mile Bright Angel Trail, up and out, from the bottom to the top of the almost-a-mile-deep Grand Canyon, past some of the oldest rock on the earth and through different climate zones from desert to pine forest. Awesome every step of the way!

DISCUSSION QUESTIONS

1. Elizabeth Cady Stanton and Susan B. Anthony used military terms to describe their fight for women's rights. Why do you think that is? What sort of language does the feminist movement use today?

2. What early childhood experiences do you think most influenced Elizabeth's and Susan's decisions to fight against entrenched gender norms of the time? How do you think Elizabeth's and Susan's differing childhoods changed the way they saw the world, and the way they became friends? Do you think their friendship would have been different had they grown up more similarly, or more differently?

3. Four-year-old Elizabeth was puzzled when people said, "What a pity it is she's a girl!" Later, she said she had been confused because she hadn't yet understood "that girls were considered an inferior order of beings" (p. 8). What does she mean by this? What are the ways that society saw her differently because she was a woman? What are some of the things society teaches young girls today?

4. What were Susan and Elizabeth's biggest arguments? How do you think they resolved their disagreements while remaining friends?

5. How was each woman changed by her friendship with the other? How are you changed by your own friendships?

6. Elizabeth wrote that "girls flock round me for a kiss, a curl, an autograph" (p. 161)—many women admired her for her work. What women, either from history or present day, do you admire and look up to?

7. Why did Elizabeth think that it was important to write a history of the women's movement?

8. What did you see as the largest challenges and barriers facing Elizabeth, Susan, and the other women in this book? How did they deal with and overcome these challenges?

9. Did reading this book change your understanding of the woman suffrage or women's rights movement? If so, what changed? Did you find that you recognized many of the influential women mentioned in the book? If not, why do you think you hadn't learned about them before?

10. What do you consider Susan's and Elizabeth's greatest achievements and contributions?

What happens to our bodies when we die? How do different cultures bury their dead? Learn all about the biology, history, and rituals of death through the centuries in *Corpses, Coffins, and Crypts: A History of Burial.*

★ "This sensitive, solid book answers a wealth of questions people have but often are too reluctant to ask." —*Booklist*, starred review

A POWERFUL LOOK AT AN INEVITABLE PART OF LIFE—DEATH

CORPSES, COFFINS, AND CRYPTS

A HISTORY OF BURIAL

PENNY COLMAN

READ ON FOR A SNEAK PEEK.

· o n e ·

Dead Is Dead:
Defining Death

My great-aunt Frieda Matousek called me with the news that her husband, Willi, was "having another attack." I wasn't surprised: Willi was eighty-six years old and he had several health problems, including heart disease.

"Call his doctor," I said. "I'm on my way."

When I arrived, Frieda met me at the door. "He's dead," she said. "Come see him."

I hugged her and kept my arm around her shoulders as we walked down the hallway to their bedroom. The bedroom was bright with sunshine and Willi lay stretched straight out on the double bed. Dressed in blue-and-white-striped pajamas, Willi's body was on top of the blankets, his head and shoulders were propped up by a pile of pillows, and his feet were bare. He looked exactly like Willi except that he was absolutely still and silent.

"Right after I talked to you, he made a noise, sat up a bit, and fell back," Frieda said. Just then the doorbell rang. I answered it.

"I'm the visiting nurse," the woman informed me. "I have an appointment to visit Mr. Willi Matousek."

"He's dead," I said. "He's in the bedroom."

"How do you know he's dead?" the nurse asked as she headed down the hallway.

This death certificate documents my brother's death. In many countries, including the United States, a death certificate is required in order to dispose of a body, settle an estate, make insurance claims, and get death benefits. The letters DOA mean Dead on Arrival.

This scene was repeated when the emergency medical technicians (EMTs) arrived at the door with all their equipment.

"He's dead," I said.

"How do you know?" they replied and rushed down the hall.

Then the police arrived.

"He's dead," I said.

"How do you know?" they replied.

At one level their question struck me as funny. "What do you mean, 'How do you know?'" I wanted to say. "He hasn't breathed or moved for at least an hour." But at another level I knew that just because Willi hadn't breathed or moved didn't necessarily mean that he was dead. Throughout history people have been declared dead when they really weren't.

In the late 1500s in England, Matthew Wall was thought to be dead until pallbearers accidentally dropped his coffin and he was revived. In the early 1600s in Scotland, Marjorie Elphinstone was supposedly dead until she groaned when grave robbers broke into her newly buried coffin to steal jewelry from her recently buried body. Forgetting about the jewelry, the robbers fled. Elphinstone climbed out of her coffin and walked home. In

Although this scene titled "Grave Robber Flees from a Corpse That Has Come to Life" was originally published in 1746, grave robbers were common in many times and places. In the case of Margaret Halcrow Erskine, a grave robber unintentionally saved her life. When Erskine appeared to have died in Chirnside, Scotland, in 1674, the sexton buried her in a shallow grave so that he could return at night and steal her jewelry. However, Erskine revived as the sexton was cutting off her finger to remove her ring. Although there's no information about what happened to the sexton, Erskine lived a long and productive life.

the 1860s passersby heard tapping coming from Philomèle Jo-
netre's grave. On exhuming her body, the director of the morgue
in Paris saw her eyelids move. She revived but died the next day,
really died. About the same time there was the case of a doctor
who cut into a supposedly dead person only to have the person
jump up and grab the doctor's throat. The "dead person" survived, but the doctor dropped dead of apoplexy. In the early
1900s a young girl had lain in her open coffin for thirty-six
hours when a relative who happened to be a physician decided
that she looked alive. He treated her and she recovered.

How can these mistakes happen? Experts have given various
explanations for erroneous declarations of death and premature
burials, including thanatomimesis, or death feigning; trances;
narcotic overdose; concussion; syncope, or fainting; and
asphyxia, or lack of oxygen. In 1884 a British medical journal,
Lancet, offered this explanation: "It is not so much the undue
haste as inexcusable carelessness that must be blamed for the
premature burying of persons who are not really dead." In 1995
Dr. Kenneth V. Iserson wrote in his book *Death to Dust: What
Happens to Dead Bodies?* that the words in *Lancet* "still ring true
today," a dreadful thought for those of us still alive. Nevertheless, mistakes are extremely rare today.

The terror of premature burial has prompted people to devise
various rituals and devices. Some ancient people waited until
the dead body began to decay before they buried or cremated it.
The Romans called out a person's name three times before
putting the body on the funeral pyre. The ancient Jews stored

The Viele Memorial, West Point, Highland Falls, New York. *Egbert Ludovicus Viele, the man who designed this memorial for himself and his wife, was terrified of being buried alive. So he rigged up a buzzer system that would ring inside the cemetery caretaker's house if he found himself alive inside the memorial. The huge memorial is patterned after an ancient Egyptian pyramid, complete with two sphinxes, the symbol of the pharaoh, which was portrayed as a lion with a human head. When Viele died in 1902, his body was placed in a sarcophagus, or stone coffin, inside the memorial. The buzzer never rang, although one caretaker reported being seriously startled until he realized that what he thought was the buzzer was only the telephone. The buzzer is no longer connected.*

dead bodies in caves and open sepulchres and regularly checked on them for a period of time. Some people stuck pins under corpses' nails. One woman instructed her doctor to stick a long metal pin in her heart before she was actually buried. A man wanted a doctor "either to sever my head or extract my heart from my body, so as to prevent any possibility of the return of vitality." In 1896 the Association for the Prevention of Premature Burial was organized in England for people who wanted to have scientific tests performed on their corpses before they were buried.

In St. Helena's Episcopal Churchyard in Beaufort, South Carolina, there's a brick vault with the remains of a Dr. Perry. According to the church history, Dr. Perry was terrified of being buried alive. So he had his friends promise to bury him with a loaf of bread, a jug of water, and a pickax. He had his slaves build a brick vault aboveground with enough room for him to swing his ax. Perry was buried with the bread, water, and pickax. He must have been truly dead because the vault still remains intact.

SOURCE NOTES

Complete information about the sources is
given in the bibliography, page 245

**Abbreviations for frequently used
sources are**
Gordon—*The Selected Papers of Elizabeth Cady
Stanton & Susan B. Anthony* (5 volumes)
Harper—*Life and Work of Susan B. Anthony* (3
volumes)
Lutz—*Created Equal: A Biography of Elizabeth
Cady Stanton*
Stanton, Anthony, Gage—*History of Woman
Suffrage* (volumes 1–3)
Stanton—*Eighty Years and More: Reminiscences
1815–1897*
Stanton and Blatch—*Elizabeth Cady Stanton* (2
volumes)

Author's Note
The use of war language appears throughout
Elizabeth's, Susan's, and their coworkers'
speeches, articles, reports, and letters.
"Night after night . . .": Stanton, p. 166.

Prologue: Imagine a Time
"Wives, submit . . .": King James Bible,
Ephesians 5:22.
"But I suffer . . .": King James Bible, I
Timothy 2:12.
"There she stood . . .": Stanton, p. 163.

PART 1

**Chapter 1: *"Ah, You Should Have Been a
Boy!"***
"keenly . . . Alps": Stanton, p. 6.
"a man . . . in all places": Stanton, p. 3.
"heard so many . . . of beings": ibid., p. 4.
"to be all . . . courageous": ibid., p. 21.
"recognize the . . . a boy!": ibid., p. 22.
"I could . . . woman's condition": ibid., p. 32.
"Again I felt . . .": ibid., pp. 33–34.

"swept over . . . of a windmill": ibid., pp.
41–42.
"Returning home . . . more happy": ibid., pp.
43–44.

Chapter 2: *"An Affectionate Family"*
"Come here . . .": Julia Taft Bayne, *Hadley
Ballads*, p. 38.
"the Anthony . . . of Anthonys": Susan B.
Anthony, *The Ghost in My Life*, p. 43.
"Although we . . .": Author's conversation
with Martin Schub, MD
"very timid . . . devotion": Harper, vol. 1, p.
232.

Chapter 3: *"Rousing Arguments"*
"The rousing . . . debate": Harper, vol. 1, pp.
53–55.
"I have brought . . . before your arrival":
Stanton, pp. 62–64.
"there was not . . . in the work": Otelia
Cromwell, *Lucretia Mott*, pp. 51, 130.
"What if . . .": Stanton, Anthony, Gage, vol.
1, p. 335.
"A pretty bold . . .": Mark Perry, *Lift Up Thy
Voice*, p. 130.
"intolerably . . .": ibid., p. 153.
"shame and dishonor . . .": ibid., p. 160.
"black and blue . . .": Andrea Moore Kerr,
Lucy Stone, p. 24.
"indignation at . . .": Perry, p. 133.
"I ask no favors . . .": Pamela R. Durso, *The
Power of Woman: The Life and Writings of Sarah
Moore Grimké*, p. 123.
"We Abolition Women . . .": Perry, p. 165.
"a passion . . . and astonishment": Stanton
and Blatch, vol. 1, pp. 57–58.
"depraved . . . conflict": ibid., p. 71.

Chapter 4: *"Hardscrabble Times"*
"the pleasure . . . Miracles": Harper, vol. 1,
p. 28.

"O, may . . .": ibid., p. 27.
"I have been guilty . . . seems worse": ibid., p. 29.
"2nd mo. . . . twelve": ibid., p. 30.
"baked 21 . . .": ibid., p. 3.
"Be the . . . had seen": ibid., p. 38.
"what a lack . . . is disgraced": ibid., pp. 39–41.
"I have no . . .": Kathleen Barry, *Susan B. Anthony*, p. 36.

Chapter 5: *"A New World"*
"own . . . rose": Gordon, vol. 1, p. 1.
"months of . . .": Stanton and Blatch, p. 67.
"much . . . blows over": ibid., p. 5.
"did not wish . . .": Stanton, p. 71.
"Yes, no doubt . . .": Wellman, *The Road to Seneca Falls*, p. 33.
"I obstinately . . . relation": Stanton, p. 72.
"Dear Friends . . .": Gordon, vol. 1, p. 10.
"had stood . . . of parting": Stanton, pp. 72–73.
"I soon . . . in this game": ibid, pp. 73–74.
"who believed . . .": ibid., p. 83.
"are constitutionally . . . whites": Dorothy Sterling, *Lucretia Mott*, p. 115.
"No shilly-shallying . . .": Lutz, p.26.
"battling so . . .": Stanton, p. 81.
"Mrs. Stanton . . .": Elisabeth Griffith, *In Her Own Right*, p. 73.
"Nobody doubted . . .": Sterling, p. 114.
"the independence . . .": Alma Lutz, *Susan B. Anthony*, p. 74.
"I sought . . .": Stanton, Anthony, Gage, vol. 1, p. 420.
"felt a new . . .": ibid., p. 422.
"resolved to hold . . .": Stanton, p. 83.
"In all my . . .": Griffith, p. 39.
"Mrs. Stanton . . . woman's rights": ibid., pp. 39–40.
"bright . . . to us": Bonnie S. Anderson, *Joyous Greetings*, p. 127.
"law . . .": Stanton, p. 111.
"The more I think . . .": Griffith, p. 37.
"dose . . . to tears": Wellman, p. 158.
"another lesson . . . earth beneath.": Stanton, p. 18.
"Let me take . . . relieve the pain": ibid., pp. 123–24.
"the Father . . .": Lutz, p. 38.

"I had . . .": Stanton, p. 107.
"did me . . .": Stanton and Blatch, vol. 2., p. 229.
"With a smile . . .": Stanton p. 144.
"solitary . . . protest and discussion": ibid., pp. 147–48.

Chapter 6: *"Sink or Swim"*
"enjoyed . . .": Harper, vol. 1, p. 44.
"I'd rather . . . both": ibid., pp. 43–44.
"seems . . . Hannah": Barry, pp. 42–43.
"line-boat . . . and home-sick": ibid., pp. 47–48.
"thinking you know it all": ibid., p. 51.
"splendid hats . . . won the victory": ibid., p. 51.
"new pearl . . . stare": ibid., p. 50.
"a fool . . .": ibid., p. 51.
"Well . . .": ibid., p. 47.
"full of . . . paper": Harper, p.38.

Chapter 7: *"To Do and Dare Anything"*
"earnest . . . rights of women": Stanton, p. 148.
"All men . . . franchise": Wellman, p. 193.
"owing to . . .": Gordon, vol. 4, p. 74.
"as vividly . . .": Wellman, p. 198.
"In due . . .": ibid., p. 203.
"so timely . . . created equal": ibid., pp. 209–10.
"with fear . . .": Stanton, p. 149.
"I have so . . . to do?": Gordon, vol. 1, pp. 123–24.
"The right . . . have begun": Wellman, p. 214.
"start women thinking . . .": Griffith, p. 58.
"a most . . .": Wellman, p. 219.
"stood aloof . . . patience": Stanton and Blatch, vol. 2, p. 39.
"has miscarried . . .": ibid., p. 169.
"What use is . . .": Lutz, p. 58.
"Depend upon it . . .": Gordon, vol. 1, p. 166.
"No men . . ." Stanton, Anthony, Gage, vol. 1, p. 110.

Chapter 8: *"Out of Sorts with the World"*
"a weariness . . . I could go!": Harper, vol. 1, p. 52.
"printed . . . Canajoharie.": ibid., p. 55.
"It is rather . . .": Gordon, vol. 1, p. 142.
"Sister . . .": Barry, p. 56.

PART 2

Chapter 9: *"An 'Intense Attraction'"*
"future friend . . .": Stanton, p. 163.
"intense attraction": Barry, p. 64.
"associated with . . .": Harper, vol. 1, p. 70.
"practical difficulties": Stanton, p. 147.
"The sisters . . . disturbers": Harper, vol. 1,
   p. 65.
"I will gladly . . .": Gordon, vol. 1, pp.
   197–98.
"anything . . . around us": Harper, vol. 1,
   p. 67.
"a hybrid . . .": ibid., pp. 69–70.
"raised . . . approval": ibid., p. 73.
"nobody who . . .": ibid., p. 72.
"the queen . . .": ibid., p. 75.
"brilliant . . . standpoint": ibid., p. 80.
"Rejoice with me . . .": Gordon, vol. 1, p. 212.
"Then you . . .": Stanton and Blatch, vol. 2, p.
   36.
"wholly . . . little I have" Stanton, p. 165.
"would modestly . . .": Stanton, Anthony,
   Gage, vol. 1, p. 494.
"plunged . . . to fry": Stanton and Blatch, vol.
   2, pp. 51–52.

Chapter 10: *"Do You Not See?"*
"I forbid . . .": Stanton and Blatch, vol. 2, p.
   51.
"the Old Fogies . . .": Harper, vol. 1, p. 96.
"grief and . . . make ourselves heard": ibid.,
   pp. 98–99.
"This convention . . . gagged": ibid., p. 102.
"shut-up" . . . be made": ibid., p. 103.
"mob convention": Stanton, Anthony, Gage,
   vol. 1, p. 570.
"from town . . . of her own": ibid., p. 104.
"I find . . . atrocious": Gordon, vol. 1, p. 237.
"generalize and . . .": Gordon, vol. 1, p. 238.
"story of . . .": Griffith, p. 81.
"a great . . .": ibid., p. 187.
"tears filling . . .": Stanton, p. 188.
"I passed . . .": Griffith, p. 84.
"daughters of . . .": Gordon, vol. 1, p. 241.
"were about . . .": Stanton, p. 190.
"unsex every . . .": Stanton, Anthony, Gage,
   vol. 1, p. 613.
"Like a captive . . . turn.": Stanton, pp.
   201–202.
"resembling . . .": Lutz, p. 78.
"let down . . .": Barry, p. 82.

"My whole soul . . .": Griffith, p. 85.
"My dear daughter . . .": collection of Coline
   Jenkins.
"She always . . .": Stanton and Blatch, vol. 1,
   p. xvii.
"Cant . . . uninterrupted": Harper, p. 122.

Chapter 11: *"Where Are You?"*
"As soon . . .": Griffith, pp. 87–88.
"the day . . .": Barry, p. 99.
"pleasing . . .": Harper, vol. 1, p. 124.
"strongly continue . . .": ibid., p. 124.
"Husbands are too critical": Griffith, p. 87.
"This is . . . thee": Beverly Wilson Palmer,
   Selected Letters of Lucretia Coffin Mott, p. 233.
"strictly confidential . . . Good night":
   Griffith, p. 84.
"rapid . . . field": Palmer, p. 233.
"great regret": Harper, vol. 1, p. 126.
"life work . . . thoughts together": ibid.,
   p. 134.
"Height, 5 ft. 5 in . . .": ibid., p. 136.
"very happy . . .": Gordon, vol. 1, p. 316.
"Imagine me . . .": ibid., p. 325.
"So for . . .": ibid., pp. 322–23.
"Come here . . .": ibid., p. 325.
"What an . . .": Griffith, p. 95.
"poor brainless . . .": Gordon, vol. 1, p. 322.
"You must . . .": ibid., p. 325.
"O, the crimes . . .": Harper, vol. 1, p. 160.
"Many a . . . heads.": Harper, p. 154.
"colored . . . social evil": Harper, p. 155.
"I did . . .": Gordon, vol. 1, pp. 351–52.
"in two . . .": Griffith, p. 93.
"How I do . . .": Gordon, vol. 1, pp. 352, 356.
"ah me!!! . . . groans": ibid., pp. 378–79.
"You need . . . see you": ibid., p. 387.
"I am . . . keep well": Lutz, p. 106.
"When you . . . from you": Gordon, vol. 1,
   p. 391.
"Where are . . .": Lutz, p. 109.

Chapter 12: *"Nevertheless You Are Right"*
"Mrs. Stanton . . . crossed": Harper, vol. 1,
   pp. 186–87.
"In thought . . .": Stanton, p. 166.
"sit far . . .": Harper, vol. 1, p. 187.
"powers . . . sacred right": Gordon, vol. 1,
   p. 408.
"She'd a great . . .": Harper, vol. 1, p. 193.
"set the . . .": ibid., p. 193.
"face was . . . sustain you": Stanton, p. 219.

Source Notes

"You are . . . slavery": Harper, vol. 1, p. 196.
"Fullest confidence . . .": Gordon, vol. 1, p. 435.
"The desire . . .": Stanton and Blatch, vol. 2, p. 80.
"He has . . .": ibid., p. 82.
"he is a man . . . code": Harper, vol. 1, pp. 195–97.
"the men . . .": Stanton and Blatch, vol. 1, p. 435.
"How can . . .": Gordon, vol. 1, p. 445.
"cautious . . . consequences": Harper, vol. 1, p. 197.
"The child belongs . . . stand by you": ibid., pp. 201–04.
"I think you . . .": Gordon, vol. 1, p. 454.
"a man of courage . . .": Stanton, p. 212.
"new life . . . hesitation": Griffith, p. 106.
"I have not yet . . .": Gordon, vol. 1, p. 468.

Chapter 13: *"Put on Your Armour and Go Forth!"*

"We have . . .": Stanton, p. 166.
"Tried to . . .": Harper, p. 216.
"I finished . . . for action": ibid., pp. 216–17.
"public work": ibid., p. 218.
"Any and every . . .": ibid., p. 221.
"While the old . . .": Gordon, vol. 1, p. 97.
"stunned and . . .": ibid., p. 224.
"not simply . . .": ibid., p. 225.
"The country . . . go forth": ibid., p. 226.
"war of ideas": Gordon, vol. 1, p. 500.
"shame on . . .": Harper, vol. 1, p. 227.
"civil and . . .": ibid., p. 229.
"go to the . . .": ibid., p. 230.
"Here's one of . . . of the republic": Stanton and Blatch, vol. 2, pp. 94–95.
"These are terrible . . .": Harper, vol. 1, p. 230.
"These petitions . . .": ibid., p. 235.
"We will have . . .": Lutz, p. 133.
"How I wish . . .": Gordon, vol. 1, p. 535.
"If that word . . .": ibid., p. 569.
"I think such . . . stand alone": Stanton and Blatch, p. 105.
"have their banners . . .": Lutz, p. 137.
"We can no . . . wholly": Gordon, vol. 1, p. 585.
"bore the double . . .": Harper, vol. 1, p. 269.
"extend the right . . . their ancestry": Harper, vol. 1, p. 268.

"emphatically the . . . perilous hour": Anderson, p. 371.
"I would gladly . . .": Gordon, vol. 1, p. 594.
"must buy . . .": Stanton, p. 115.
"two dozen unknown friends": Griffith, p. 126.
"I was convinced . . .": Stanton, p. 254.

PART 3

Chapter 14: *"Keep the Thing Stirring"*

"There is . . .": Stanton, Anthony, Gage, vol. 2, pp. 193–94.
"Women and colored men . . .": ibid., p. 227.
"With the help . . .": Gordon, vol. 2, p. 69.
"I could . . .": Kerr, p. 125.
"a finger's length": ibid., p. 125.
"The best . . . the constitution": Harper, vol. 1, pp. 278–79.
"most . . . Stanton": Stanton, pp. 117–18.
"so much . . .": Harper, vol. 1, pp. 282–83.
"All were . . . rapidly reduced": ibid., pp. 284–85.
"bushel . . . degree of cheerfulness": Stanton, pp. 246–52.
"come to . . .": Ellen Carol DuBois, *Feminism and Suffrage*, p. 94.
"shut out . . . Democrats": Stanton, Anthony, Gage, vol. 2, p. 264.
"a lunatic . . .": Griffith, p. 130.
"Kansas Suffrage Song": *Hurrah for Woman Suffrage* recording by Miriam Reed, Miriam Reed Productions, www.miriamreed.com.
"narrow policy . . .": Stanton, p. 254.
"first ever . . .": Harper, vol. 1, p. 291.
"I take . . . influence": ibid., p. 293.
"The agitation . . .": Stanton, p. 256.
"solemnly vowed . . .": Stanton, Anthony, Gage, vol. 2, pp. 267–68.

Chapter 15: *"Male Versus Female"*

"charged to . . . pretty baby": Harper, vol. 1, pp. 295–97.
"In quite . . .": Stanton, p. 123.
"her usual . . .": Harper, vol. 1, p. 314.
"Woman will . . .": Ellen DuBois, *Feminism & Suffrage*, p. 175.
"The are two . . .": Kerr, p. 140.
"like magic . . .": Lutz, p. 170.
"will be memorable . . .": Gordon, vol. 2, p. 236.

"I wish . . .": DuBois, p. 185.

"Feeling . . .": Harper, vol. 1, p. 319.

"who cannot . . .": Geoffrey C. Ward and Ken Burns, *Not For Ourselves Alone*, p. 123.

"division in . . .": Lutz, p. 180.

"I did my . . .": ibid., pp. 182–83.

"merge their . . .": Palmer, p. 437.

"So, I say . . .": Gordon, vol. 2, p. 284.

"deplored . . . public sentiment": Barry, p. 205.

"You and I . . .": Harper, vol. 1, p. 357.

"My paper . . . business": ibid., 351.

"My Dear Susan . . . mean *ever*": Stanton, pp. 123–25.

"already Free": Gordon, vol. 2, p. 407.

Chapter 16: *"The Crowning Insult"*

"golden . . . a ribbon": Harper, vol. 1, p. 353.

"It was . . .": ibid., p. 362.

"Our *Revolution* . . .": Stanton and Blatch, vol. 2, p. 126.

"I never . . . my retreat": Gordon, vol. 2, pp. 359–60.

"At a dead lock . . . yoke of bondage": Harper, vol. 1, p. 366.

"Dearest Susan . . . blessed Susan": Stanton and Blatch, vol. 2, pp. 127–28.

"Met Mrs. S . . . tired out": Gordon, vol. 2, pp. 363, 367.

"I send . . . good to eat": ibid., p. 375.

"I loved . . . life's threads": Harper, vol. 1, p. 369.

"I think her . . .": Barbara A. White, *The Beecher Sisters*, p. 163.

"declined to be . . . displaced": Harper, vol. 1, p. 373.

"O, how I have . . . understand": Gordon, vol. 2, pp. 401–02.

"you see . . .": ibid., p. 402.

"on account . . . to races": Stanton, Anthony, Gage, vol. 2, p. 445.

"new, fresh . . . advocating": Harper, vol. 1, p. 367.

"Do not . . . Woodhull": Griffith, p. 148.

"When men . . . chaste": Harper, vol. 1, p. 379.

"I feel . . .": Gordon, vol. 2, p. 407.

"the crowning . . . and friction": Stanton and Blatch, vol. 2, p. 130.

"feeble health, to identify": Palmer, p. 460.

"We mean . . . social principles": Lutz, *Susan B. Anthony*, pp. 184–85.

Chapter 17: "I Have Been & Gone & Done It!"

"We have . . . spirit of love": Harper, vol. 1, p. 388.

"women alone . . .": Stanton and Blatch, vol. 2, pp. 132–33.

"press sneers . . . for it": Harper, vol. 1, p. 387.

"Mrs. Stanton . . .": Stanton and Blatch, vol. 2, p. 134.

"a very pretty . . . children": Stanton, pp. 288–89.

"Never in . . . cut down": Harper, vol. 1, p. 392.

"piled one above another . . .": Stanton, p. 290.

"fat": ibid., p. 393.

"Trust one's . . . jelly": ibid., pp. 292–93.

"grand brave woman": Griffith, p. 151.

"Strong . . . on land again": Harper, vol. 1, p. 395.

"The first fire . . . clear for her": ibid., pp. 396–97.

"seize their . . .": ibid., p. 402.

"Remember that . . . quicksand": Gordon, vol. 2, p. 449.

"Thus closes . . .": Harper, vol. 1, p. 407.

"looking over . . .": Gordon, vol. 2, p. 487.

"All our time . . .": Harper, vol. 1, p. 413.

"narrow, bigoted . . .": Ward and Burns, p. 141.

"A sad day . . .": ibid., p. 415.

"oldest and . . .": Barry, p. 247.

"equal rights . . . politicians": Harper, vol. 1, p. 416.

"a splinter . . . nothing": ibid., p. 420.

"dreadfully . . . vocabulary": Stanton and Blatch, p. 141.

"Now register . . .": Harper, vol. 1, p. 423.

"should be . . . right to vote": ibid., pp. 424–26.

Chapter 18: *"Our Friendship Is Too Long Standing"*

"hardly find . . . the fine is paid": Harper, vol. 1, pp. 436–41.

"my continuous . . .": Stanton and Blatch, vol. 2, p. 143.

"It is as you say . . .": Gordon, vol. 2, p. 592.

"Constitution . . .": Harper, vol. 1, p. 453.

"a great social . . .": Gordon, vol. 3, p. 102.

"free love": ibid., p. 462.

"a friend . . . the subject": Griffith, p. 158.

"Offended, Susan . . .": Stanton and Blatch, p. 145.

"one-half . . .": Harper, vol., p. 475.

"found them . . . her strength": Barry, p. 269.

"We ask . . .": Lutz, *Susan B. Anthony*, p. 228.

"working for . . .": Harper, vol. 1, p. 430.

"wonderful head . . .": Stanton, p. 325.

"our children . . . my heart": Harper, vol. 1, pp. 488–89.

"with innumerable . . . people do": Gordon, vol. 4, pp. 560–61.

"I am immersed . . .": Harper, vol. 1, p. 480.

"Do be . . .": Harper, p. 488.

"I sit . . .": Stanton and Blatch, p. 150.

"You would . . .": Lutz, *Susan B. Anthony*, p. 202.

"withered beldames . . . go home": Harper, vol. 2, p. 517.

"newspaper ridicule . . . suffrage": Harper, vol. 1, p. 505.

"Our friendshship . . .": Harper, vol.1, p. 633.

PART 4

Chapter 19: *"We Stood Appalled"*
"the rousingest . . . and lightning": Gordon, vol. 2, p. 527.

"had not . . . neck of woman": ibid., p. 518.

"large room . . . squabbling": Stanton and Blatch, vol. 2, p. 187.

"go down . . . present had": ibid., p. 172.

"bright sunny . . . example": ibid., pp. 177–78.

"stood appalled . . .": Stanton, p. 374.

"I am just sick . . .": Griffith, p. 177.

"We are . . .": Stanton and Blatch, p. 181.

"I welcomed . . .": Stanton, p. 276.

"It is . . .": Harper, vol. 1, p. 535.

"a little . . . the fort": Kerr, p. 208.

"leave these . . .": Gordon, vol. 2, p. 552.

"union of . . . fresh power": Stanton and Blatch, vol. 2, p. 169.

"It is so easy . . .": Harper, vol. 2, p. 537.

"The year . . . for the cause": Harper, vol. 2, p. 539.

"mischief . . . families": Stanton, Anthony, Gage, vol. 3, p. 199.

"thrilled . . . and blest": ibid., p. 228.

"O, how I . . .": Harper, vol. 2, p. 542.

"while the . . .": Kerr, p. 194.

"do credit . . .": Ward and Burns, p. 162.

"tall, dark . . .": Ellen Carol DuBois, *Harriot Stanton Blatch and the Winning of Woman Suffrage*, p. 40.

"one of . . . guard her": Stanton and Blatch, vol. 2, p. 200.

"Only think . . .": Harper, vol. 2, p. 544.

"an extra . . . Anthony": ibid., p. 547.

"stormy periods . . . in the wind": ibid., p. 549.

"the tiptoe . . .": Harper, vol. 2, p. 553.

"Our friends . . .": Stanton and Blatch, vol. 2, p. 208.

"Even the . . .": Harper, vol. 2, p. 265.

"the first . . .": DuBois, *Harriet Stanton Blatch*, p. 58.

"As I sit . . .": Stanton and Blatch, vol. 2, p. 217.

"more worlds . . .": Barry, p. 282.

"I prefer . . . of my own": Harper , vol. 2, p. 667.

"When Hattie and I . . .": Stanton and Blatch, vol. 2, p. 212.

Chapter 20: *"Brace Up and Get Ready"*
"amalgamation . . . yours": Harper, vol. 2, p. 586.

"number of . . . great world": Stanton and Blatch, vol. 2, pp. 216–17.

"to keep . . . to vote": ibid., p. 219.

"I really think . . .": Harper, vol. 2, p. 600.

"was enough . . . dead standstill": Stanton and Blatch, vol. 2, p. 226.

"week . . . accomplish this": ibid., pp. 228–30.

"As to . . . cisterns": Carol Lasser and Marlene Deahl Merrill, *Friends and Sisters*, p. 250.

"Death . . . beyond": Stanton and Blatch, vol. 2, p. 236.

"I fear . . . no doubt.": Gordon, vol. 2, pp. 263–64.

"our beloved . . . a century": Gordon, vol. 4, p. 550.

"the rights . . .": Harper, vol. 4, p. 617.

"unsex . . .": ibid., p. 620.

"That we . . .": Anthony and Harper, vol. 4, p. 122.

"Oh dear . . .": Barry, p. 285.

"Put every . . .": Gordon, vol. 5, p. 10.

"all the women . . .": Stanton and Blatch, vol. 2, p. 237.

"We have . . . back": Harper, vol. 2, p. 635.

"the faithful . . . must go": Stanton and Blatch, vol. 2, p. 248.

"I am ablaze . . . permitted": Harper, vol. 2, p. 636.

"splendid agitation": Stanton and Blatch, p. 250.

"gay-hearted . . . minutes": ibid., pp. 637–38.

"Even the preamble . . . violence": Anthony and Harper, vol. 4, p. 138.

"up hill . . . weather": Stanton and Blatch, p. 320.

"mission to . . . seventh heaven": Stanton and Blatch, vol. 2, p. 259.

Chapter 21: *"Under Your Thumb"*

"tempted . . . February": Stanton and Blatch, vol. 2, p. 260.

"Would . . . close of the war": ibid., p. 261.

"I am very . . . at my right hand": Harper, vol 2, pp. 667–68.

"utmost liberty . . . vote for Mrs. Stanton": Gordon, vol. 5, pp. 246–47.

"greater . . . demonstration": Stanton and Blatch, vol. 2, p. 261.

"showed . . . for me": Gordon, vol. 5, p. 268.

"Saint-Susan . . . meeting": Anthony and Harper, vol. 4, p. 173.

"unalterably . . . without woman suffrage": ibid., pp. 999–1,000.

"I cannot . . . soul": Stanton and Blatch, p. 265.

"very . . . green grapes": Harper, vol. 2, pp. 689, 691.

"My advice . . . desire": Harper, vol. 2, p. 707.

"anchored": ibid., p. 712.

"filled with sadness . . . as possible": Stanton, p. 359.

"they might . . . utterances": Harper, vol. 2, p. 712.

"eyrie": Stanton, p. 433.

"summoned . . . command": ibid., pp. 433–34.

"I felt . . . mittens": Harper, vol. 2, p. 715.

"to think . . . years": Stanton and Blatch, vol. 2, p. 281.

"The point . . .": Estelle B. Freedman, *The Essential Feminist Reader*, p. 123.

"To Elizabeth . . .": Lutz, *Elizabeth Cady Stanton*, p. 290.

"clamber up . . . me": Stanton and Blatch, vol. 2, p. 290.

"general reading . . . into": Lutz, *Elizabeth Cady Stanton*, p. 297.

"Susan is . . . read them": Stanton and Blatch, p. 287.

"whole matter . . .": Harper, vol. 2, p. 729.

"simply overwhelmed": ibid., p. 737.

"She came . . .": Stanton, p. 375.

"he'd learn . . .": Rheta Childe Dorr, *Susan B. Anthony*, p. 306.

"Now we . . . moves": Stanton and Blatch, vol. 2, p. 301.

"the happiest . . .": Harper, vol. 2, p. 753.

"an insurrection . . . judgment": Harper, vol. 2, pp. 769–70.

"I seem . . . other": Stanton and Blatch, p. 304.

"great . . . oligarchy": ibid., p. 307.

"If the . . . South": Harper, vol. 2, p. 815.

"literally buried . . .": ibid., p. 827.

"thinner . . . if dead": ibid., p. 840–41.

"I never . . . the mend": ibid., p. 842.

"Surely . . . dream": ibid., p. 846.

"pioneers . . . Anthony": ibid., p. 848.

"able to . . .": Lutz, p. 293.

"Do all . . . think": Stanton and Blatch, p. 252.

"may feel . . . despair": "Elizabeth Cady Stanton," *The New York Times*, November 13, 1895, p. 1.

"Church and . . . man": Stanton et al., introduction.

"Women have . . .": Lutz, *Susan B. Anthony*, p. 304.

"Get political . . .": Harper, vol. 1, p. 857.

Chapter 22: *"To Stir You and Others Up"*

"I could cry . . . narrow action": Lutz, *Susan B. Anthony*, pp. 279–80.

"Won't it . . . your help": Harper, vol. 2, p. 879.

"A great loss . . . on one subject": Stanton and Blatch, vol. 2, pp. 320–21.

"It is not . . . successes than any": Harper, vol. 2, p. 903.

"natural and . . .": Stanton, Anthony, Gage, vol. 2, p. 626.

"dimmer and dimmer": Stanton and Blatch, vol. 2, p. 325.

"would she . . . affairs": Harper, vol. 2, p. 914.

"It was a . . .": ibid., p. 917.

"The first . . . its own": Stanton and Blatch, vol. 2, p. 327.

"the prime . . . strong as ever": ibid.,
 pp. 328–29.
"You will . . .": Stanton, Anthony, Gage, vol.
 4, p. 288.
"Spring is . . . no report": Harper, vol. 3,
 p. 1,113.
"her Queenmother . . . subjection": DuBois,
 Harriot Stanton Blatch, p. 58.
"I really believe . . .": Barry, p. 327.
"I am as . . .": Stanton and Blatch, vol. 2,
 p. 337.
"Though she . . .": Barry, p. 330.
"failing . . . planet": Stanton and Blatch,
 vol. 2, p. 335.
"a warm . . .": ibid., p. 344.
"She accepted . . . to wait": ibid., p. 337.

Chapter 23: *"Oh, This Awful Hush"*
"ought to be done . . . of the nation": Stanton
 and Blatch, vol. 2, p. 346.
"The hardships . . .": Harper, vol. 3, p. 1163.
"seem to know . . .": Stanton and Blatch,
 vol. 2, p. 358.
"I am . . . do it well": Harper, vol. 3, p. 1170.
"You have . . . there again": Stanton,
 Anthony, Gage, vol. 4, p. 389.
"The friendship . . .": Harper, vol. 3, p. 1186.
"As I was . . .": ibid., p. 1269.
"Give it . . . and Courage": ibid., pp.
 1223–26.
"There is no . . . A-MEN!": Barry, p. 337.
"I thought . . . be seen": Harper, vol. 3,
 p. 1,228.

"persuaded not . . . always well": Stanton and
 Blatch, vol. 2, p. 354.
"But it . . .": ibid., p. 358.
"loyalty . . . convention": Harper, vol. 3,
 p. 1232.
"had earned . . .": Stanton and Blatch, p. 358.
"magnificent view . . .": ibid., p. 1241.
"He said . . .": Stanton and Blatch, vol. 2,
 p. 358.
"crept along . . .": Harper, vol. 3, p. 1244.
"though Mrs. Stanton . . . still strong": ibid.
 p. 1255.
"Shall I . . . know it": ibid., p. 1256.
"sure there . . .": Lutz, *Elizabeth Cady Stanton*,
 p. 318.
"It is fifty- one . . .": Ida Husted Harper,
 History of Woman Suffrage, vol. 5,
 pp. 741–42.
"Mother passed . . . who dies!": Harper, vol.
 3, pp. 1262–64.
"Dear Mr. Roosevelt . . .": ibid., p. 1275.
"The pioneers . . .": ibid., p. 1289.
"We have . . .": ibid., p. 1308.
"Why not . . .": ibid. , p. 1306.
"because of deeds . . .": ibid., p. 1365.
"The fight . . . endlessly!": ibid., 1397.
"There have been . . . is impossible": ibid.,
 p. 1408.
"So dear Susan . . .": ibid., p. 1453.

Epilogue
"Three ladies . . ." Author's conversation
 with tour guides.

SELECTED BIBLIOGRAPHY

Additional sources, a reading guide, and podcasts are at www.pennycolman.com.

Anderson, Bonnie, S. *Joyous Greetings: The First International Women's Movement, 1830–1860* (New York: Oxford University Press, 2000).

Anthony, Susan B. *The Ghost in My Life* (Old Tappan, NJ: Fleming H. Revell, 1971).

Banner, Lois W. *Elizabeth Cady Stanton: A Radical for Woman's Rights* (Boston: Little, Brown, 1980).

Barry, Kathleen. *Susan B. Anthony: A Biography of a Singular Feminist* (New York: Ballantine Books, 1988).

Bayne, Julia Taft. *Hadley Ballads* (Kila, TN: Kessinger Publishing, 2009).

Blatch, Harriot Stanton, and Alma Lutz. *Challenging Years: The Memoirs of Harriot Stanton Blatch* (New York: G. P. Putnam's Sons, 1940).

Buhle, Mari Jo, and Paul Buhle, eds. *The Concise History of Woman Suffrage: Selections from the Classic Work of Stanton, Gage, and Harper* (Urbana, IL: University of Illinois Press, 1978).

Cromwell, Otelia. *Lucretia Mott* (Cambridge, MA: Harvard University Press, 1958).

Dorr, Rheta Childe. *Susan B. Anthony: The Woman Who Changed the Mind of a Nation* (New York: Frederick A. Stokes, 1928).

DuBois, Ellen Carol. *Feminism & Suffrage* (Ithaca, NY: Cornell University Press, 1999).

———. *Harriot Stanton Blatch and the Winning of Woman Suffrage* (New Haven, CT: Yale University Press, 1997).

DuBois, Ellen Carol, ed. *Elizabeth Cady Stanton/Susan B. Anthony: Correspondence, Writings, Speeches* (New York: Schocken Books, 1981).

DuBois, Ellen Carol, and Richard Cándida Smith, eds. *Elizabeth Cady Stanton, Feminist as Thinker: A Reader in Documents and Essays* (New York: New York University Press, 2007).

Flexner, Eleanor, and Ellen Fitzpatrick. *Century of Struggle: The Woman's Rights Movement in the United States*, enlarged edition (Cambridge, MA: Harvard University Press, 1996).

Foner, Philip S., ed. *Frederick Douglass on Women's Rights* (New York: Da Capo Press, 1992).

Freedman, Estelle B., ed. *The Essential Feminist Reader* (New York: The Modern Library, 2007).

Frost, Elizabeth, and Kathryn Cullen-DuPont. *Women's Suffrage in America* (New York: Facts On File, 1992).

Ginzberg, Lori D. *Elizabeth Cady Stanton: An American Life* (New York: Hill and Wang, 2009).

Gordon, Ann D., ed. *The Selected Papers of Elizabeth Cady Stanton & Susan B. Anthony*, volumes 1–5 (New Brunswick, NJ: Rutgers University Press, 1997–2009).

Griffith, Elisabeth. *In Her Own Right: The Life of Elizabeth Cady Stanton* (New York: Oxford University Press, 1984).

Gurko, Miriam. *The Ladies of Seneca Falls: The Birth of the Woman's Rights Movement* (New York: Schocken Books, 1974).

Harper, Ida Husted. *The Life and Work of Susan B. Anthony: Including Public Addresses, Her Own Letters and Many from Her Contemporaries During Fifty Years*, 3 volumes (Indianapolis, IN: The Hollenbeck Press, vols. 1 and 2, 1898; vol. 3, 1908).

Holland, Patricia G., and Ann D. Gordon, eds. *The Papers of Elizabeth Cady Stanton and Susan B. Anthony*, microfilm edition (Wilmington, DE: Scholarly Resources, 1991).

———. *Guide and Index to the Microfilm Edition* (Wilmington, DE: Scholarly Resources, 1992).

Jones, Martha S. *All Bound Up Together: The Woman Question in African American Public Culture, 1830–1900* (Chapel Hill: University of North Carolina Press, 2006).

Kerr, Andrea Moore. *Lucy Stone: Speaking Out for Equality* (New Brunswick, NJ: Rutgers University Press, 1992).

Keyssar, Alexander. *The Right to Vote: The Contested History of Democracy in the United States* (New York: Basic Books, 2000).

Lasser, Carol, and Marlene Deahl Merrill, eds. *Friends and Sisters: Letters Between Lucy Stone and Antoinette Brown Blackwell 1846–93.* (Chicago: University of Illinois Press, 1987.)

Lutz, Alma. *Created Equal: A Biography of Elizabeth Cady Stanton, 1815–1902* (New York: The John Day Company, 1940).

———. *Susan B. Anthony: Rebel, Crusader, Humanitarian* (Boston: Beacon Press, 1959).

Mayer, Henry. *All on Fire: William Lloyd Garrison and the Abolition of Slavery* (New York: St. Martin's Griffin, 1998).

McMillen, Sally G. *Seneca Falls and the Origins of the Women's Rights Movement* (New York: Oxford University Press, 2008).

Painter, Nell Irvin. *Sojourner Truth: A Life, a Symbol* (New York: W. W. Norton, 1996).

Palmer, Beverly Wilson, ed. *Selected Letters of Lucretia Coffin Mott* (Urbana and Chicago: University of Illinois Press, 2002).

Parton, James, et al. *Eminent Women of the Age: Being Narratives of the Lives and Deeds of the Most Prominent Women of the Present Generation* (Hartford, CT: S. M. Betts & Co., 1869).

Penney, Sherry H., and James D. Livingston. *A Very Dangerous Woman: Martha Wright and Women's Rights* (Amherst: University of Massachusetts Press, 2004).

Perry, Mark. *Lift Up Thy Voice: The Grimké Family's Journey from Slaveholders to Civil Rights Leaders* (New York: Penguin Books, 2001).

Russo, Ann, and Cheris Kramarae, eds. *The Radical Women's Press of the 1850s* (New York: Routledge, 1991).

Sherr, Lynn. *Failure Is Impossible: Susan B. Anthony in Her Own Words* (New York: Times Books, 1995).

Sklar, Kathryn Kish. *Women's Rights Emerges Within the Antislavery Movement 1830–1870: A Brief History with Documents* (Boston: Bedford/St. Martin's, 2000).

Stanton, Elizabeth Cady. *Eighty Years and More: Reminiscences 1815–1897* (New York: Shocken Books, 1971; reprinted from T. Fisher Urwin edition, 1898).

——— *The Woman's Bible* (Boston: Northeastern University Press, 1993; first published 1895).

Stanton, Elizabeth Cady, Susan B. Anthony, and Matilda Joslyn Gage, eds. *History of Woman Suffrage*, volumes 1–3 (New York: Fowler and Wells, 1881, 1882; Rochester, NY: Susan B. Anthony, 1886).

Stanton, Theodore, and Harriet Stanton Blatch, eds. *Elizabeth Cady Stanton as Revealed in Her Letters, Diary, and Reminiscences*, 2 volumes (New York: Harper & Brothers, 1922).

Sterling, Dorothy. *Lucretia Mott, Gentle Warrior* (New York: The Feminist Press, 1999).

Ulrich, Laurel Thatcher. *Well-Behaved Women Seldom Make History* (New York: Alfred A. Knopf, 2007).

Ward, Geoffrey C., and Ken Burns. *Not for Ourselves Alone: The Story of Elizabeth Cady Stanton and Susan B. Anthony* (New York: Alfred A. Knopf, 1999).

Wellman, Judith. *The Road to Seneca Falls: Elizabeth Cady Stanton and the First Woman's Rights Convention* (Urbana: University of Illinois Press, 2004).

White, Barbara Anne. *The Beecher Sisters* (New Haven, CT: Yale University Press, 2003).

WEBLIOGRAPHY

Elizabeth Cady Stanton Trust is online at www.elizabethcadystanton.org.

The Elizabeth Cady Stanton & Susan B. Anthony Papers Project, Rutgers, the State University of New Jersey, and the National Historical Publications and Records Commission, online at http://ecssba.rutgers.edu/.

"George Francis Train and the Woman Suffrage Movement, 1867–70," Patricia G. Holland, from *Books at Iowa* 46 (April 1987) online at www.lib.uiowa.edu/spec-coll/bai/holland.htm.

The Lucretia Coffin Mott Papers Project is online at http://Mott.pomona.edu.

"This Shall be the Land for Women: The Struggle for Western Women's Suffrage, 1860–1920," Women of the West Museum, online at http://theautry.org/explore/exhibits/suffrage.

"Susan B. Anthony: Celebrating 'A Heroic Life,'" includes many images, is online at http://www.lib.rochester.edu/index.cfm?page=4119.

"Susan B. Anthony House Virtual Tour," featuring her home in Rochester, is online at www.susanbanthonyhouse.org/tour0.shtml.

"Susan B. Anthony in Nebraska, late August–October 14, 1882," part of Women on the Rails: Nebraska Suffragists and the Railroad, is online at http://segonku.unl.edu/~lworking/SBA_TourMovie.html.

The Susan B. Anthony Manuscript Collection, including the entire poem Elizabeth wrote for Susan's eightieth birthday celebration, can be read at http://www.libraryweb.org/rochimag/SBA/ephemera.htm.

"Votes for Women: Selections from the National American Woman Suffrage Association Collection, 1848–1921," Library of Congress, is online at http://memory.loc.gov/ammem/naw/nawshome.html.

"Votes for Women: Suffrage Pictures, 1850–1920," Library of Congress, is online at http://memory.loc.gov/ammem/vfwhtml/vfwhome.html.

"Western New York Suffragists: Winning the Vote" online resource at www.winningthevote.org.

The Women's Rights National Historical Park is online at www.nps.gov/wori.

Note: The following books can all be read online at http://books.google.com: *Elizabeth Cady Stanton as Revealed in Her Letters, Diary, and Reminiscences,* edited by Theodore Stanton and Harriot Stanton Blatch; *The History of Woman Suffrage* by Elizabeth Cady Stanton, Susan B. Anthony, and Matilda Joslyn Gage; *The Life and Work of Susan B. Anthony* by Ida Husted Harper; *The Solitude of Self* by Elizabeth Cady Stanton; *The Woman's Bible* by Elizabeth Cady Stanton; and the novel *Adam Bede* by George Eliot, which Elizabeth and Susan discussed.

INDEX

Index